BLACKWOOD

BLACKWOOD

Written by **EVAN DORKIN**

Art by **VERONICA** and **ANDY FISH**

Cover by **VERONICA FISH**

Chapter breaks by **VERONICA FISH**

DARK HORSE BOOKS

President & Publisher **MIKE RICHARDSON**

Editor **DANIEL CHABON**

Assistant Editor **BRETT ISRAEL**

Designer **SARAH TERRY**

Digital Art Technician **JOSIE CHRISTENSEN**

BLACKWOOD

Collects issues #1–#4 of the Dark Horse Comics series *Blackwood*.

Published by Dark Horse Books, a division of Dark Horse Comics, Inc.
10956 SE Main Street, Milwaukie, OR 97222

DarkHorse.com
To find a comics shop in your area, visit comicshoplocator.com

First edition: December 2018 ◆ ISBN 978-1-50670-742-6
Digital ISBN 978-1-50670-756-3

13 5 7 9 10 8 6 4 2
Printed in China

Library of Congress Cataloging-in-Publication Data

Names: Dorkin, Evan, writer. | Fish, Veronica, artist. | Fish, Andy, artist. | Cloonan, Becky, artist. | Shalvey, Declan, artist. | Bellaire, Jordie, artist. | Crook, Tyler, artist. | Rubin, David, 1977- artist.
Title: Blackwood / written by Evan Dorkin ; art by Veronica and Andy Fish ; cover by Veronica Fish ; chapter breaks by Veronica Fish, Becky Cloonan, Declan Shalvey and Jordie Bellaire, Tyler Crook, and David Rubin.
Description: First edition. | Milwaukie, OR : Dark Horse Books, December 2018. | "Collects issues #1-#4 of the Dark Horse Comics series Blackwood."
Identifiers: LCCN 2018029929 | ISBN 9781506707426 (paperback)
Subjects: | BISAC: COMICS & GRAPHIC NOVELS / Horror. | COMICS & GRAPHIC NOVELS / Fantasy. | COMICS & GRAPHIC NOVELS / General.
Classification: LCC PN6728.B524 D67 2018 | DDC 741.5/973--dc23
LC record available at https://lccn.loc.gov/2018029929

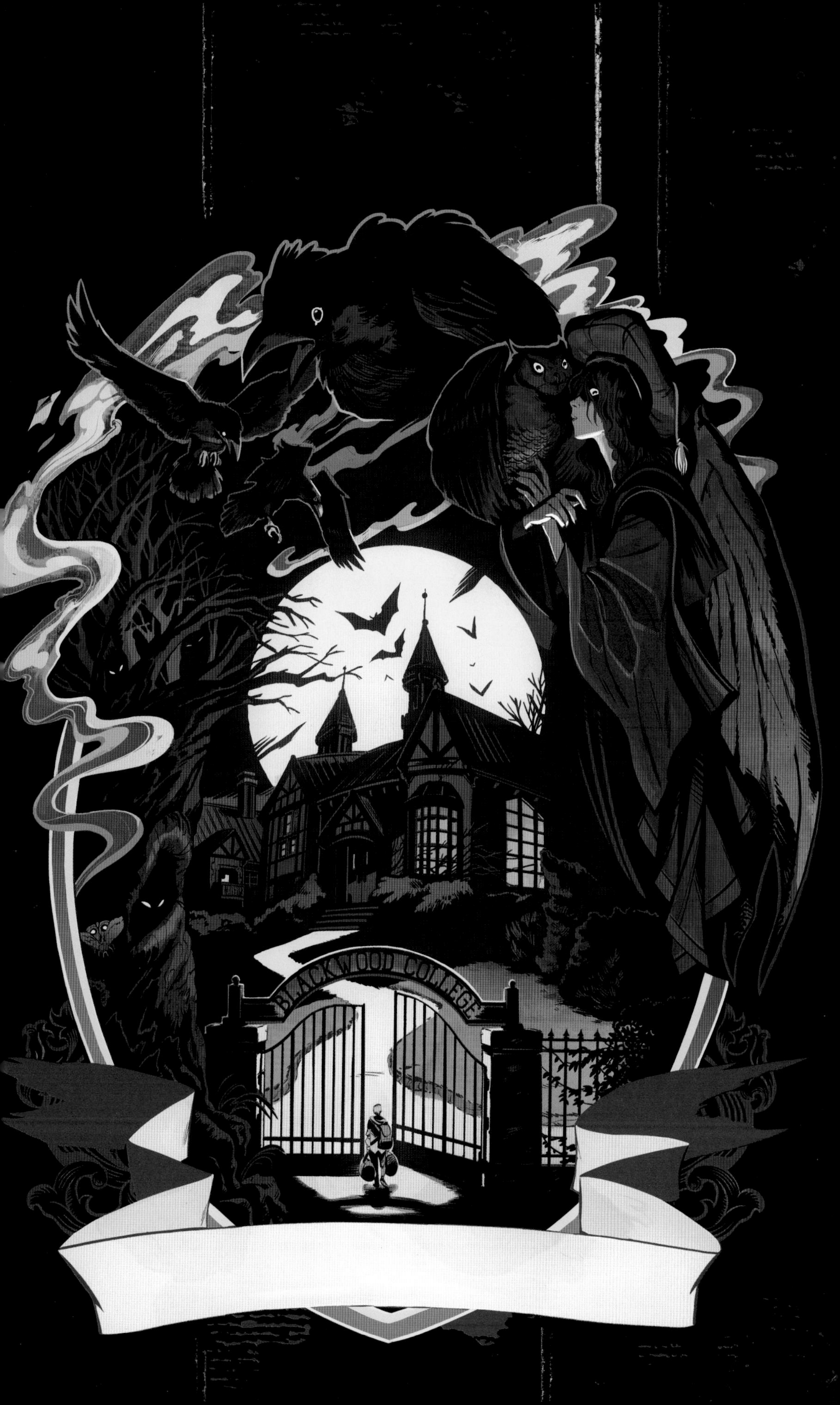
BLACKWOOD COLLEGE

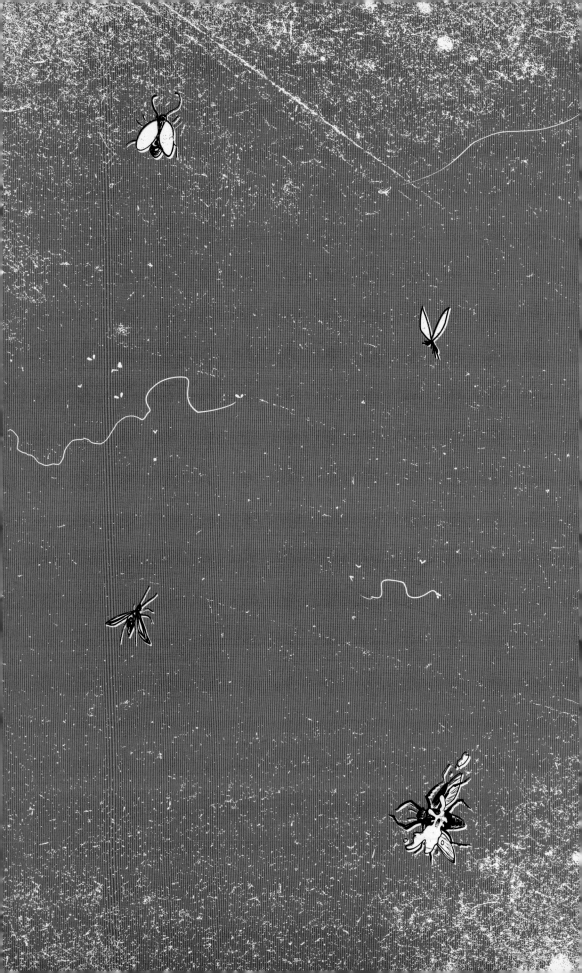

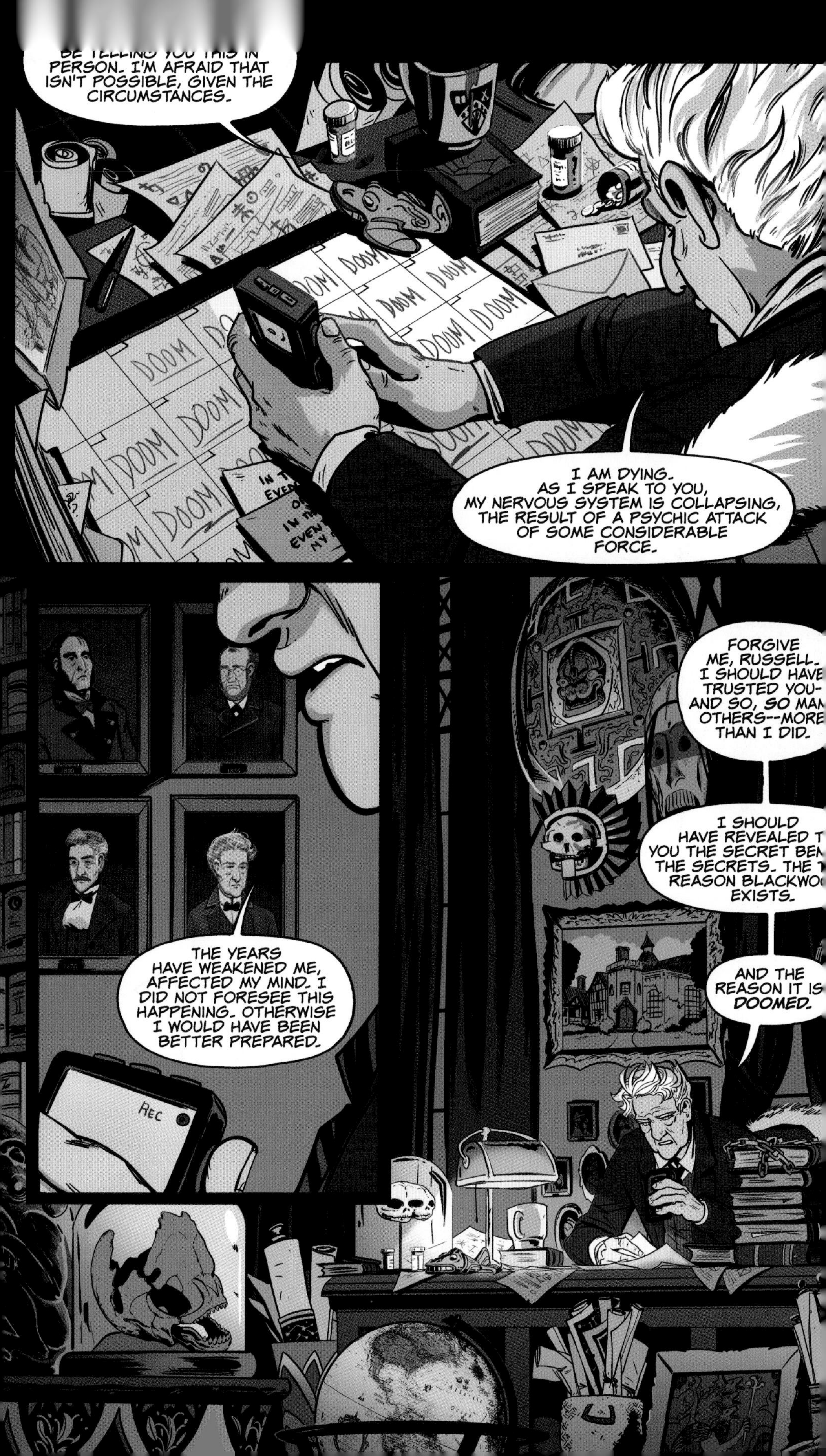

BE TELLING YOU THIS IN PERSON. I'M AFRAID THAT ISN'T POSSIBLE, GIVEN THE CIRCUMSTANCES.
I AM DYING. AS I SPEAK TO YOU, MY NERVOUS SYSTEM IS COLLAPSING, THE RESULT OF A PSYCHIC ATTACK OF SOME CONSIDERABLE FORCE.
THE YEARS HAVE WEAKENED ME, AFFECTED MY MIND. I DID NOT FORESEE THIS HAPPENING. OTHERWISE I WOULD HAVE BEEN BETTER PREPARED.
REC
FORGIVE ME, RUSSELL. I SHOULD HAVE TRUSTED YOU-- AND SO, SO MAN OTHERS--MORE THAN I DID.
I SHOULD HAVE REVEALED T YOU THE SECRET BEH THE SECRETS. THE T REASON BLACKWOO EXISTS.
AND THE REASON IT IS DOOMED.

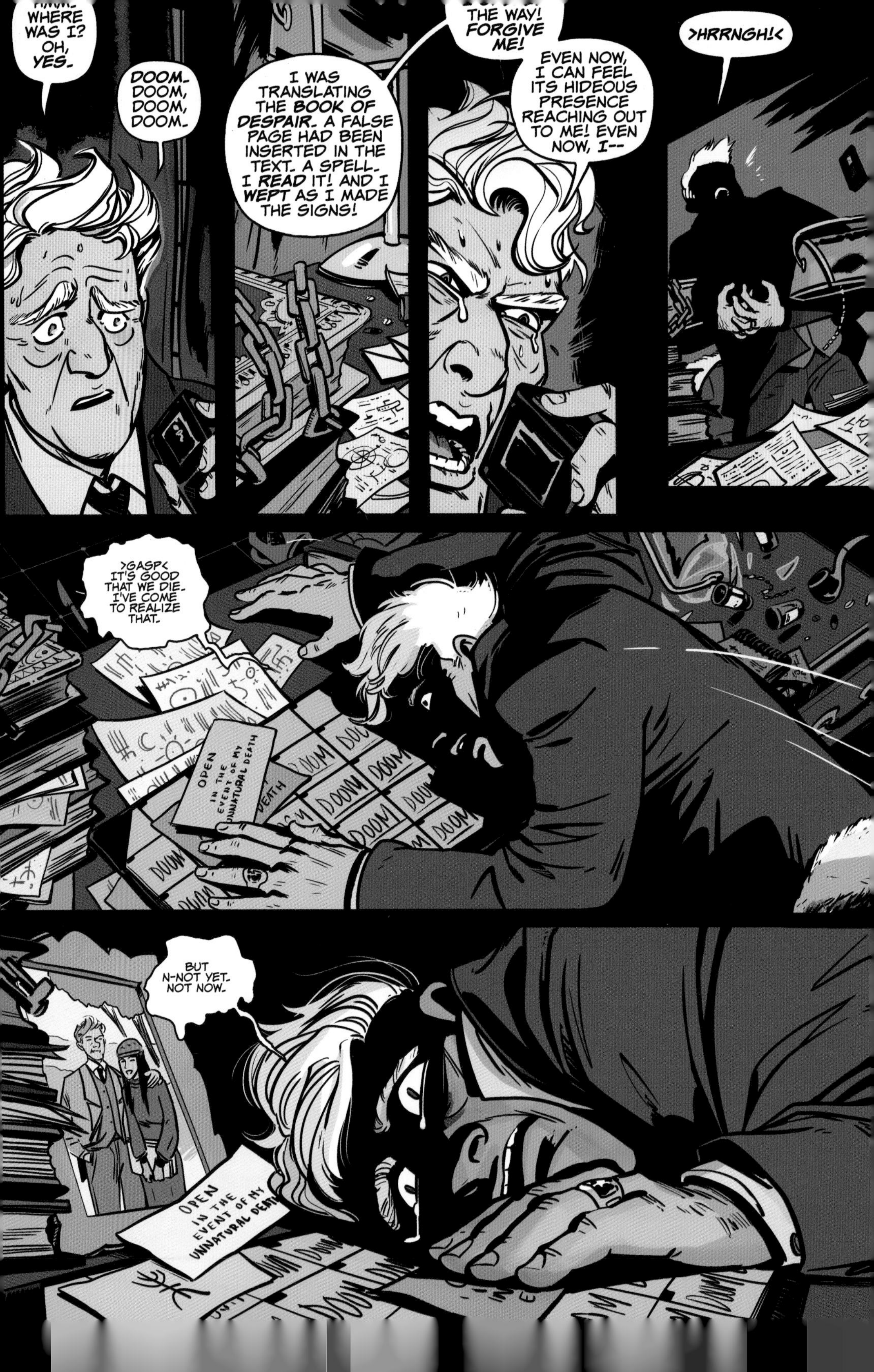

WHERE WAS I? OH, YES.
DOOM. DOOM, DOOM, DOOM.
I WAS TRANSLATING THE BOOK OF DESPAIR. A FALSE PAGE HAD BEEN INSERTED IN THE TEXT. A SPELL. I READ IT! AND I WEPT AS I MADE THE SIGNS!
THE WAY! FORGIVE ME!
EVEN NOW, I CAN FEEL ITS HIDEOUS PRESENCE REACHING OUT TO ME! EVEN NOW, I--
>HRRNGH!<
>GASP< IT'S GOOD THAT WE DIE. I'VE COME TO REALIZE THAT.
OPEN IN THE EVENT OF MY UNNATURAL DEATH
DOOM
BUT N-NOT YET. NOT NOW.
OPEN IN THE EVENT OF MY UNNATURAL DEATH

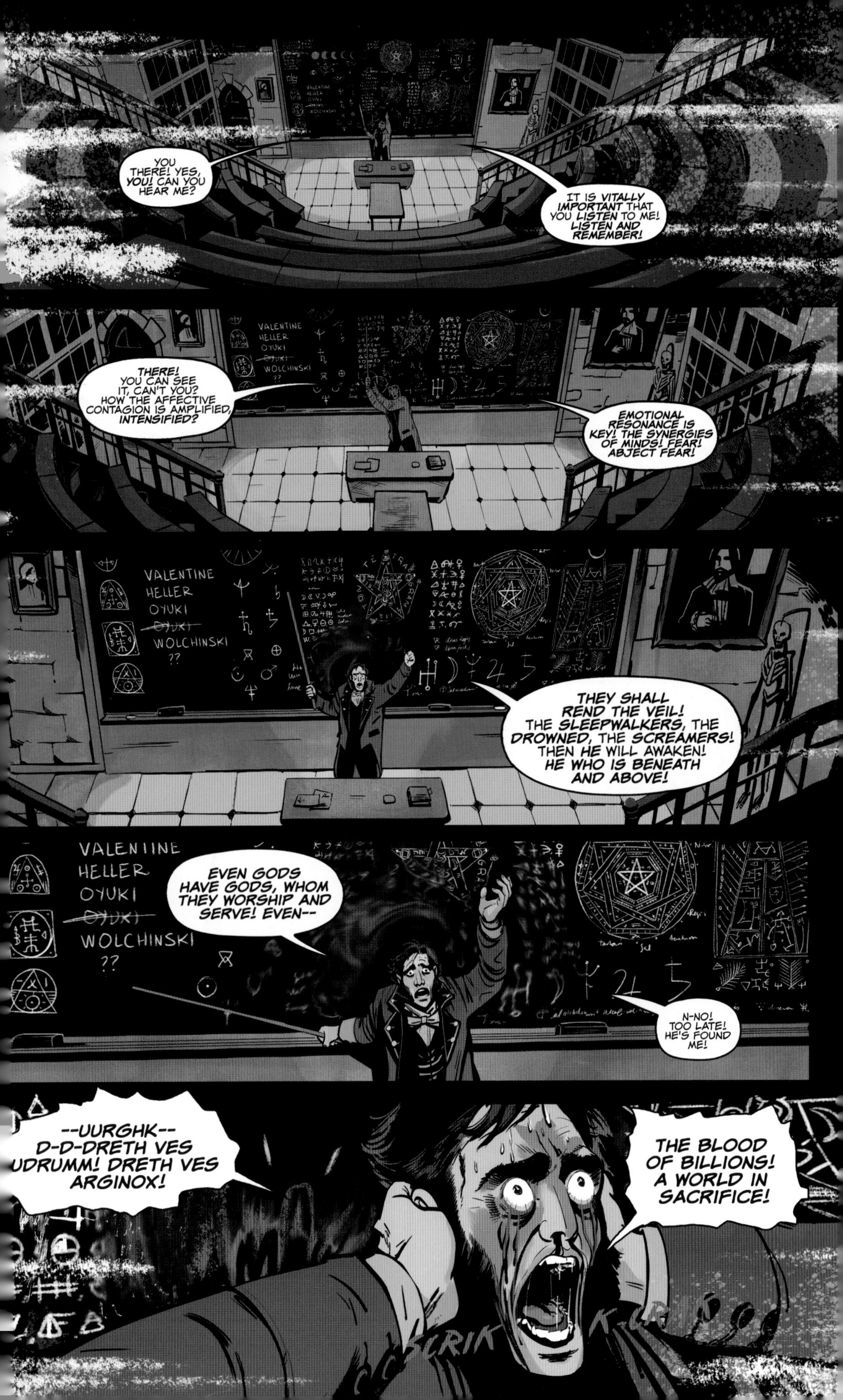
YOU THERE! YES, YOU! CAN YOU HEAR ME?
IT IS VITALLY IMPORTANT THAT YOU LISTEN TO ME! LISTEN AND REMEMBER!
VALENTINE
HELLER
OYUKI
~~OYUKI~~
WOLCHINSKI
??
THERE! YOU CAN SEE IT, CAN'T YOU? HOW THE AFFECTIVE CONTAGION IS AMPLIFIED, INTENSIFIED?
EMOTIONAL RESONANCE IS KEY! THE SYNERGIES OF MINDS! FEAR! ABJECT FEAR!
THEY SHALL REND THE VEIL! THE SLEEPWALKERS, THE DROWNED, THE SCREAMERS! THEN HE WILL AWAKEN! HE WHO IS BENEATH AND ABOVE!
EVEN GODS HAVE GODS, WHOM THEY WORSHIP AND SERVE! EVEN--
N-NO! TOO LATE! HE'S FOUND ME!
--UURGHK-- D-D-DRETH VES UDRUMM! DRETH VES ARGINOX!
THE BLOOD OF BILLIONS! A WORLD IN SACRIFICE!
SKRIK
KRR

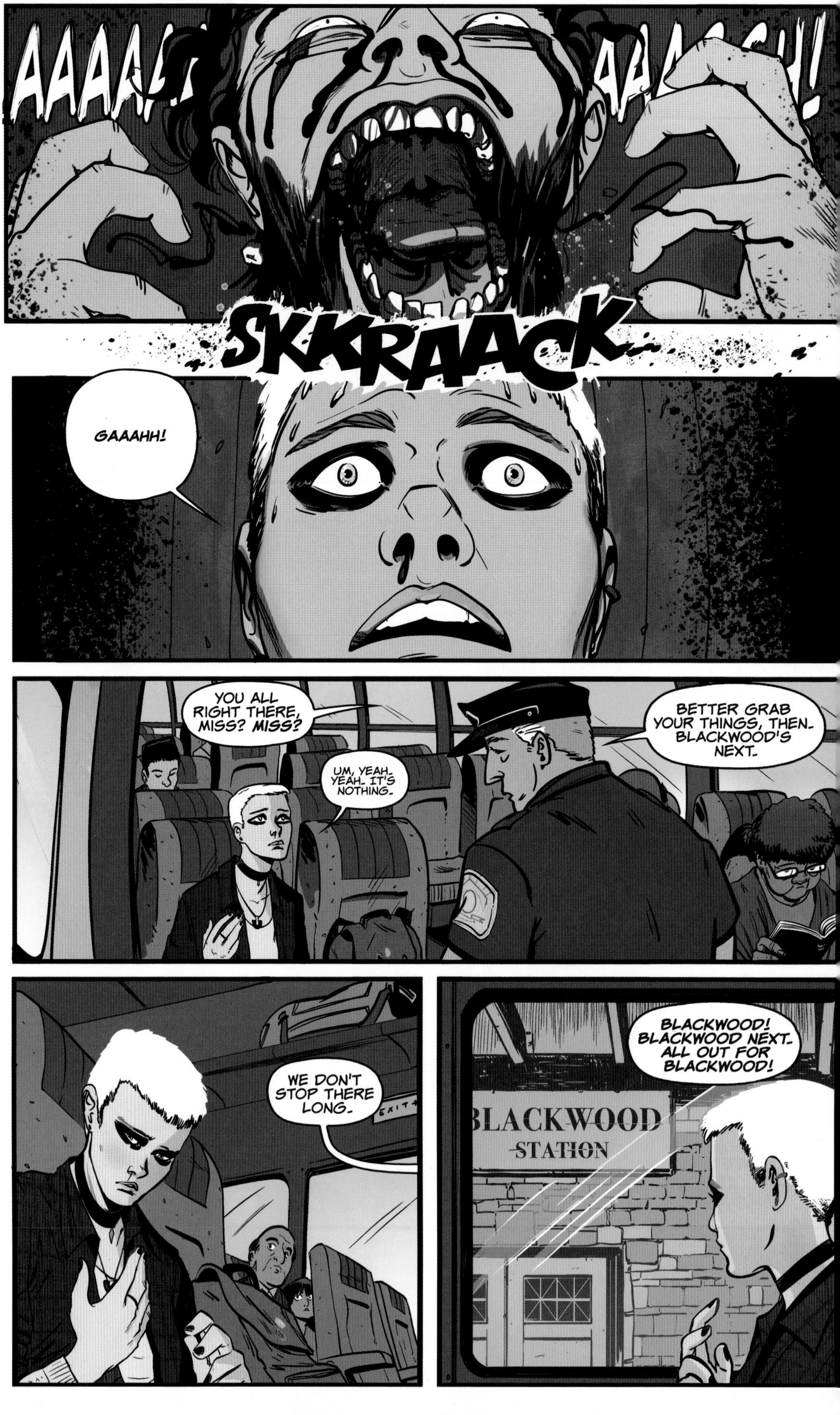
AAAAAAAAAGH!
SKKRAACK
GAAAHH!
YOU ALL RIGHT THERE, MISS? MISS?
UM, YEAH. YEAH. IT'S NOTHING.
BETTER GRAB YOUR THINGS, THEN. BLACKWOOD'S NEXT.
WE DON'T STOP THERE LONG.
BLACKWOOD! BLACKWOOD NEXT. ALL OUT FOR BLACKWOOD!
BLACKWOOD STATION

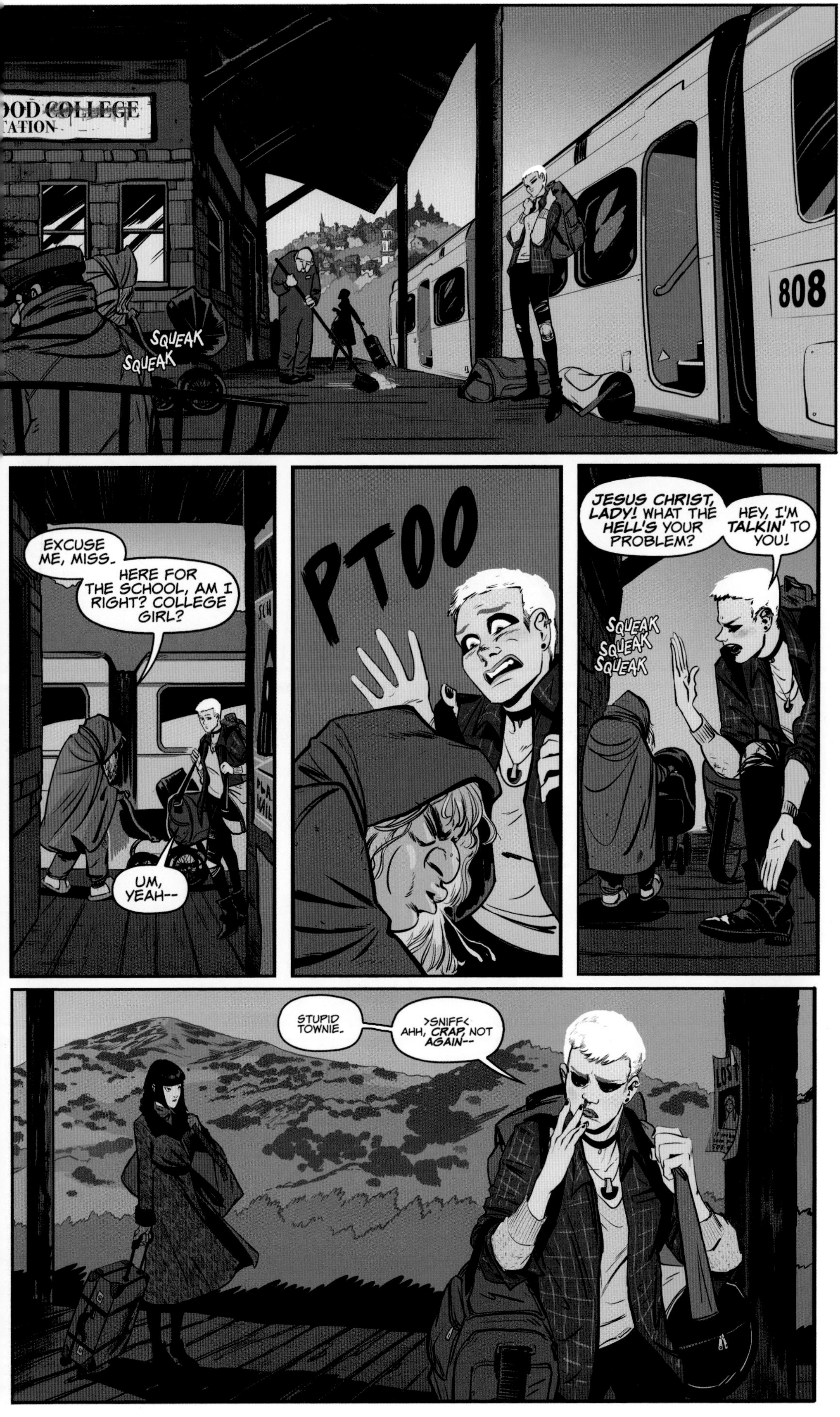

OOD COLLEGE
TATION
SQUEAK
SQUEAK
808
EXCUSE ME, MISS.
HERE FOR THE SCHOOL, AM I RIGHT? COLLEGE GIRL?
UM, YEAH--
PTOO
JESUS CHRIST, LADY! WHAT THE HELL'S YOUR PROBLEM?
HEY, I'M TALKIN' TO YOU!
SQUEAK
SQUEAK
SQUEAK
STUPID TOWNIE.
>SNIFF< AHH, CRAP, NOT AGAIN--
LOST

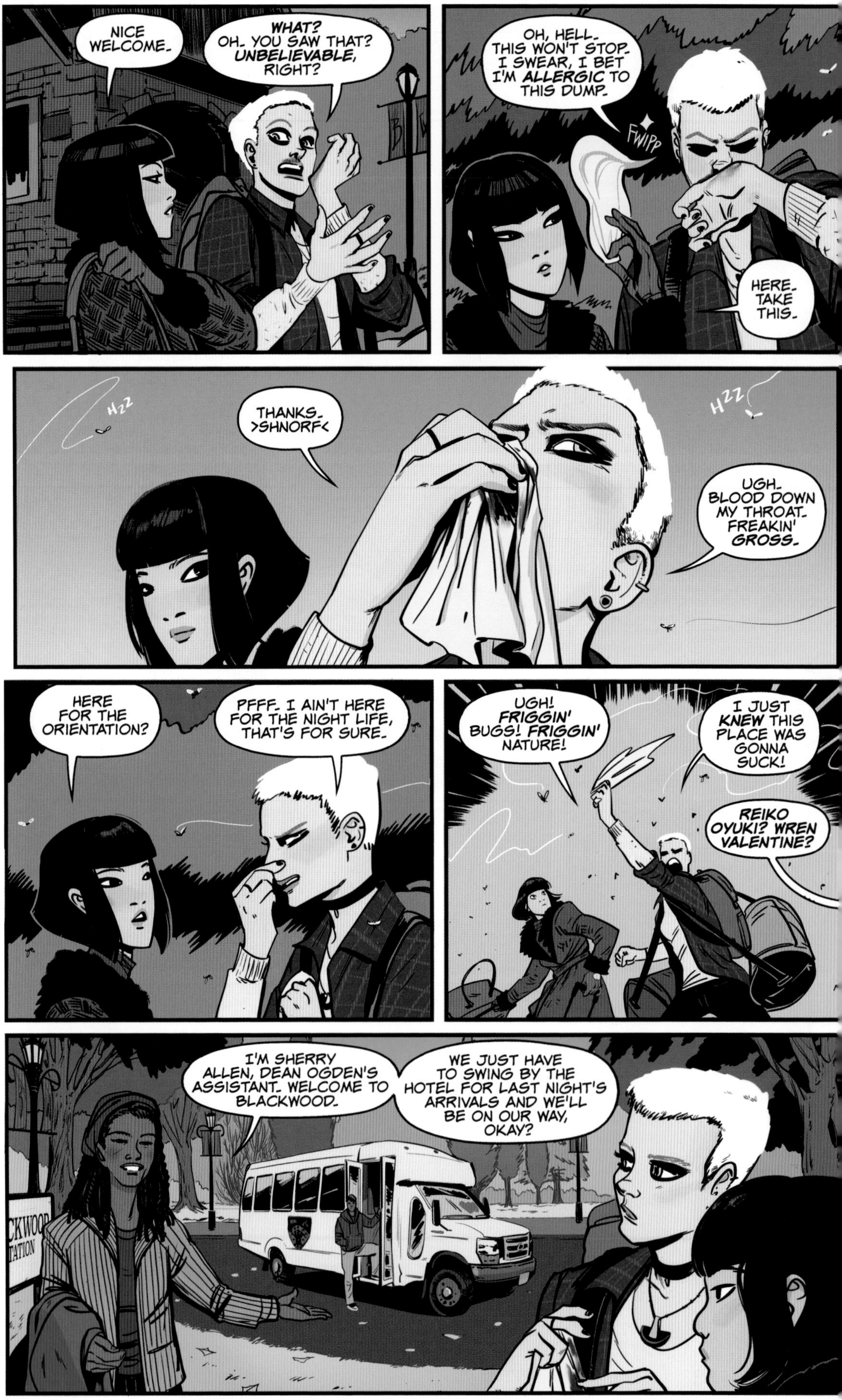

NICE WELCOME.
WHAT? OH. YOU SAW THAT? UNBELIEVABLE, RIGHT?
OH, HELL. THIS WON'T STOP. I SWEAR, I BET I'M ALLERGIC TO THIS DUMP.
FWIPP
HERE. TAKE THIS.
HZZ
THANKS. >SHNORF<
HZZ
UGH. BLOOD DOWN MY THROAT. FREAKIN' GROSS.
HERE FOR THE ORIENTATION?
PFFF. I AIN'T HERE FOR THE NIGHT LIFE, THAT'S FOR SURE.
UGH! FRIGGIN' BUGS! FRIGGIN' NATURE!
I JUST KNEW THIS PLACE WAS GONNA SUCK!
REIKO OYUKI? WREN VALENTINE?
I'M SHERRY ALLEN, DEAN OGDEN'S ASSISTANT. WELCOME TO BLACKWOOD.
WE JUST HAVE TO SWING BY THE HOTEL FOR LAST NIGHT'S ARRIVALS AND WE'LL BE ON OUR WAY, OKAY?

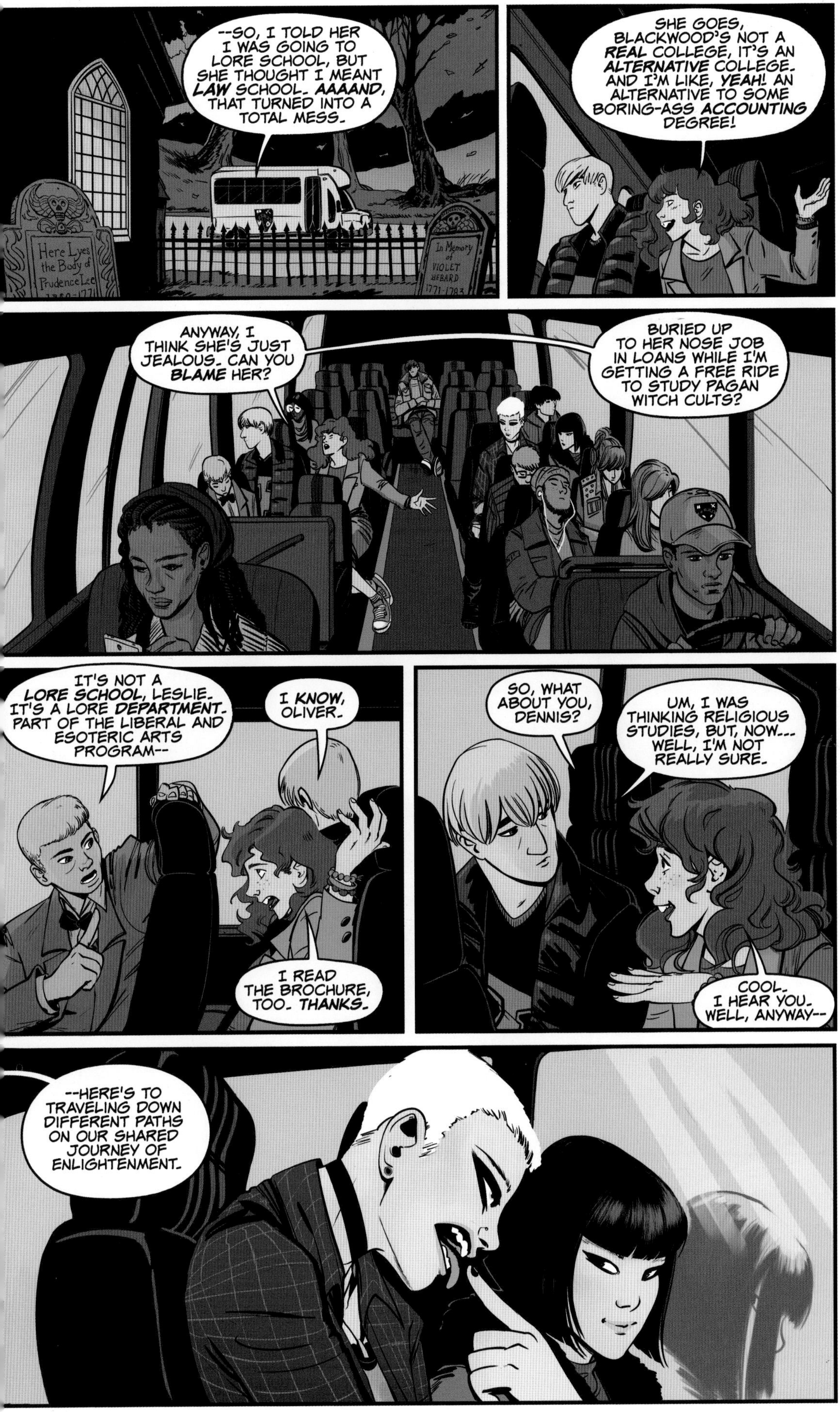
--SO, I TOLD HER I WAS GOING TO LORE SCHOOL, BUT SHE THOUGHT I MEANT LAW SCHOOL. AAAAND, THAT TURNED INTO A TOTAL MESS.
Here Lyes the Body of Prudence Lee
In Memory of VIOLET HEBARD 1771-1783
SHE GOES, BLACKWOOD'S NOT A REAL COLLEGE, IT'S AN ALTERNATIVE COLLEGE. AND I'M LIKE, YEAH! AN ALTERNATIVE TO SOME BORING-ASS ACCOUNTING DEGREE!
ANYWAY, I THINK SHE'S JUST JEALOUS. CAN YOU BLAME HER?
BURIED UP TO HER NOSE JOB IN LOANS WHILE I'M GETTING A FREE RIDE TO STUDY PAGAN WITCH CULTS?
IT'S NOT A LORE SCHOOL, LESLIE. IT'S A LORE DEPARTMENT. PART OF THE LIBERAL AND ESOTERIC ARTS PROGRAM--
I KNOW, OLIVER.
I READ THE BROCHURE, TOO. THANKS.
SO, WHAT ABOUT YOU, DENNIS?
UM, I WAS THINKING RELIGIOUS STUDIES, BUT, NOW... WELL, I'M NOT REALLY SURE.
COOL. I HEAR YOU. WELL, ANYWAY--
--HERE'S TO TRAVELING DOWN DIFFERENT PATHS ON OUR SHARED JOURNEY OF ENLIGHTENMENT.

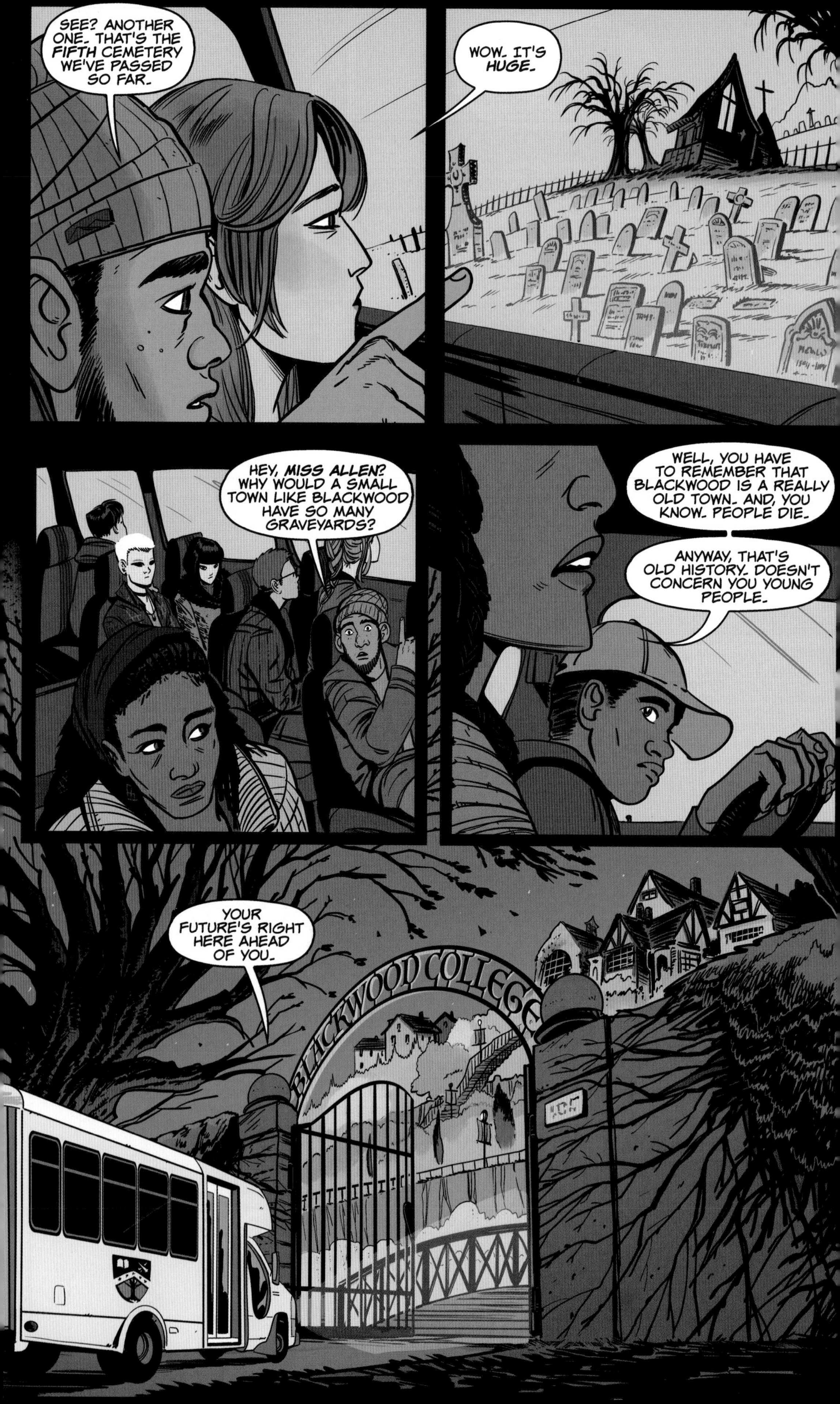
SEE? ANOTHER ONE. THAT'S THE FIFTH CEMETERY WE'VE PASSED SO FAR.
WOW. IT'S HUGE.
HEY, MISS ALLEN? WHY WOULD A SMALL TOWN LIKE BLACKWOOD HAVE SO MANY GRAVEYARDS?
WELL, YOU HAVE TO REMEMBER THAT BLACKWOOD IS A REALLY OLD TOWN. AND, YOU KNOW. PEOPLE DIE.
ANYWAY, THAT'S OLD HISTORY. DOESN'T CONCERN YOU YOUNG PEOPLE.
YOUR FUTURE'S RIGHT HERE AHEAD OF YOU.
BLACKWOOD COLLEGE

OKAY, FOLKS, TOMORROW'S THE GRAND TOUR.

TODAY WE'LL JUST GET YOU IN YOUR ROOMS, MEET WITH DEAN OGDEN, GET SOME FOOD IN YOU, AND LET YOU RELAX. HOW'S THAT SOUND?

OH, HELL. CROWTHER HALL. WE GOT THE OLD DORM. THE REALLY OLD DORM.

HZZ

BET THE WI-FI SUCKS WORSE HERE THAN ANYWHERE ELSE ON CAMPUS.

HEY. DON'T GO INTO TOWN TONIGHT, OKAY, JAMAR?

WHAT? WHY NOT?

YOU KNOW HOW IT CAN GET WITH NEW ARRIVALS, EVEN JUST A FEW. THEY WERE WATCHING AT THE STATION.

YEAH, YEAH. NO PROBLEM.

GOOD. SEE YOU LATER, OKAY, SWEETIE?

OKAY, MOM. LOVE YOU.

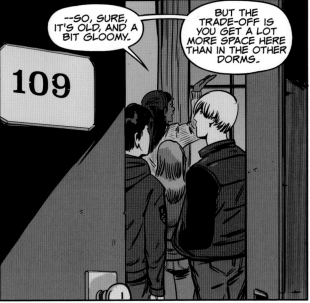

109

--SO, SURE, IT'S OLD, AND A BIT GLOOMY.

BUT THE TRADE-OFF IS YOU GET A LOT MORE SPACE HERE THAN IN THE OTHER DORMS.

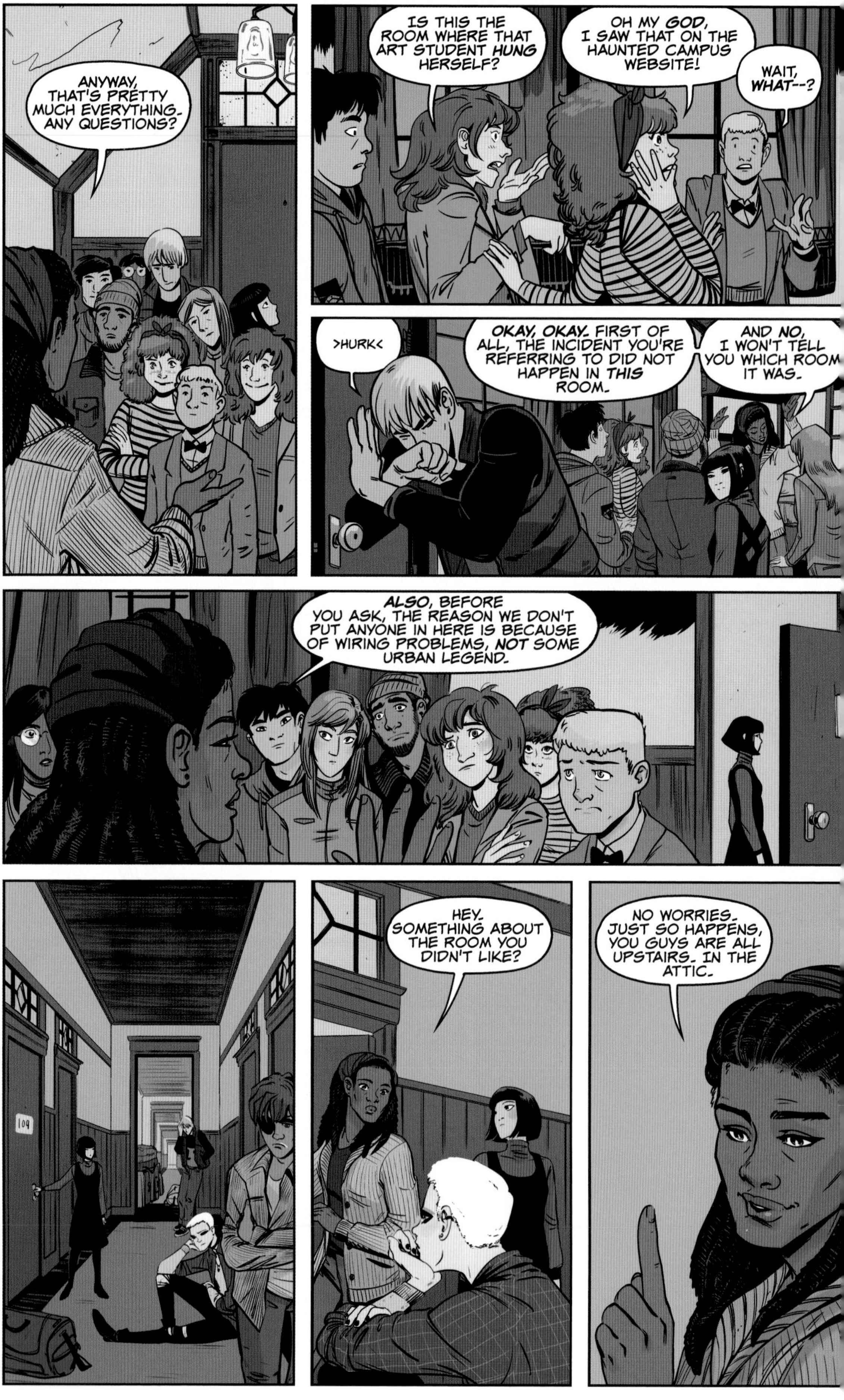
ANYWAY, THAT'S PRETTY MUCH EVERYTHING. ANY QUESTIONS?
IS THIS THE ROOM WHERE THAT ART STUDENT HUNG HERSELF?
OH MY GOD, I SAW THAT ON THE HAUNTED CAMPUS WEBSITE!
WAIT, WHAT--?
>HURK<
OKAY, OKAY. FIRST OF ALL, THE INCIDENT YOU'RE REFERRING TO DID NOT HAPPEN IN THIS ROOM.
AND NO, I WON'T TELL YOU WHICH ROOM IT WAS.
ALSO, BEFORE YOU ASK, THE REASON WE DON'T PUT ANYONE IN HERE IS BECAUSE OF WIRING PROBLEMS, NOT SOME URBAN LEGEND.
109
HEY. SOMETHING ABOUT THE ROOM YOU DIDN'T LIKE?
NO WORRIES. JUST SO HAPPENS, YOU GUYS ARE ALL UPSTAIRS. IN THE ATTIC.

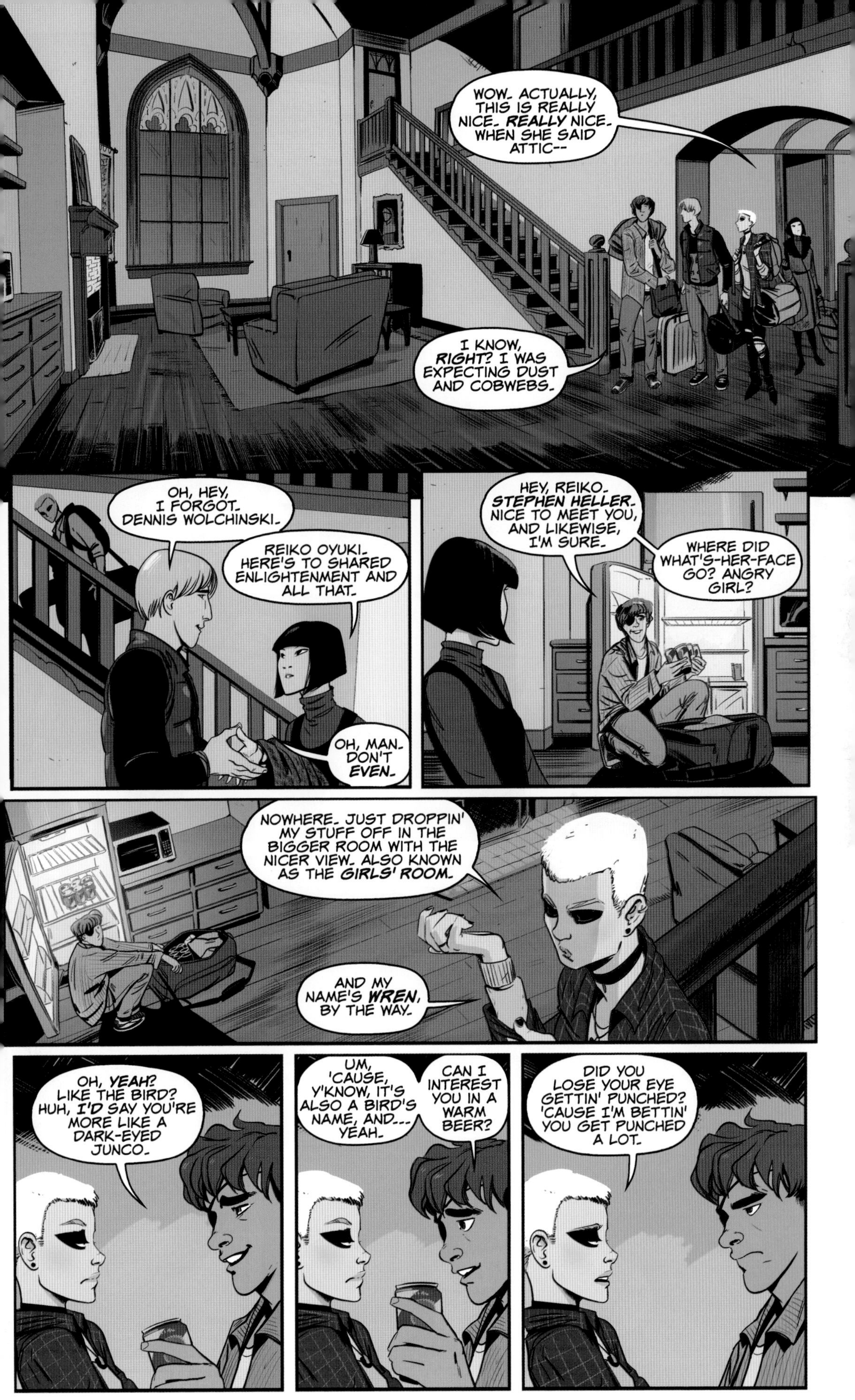
WOW. ACTUALLY, THIS IS REALLY NICE. REALLY NICE. WHEN SHE SAID ATTIC--
I KNOW, RIGHT? I WAS EXPECTING DUST AND COBWEBS.
OH, HEY, I FORGOT. DENNIS WOLCHINSKI.
REIKO OYUKI. HERE'S TO SHARED ENLIGHTENMENT AND ALL THAT.
OH, MAN. DON'T EVEN.
HEY, REIKO. STEPHEN HELLER. NICE TO MEET YOU, AND LIKEWISE, I'M SURE.
WHERE DID WHAT'S-HER-FACE GO? ANGRY GIRL?
NOWHERE. JUST DROPPIN' MY STUFF OFF IN THE BIGGER ROOM WITH THE NICER VIEW. ALSO KNOWN AS THE GIRLS' ROOM.
AND MY NAME'S WREN, BY THE WAY.
OH, YEAH? LIKE THE BIRD? HUH, I'D SAY YOU'RE MORE LIKE A DARK-EYED JUNCO.
UM, 'CAUSE, Y'KNOW, IT'S ALSO A BIRD'S NAME, AND... YEAH.
CAN I INTEREST YOU IN A WARM BEER?
DID YOU LOSE YOUR EYE GETTIN' PUNCHED? 'CAUSE I'M BETTIN' YOU GET PUNCHED A LOT.

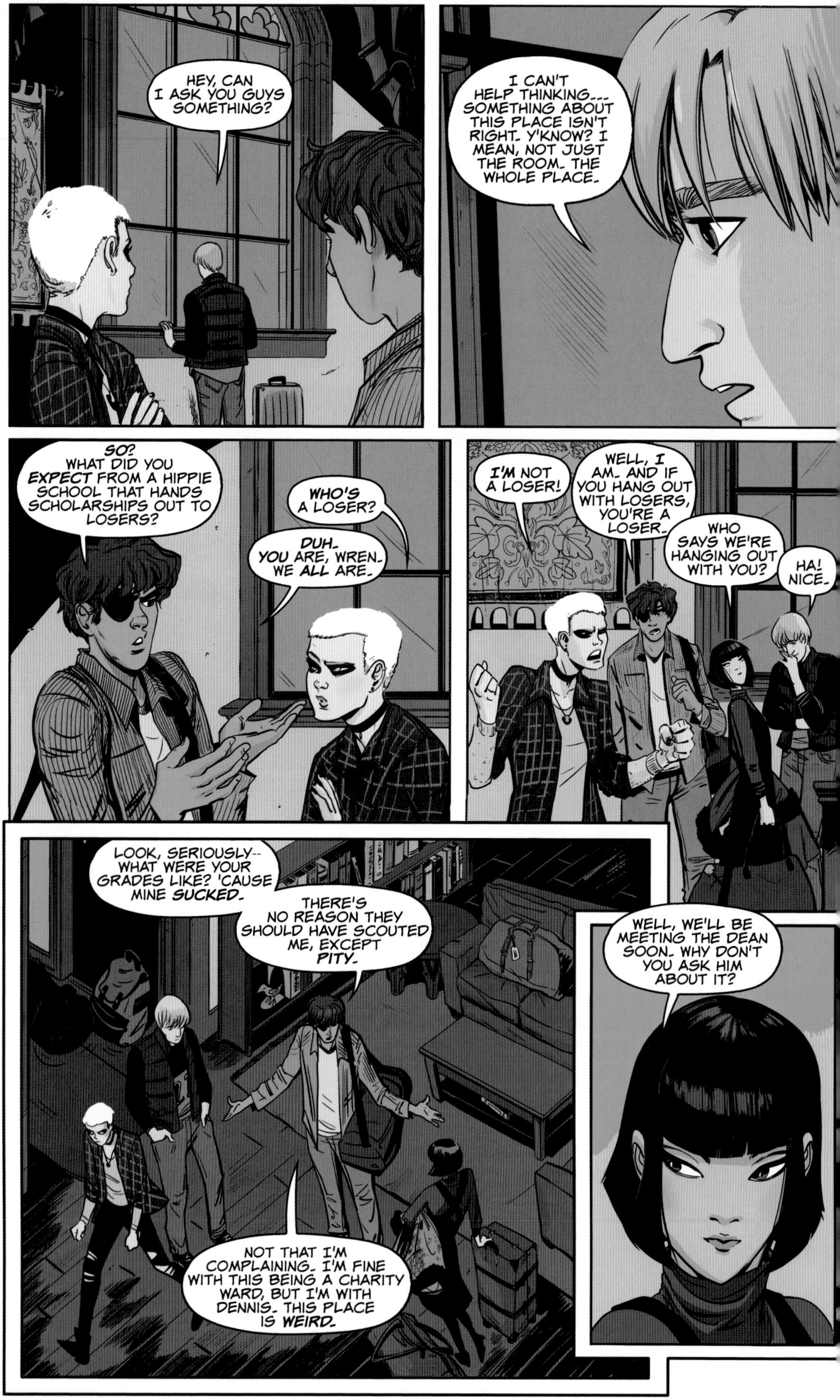

HEY, CAN I ASK YOU GUYS SOMETHING?
I CAN'T HELP THINKING... SOMETHING ABOUT THIS PLACE ISN'T RIGHT. Y'KNOW? I MEAN, NOT JUST THE ROOM. THE WHOLE PLACE.
SO? WHAT DID YOU EXPECT FROM A HIPPIE SCHOOL THAT HANDS SCHOLARSHIPS OUT TO LOSERS?
WHO'S A LOSER?
DUH. YOU ARE, WREN. WE ALL ARE.
I'M NOT A LOSER!
WELL, I AM. AND IF YOU HANG OUT WITH LOSERS, YOU'RE A LOSER.
WHO SAYS WE'RE HANGING OUT WITH YOU?
HA! NICE.
LOOK, SERIOUSLY-- WHAT WERE YOUR GRADES LIKE? 'CAUSE MINE SUCKED.
THERE'S NO REASON THEY SHOULD HAVE SCOUTED ME, EXCEPT PITY.
NOT THAT I'M COMPLAINING. I'M FINE WITH THIS BEING A CHARITY WARD, BUT I'M WITH DENNIS. THIS PLACE IS WEIRD.
WELL, WE'LL BE MEETING THE DEAN SOON. WHY DON'T YOU ASK HIM ABOUT IT?

BANG BANG BANG

OGDEN!

DEAN HOWARD OGDEN

OPEN THE DOOR, YOU OLD BASTARD! I CAN'T HOLD THE COUNCIL OFF ANY LONGER! AND THAT GODDAMN BUSIRUS TROPHY'S GONE MISSING AGAIN!

PROBLEM, MR. COLBY?

OH, NO! NO PROBLEM. JUST A FULL-BLOWN CRISIS! I--

CLICK SHHHHK KCHAK

CREEEE EEEE EEEEEAAAK

OH! OHHH! FOR GOD'S SAKE, HOWARD!

DEAN HOWARD OGDEN

>COUGH COUGH< SOMEONE GET A CUSTODIAN! TELL THEM TO BRING A FLAMETHROWER AND A BIBLE!

I TOLD YOU NOT TO BOTHER ME. GO AWAY. ALL OF YOU.

BUT, SIR, YOU ASKED TO SEE THE SCHOLARSHIP GROUP--

I'VE SEEN THEM. NOW I HAVE WORK TO DO.

BRUMP!

SOOOO, YEAH. THAT'S OUR DEAN.

ANYBODY HUNGRY?

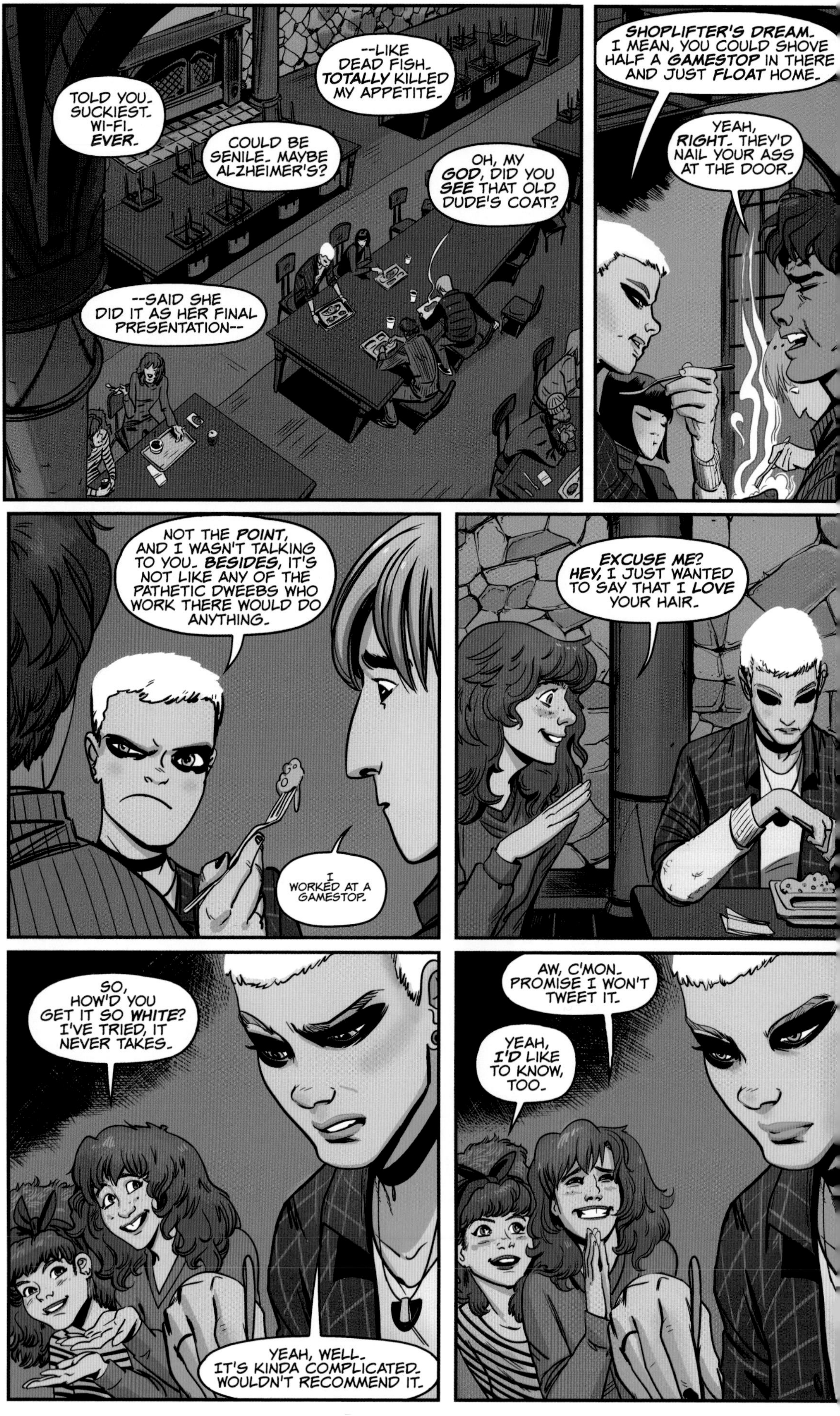
TOLD YOU. SUCKIEST. WI-FI. EVER.
COULD BE SENILE. MAYBE ALZHEIMER'S?
--LIKE DEAD FISH. TOTALLY KILLED MY APPETITE.
OH, MY GOD, DID YOU SEE THAT OLD DUDE'S COAT?
--SAID SHE DID IT AS HER FINAL PRESENTATION--
SHOPLIFTER'S DREAM. I MEAN, YOU COULD SHOVE HALF A GAMESTOP IN THERE AND JUST FLOAT HOME.
YEAH, RIGHT. THEY'D NAIL YOUR ASS AT THE DOOR.
NOT THE POINT, AND I WASN'T TALKING TO YOU. BESIDES, IT'S NOT LIKE ANY OF THE PATHETIC DWEEBS WHO WORK THERE WOULD DO ANYTHING.
I WORKED AT A GAMESTOP.
EXCUSE ME? HEY, I JUST WANTED TO SAY THAT I LOVE YOUR HAIR.
SO, HOW'D YOU GET IT SO WHITE? I'VE TRIED, IT NEVER TAKES.
YEAH, WELL. IT'S KINDA COMPLICATED. WOULDN'T RECOMMEND IT.
AW, C'MON. PROMISE I WON'T TWEET IT.
YEAH, I'D LIKE TO KNOW, TOO.

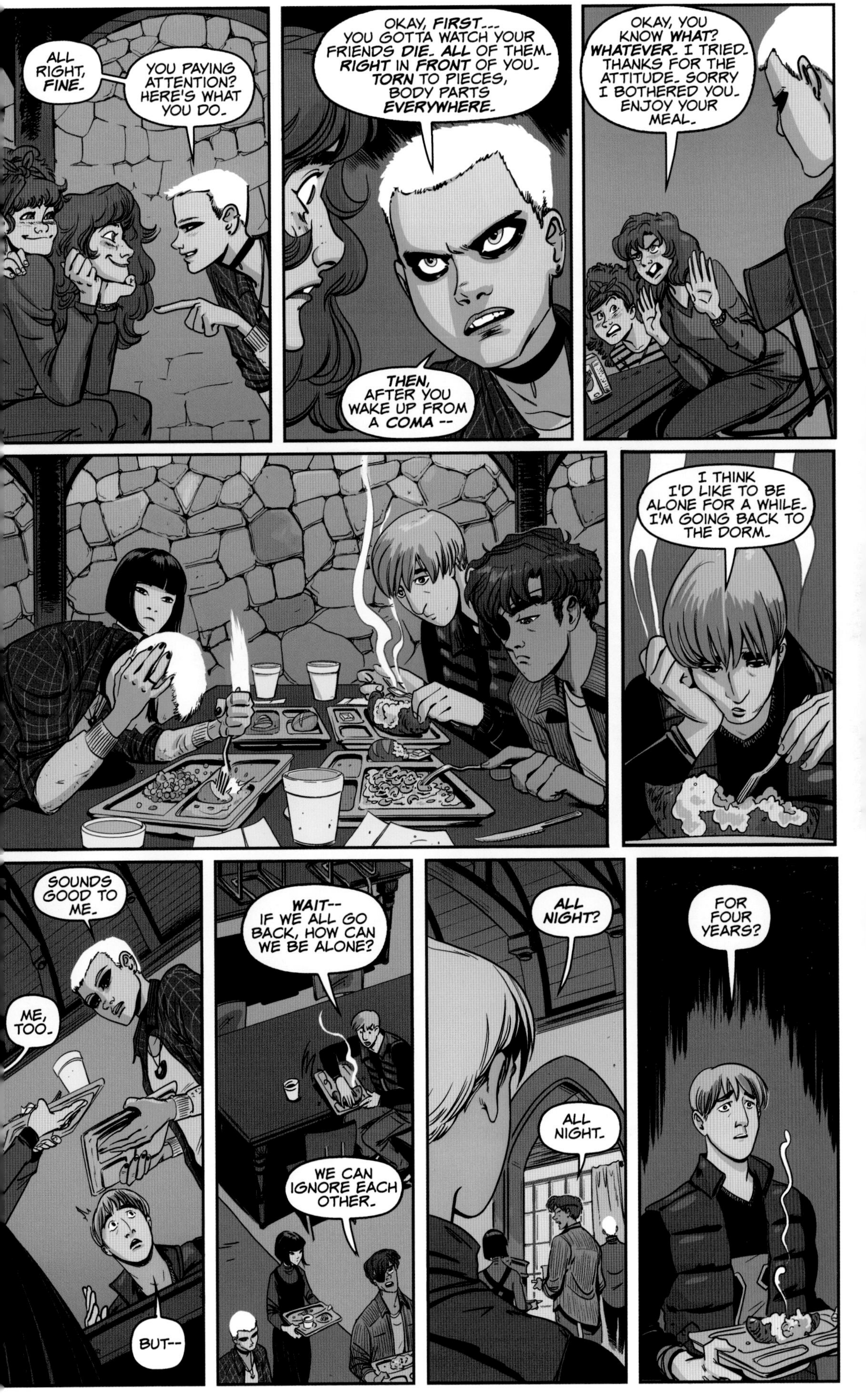
ALL RIGHT, FINE.
YOU PAYING ATTENTION? HERE'S WHAT YOU DO.
OKAY, FIRST... YOU GOTTA WATCH YOUR FRIENDS DIE. ALL OF THEM. RIGHT IN FRONT OF YOU. TORN TO PIECES, BODY PARTS EVERYWHERE.
THEN, AFTER YOU WAKE UP FROM A COMA --
OKAY, YOU KNOW WHAT? WHATEVER. I TRIED. THANKS FOR THE ATTITUDE. SORRY I BOTHERED YOU. ENJOY YOUR MEAL.
I THINK I'D LIKE TO BE ALONE FOR A WHILE. I'M GOING BACK TO THE DORM.
SOUNDS GOOD TO ME.
ME, TOO.
BUT--
WAIT-- IF WE ALL GO BACK, HOW CAN WE BE ALONE?
WE CAN IGNORE EACH OTHER.
ALL NIGHT?
ALL NIGHT.
FOR FOUR YEARS?

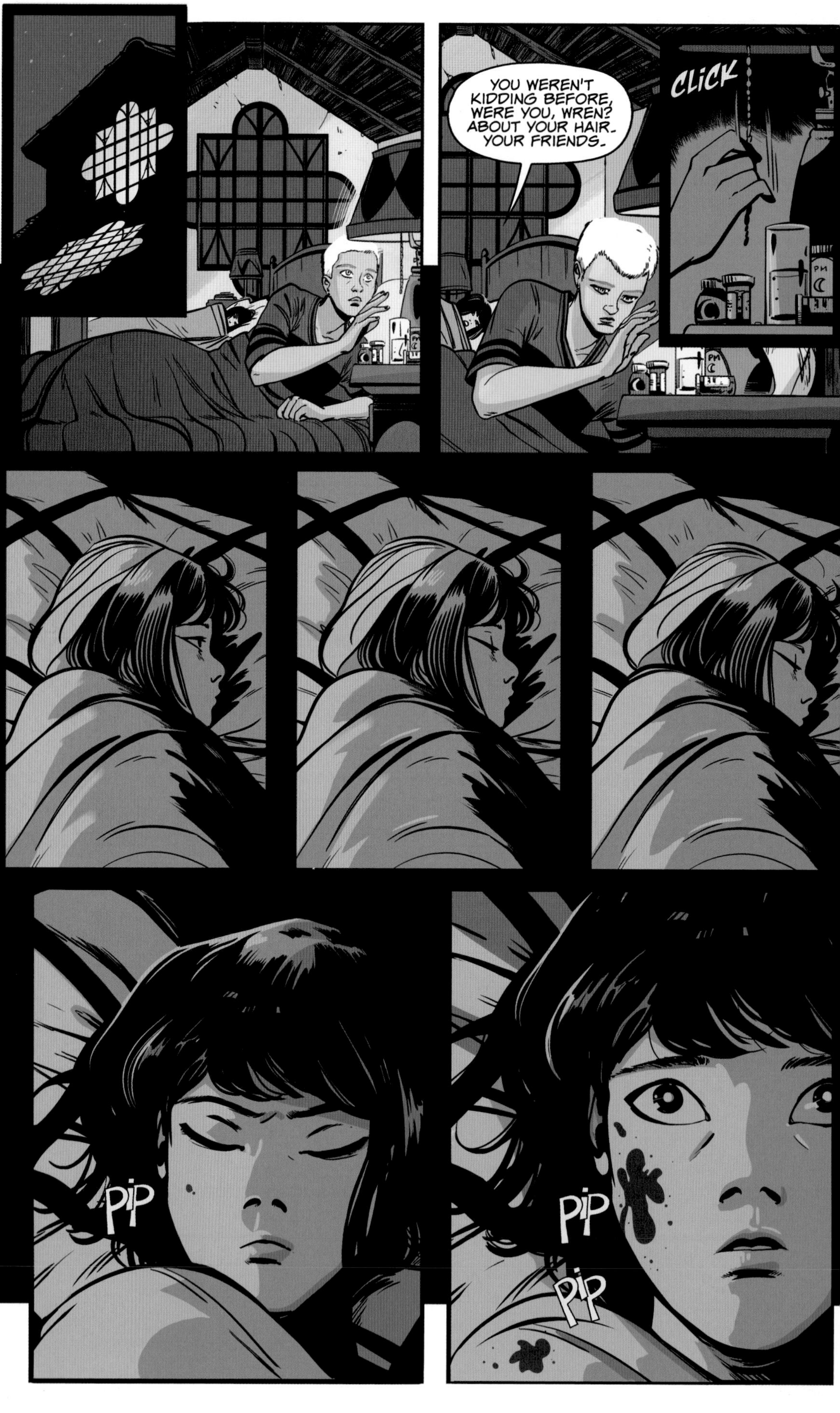
YOU WEREN'T KIDDING BEFORE, WERE YOU, WREN? ABOUT YOUR HAIR. YOUR FRIENDS.
CLICK
PIP
PIP
PIP

HELP ME. I'M DEAD. WE'RE ALL DEAD.

THEY WILL REND THE VEIL, AND HE WILL AWAKEN.

YOU CANNOT ALLOW THIS. YOU MUSTN'T! WE WILL NOT LET YOU!

DRETH VES UDRUMM!

DRETH VES ARGINOX!

!

LOOK, I SAID I DON'T WANT TO TALK ABOUT IT. I JUST WANT TO GET--

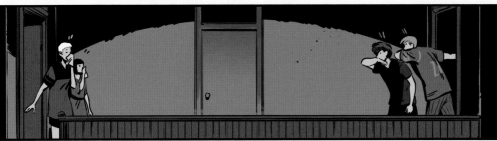

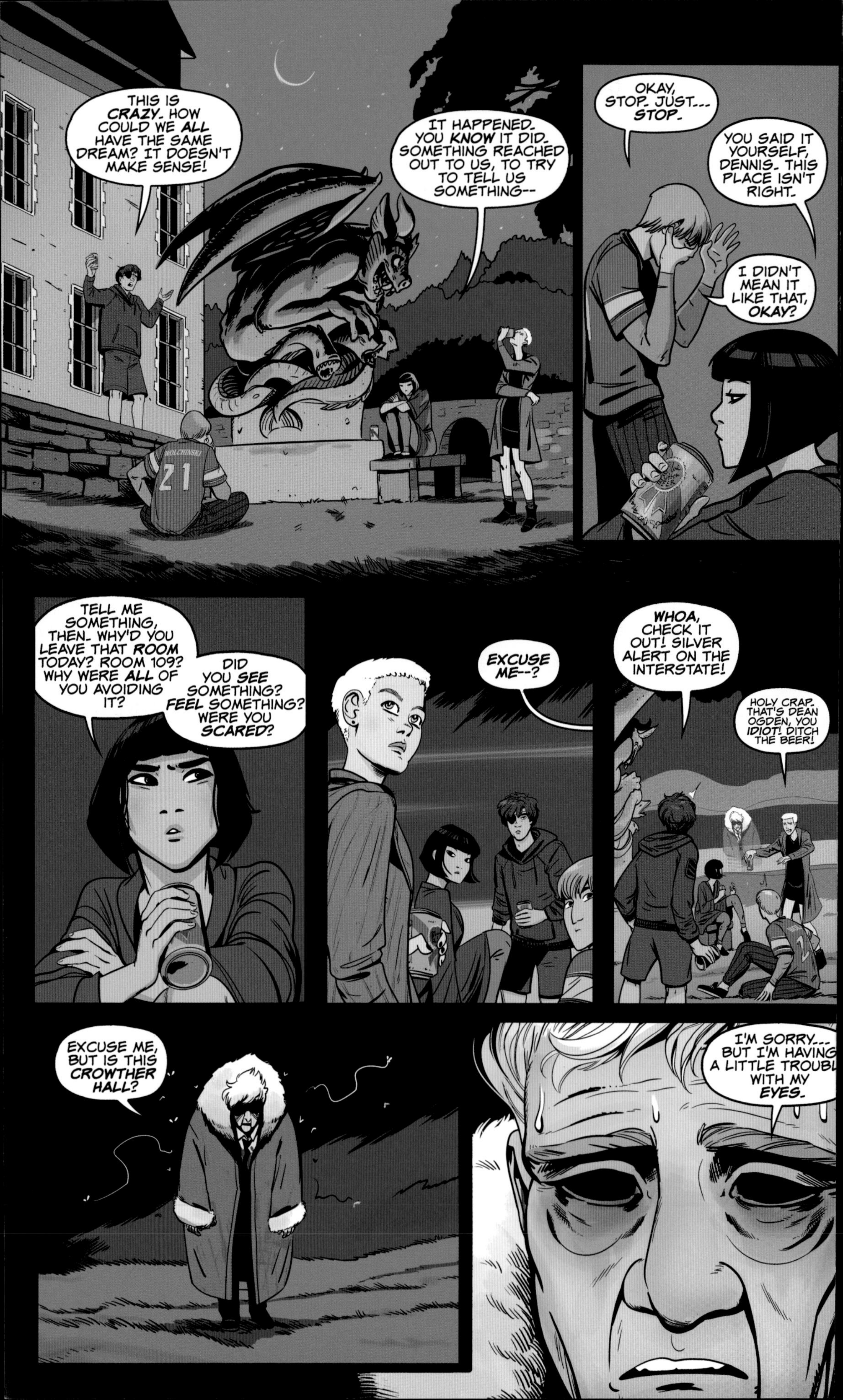
THIS IS CRAZY. HOW COULD WE ALL HAVE THE SAME DREAM? IT DOESN'T MAKE SENSE!
IT HAPPENED. YOU KNOW IT DID. SOMETHING REACHED OUT TO US, TO TRY TO TELL US SOMETHING--
WOLCHINSKI
21
OKAY, STOP. JUST... STOP.
YOU SAID IT YOURSELF, DENNIS. THIS PLACE ISN'T RIGHT.
I DIDN'T MEAN IT LIKE THAT, OKAY?
TELL ME SOMETHING, THEN. WHY'D YOU LEAVE THAT ROOM TODAY? ROOM 109? WHY WERE ALL OF YOU AVOIDING IT?
DID YOU SEE SOMETHING? FEEL SOMETHING? WERE YOU SCARED?
EXCUSE ME--?
WHOA, CHECK IT OUT! SILVER ALERT ON THE INTERSTATE!
HOLY CRAP. THAT'S DEAN OGDEN, YOU IDIOT! DITCH THE BEER!
EXCUSE ME, BUT IS THIS CROWTHER HALL?
I'M SORRY... BUT I'M HAVING A LITTLE TROUBL WITH MY EYES.

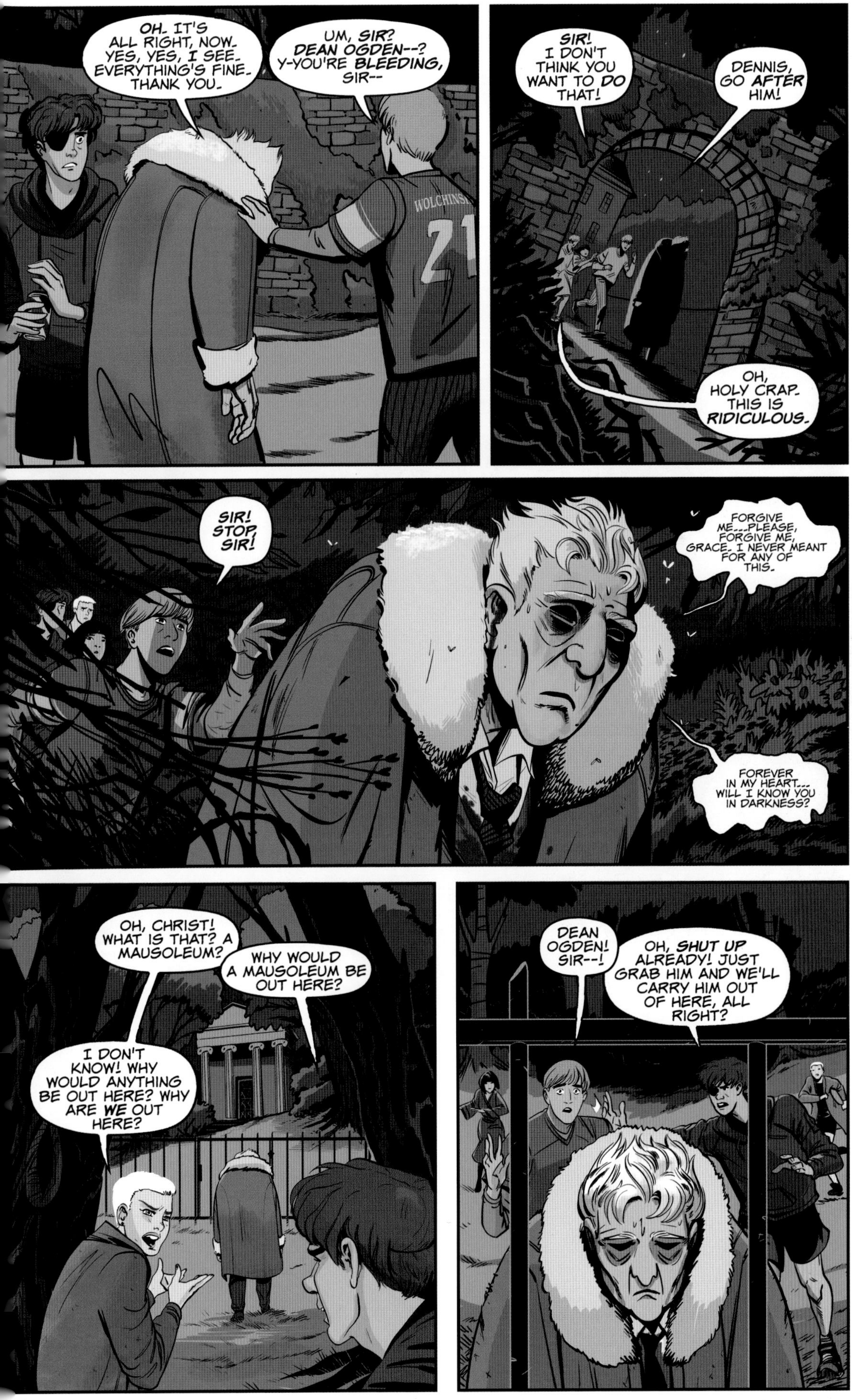
OH. IT'S ALL RIGHT, NOW. YES, YES, I SEE. EVERYTHING'S FINE. THANK YOU.
UM, SIR? DEAN OGDEN--? Y-YOU'RE BLEEDING, SIR--
WOLCHINSK 21
SIR! I DON'T THINK YOU WANT TO DO THAT!
DENNIS, GO AFTER HIM!
OH, HOLY CRAP. THIS IS RIDICULOUS.
SIR! STOP, SIR!
FORGIVE ME...PLEASE, FORGIVE ME, GRACE. I NEVER MEANT FOR ANY OF THIS.
FOREVER IN MY HEART... WILL I KNOW YOU IN DARKNESS?
OH, CHRIST! WHAT IS THAT? A MAUSOLEUM?
WHY WOULD A MAUSOLEUM BE OUT HERE?
I DON'T KNOW! WHY WOULD ANYTHING BE OUT HERE? WHY ARE WE OUT HERE?
DEAN OGDEN! SIR--!
OH, SHUT UP ALREADY! JUST GRAB HIM AND WE'LL CARRY HIM OUT OF HERE, ALL RIGHT?

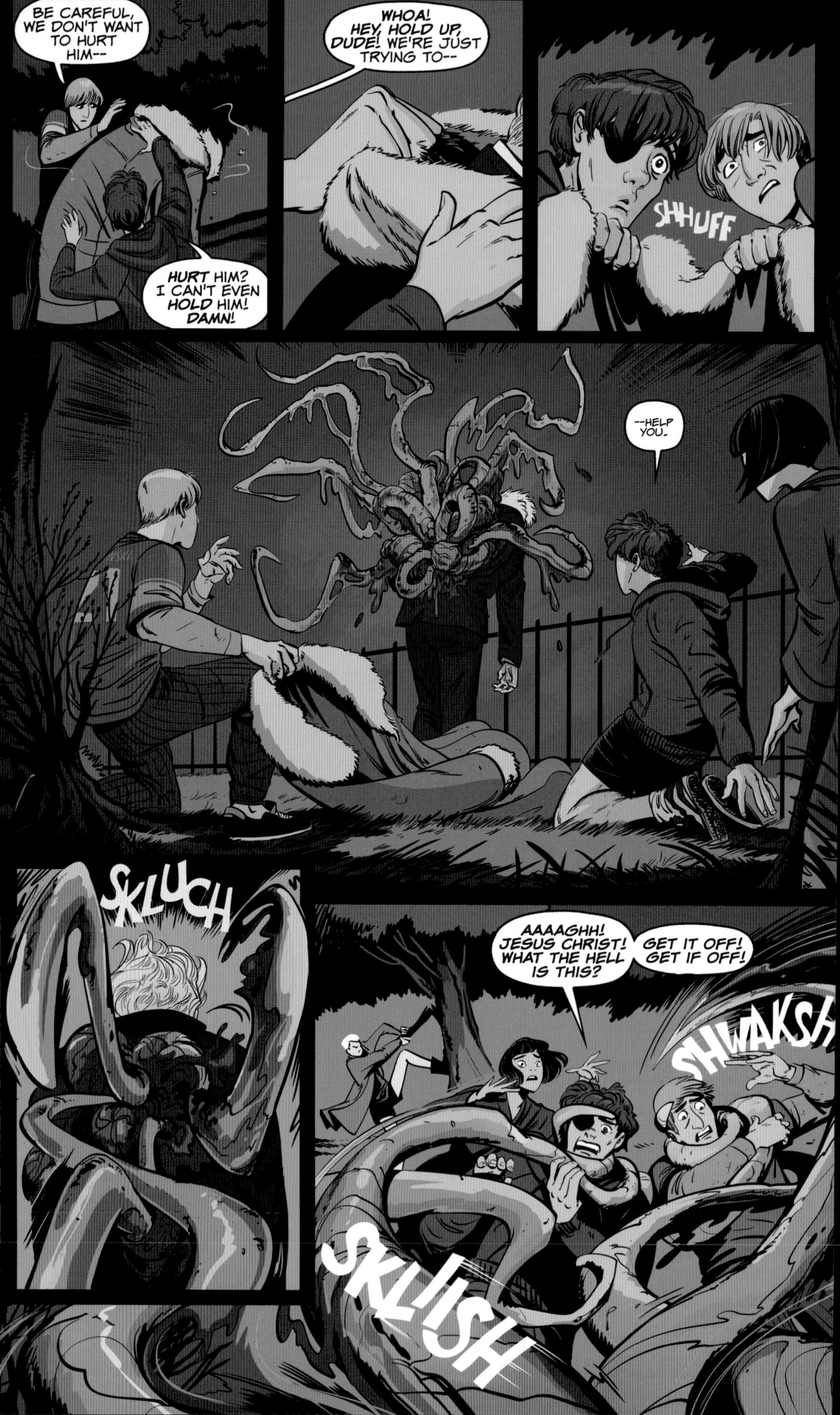
BE CAREFUL, WE DON'T WANT TO HURT HIM--
HURT HIM? I CAN'T EVEN HOLD HIM! DAMN!
WHOA! HEY, HOLD UP, DUDE! WE'RE JUST TRYING TO--
SHHUFF
--HELP YOU.
SKLUCH
AAAAGHH! JESUS CHRIST! WHAT THE HELL IS THIS?
GET IT OFF! GET IF OFF!
SHWAKSH
SKLISH

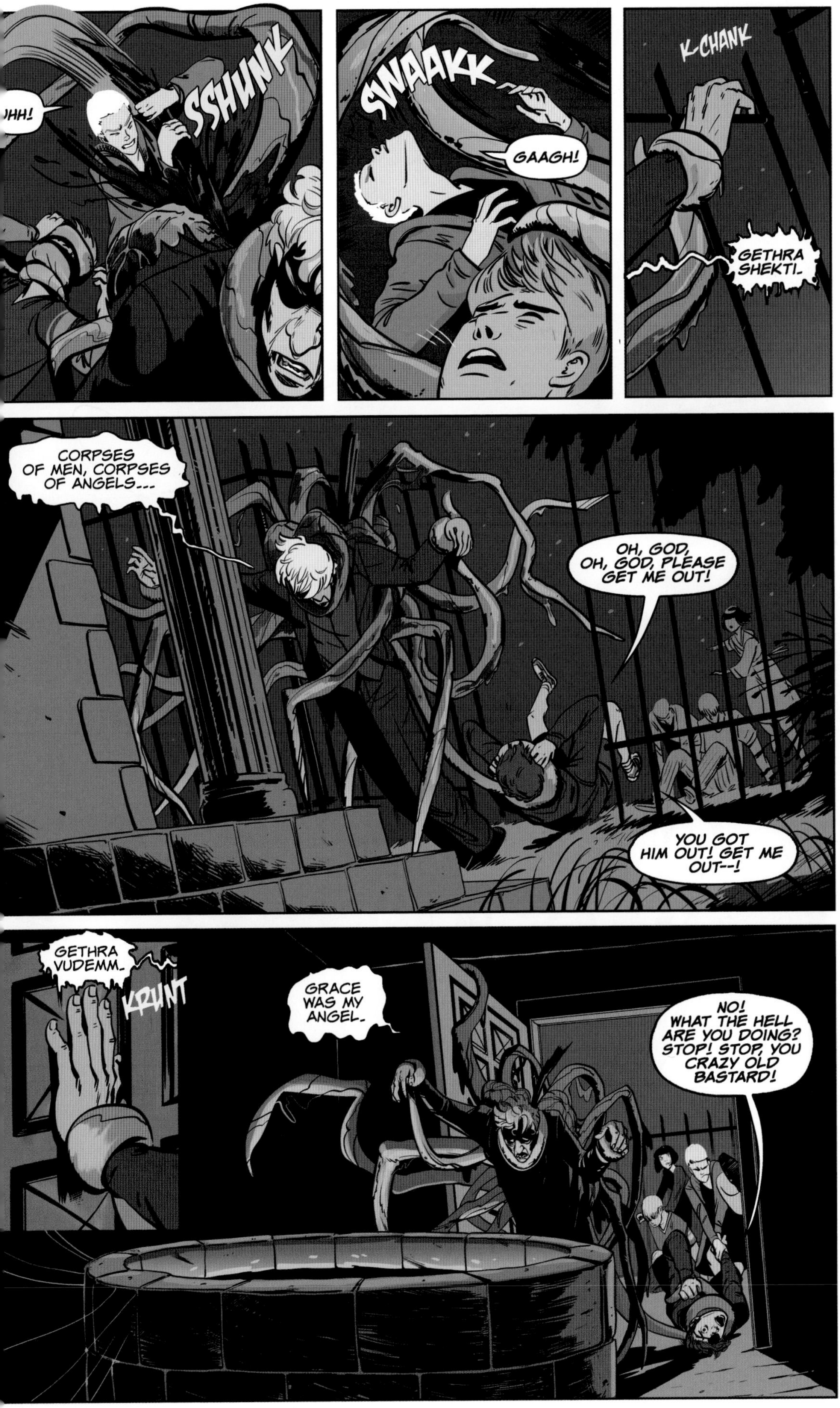
HH!
SSHUNK
SWAAKK
GAAGH!
K-CHANK
GETHRA SHEKTI.
CORPSES OF MEN, CORPSES OF ANGELS...
OH, GOD, OH, GOD, PLEASE GET ME OUT!
YOU GOT HIM OUT! GET ME OUT--!
GETHRA VUDEMM.
KRUNT
GRACE WAS MY ANGEL.
NO! WHAT THE HELL ARE YOU DOING? STOP! STOP, YOU CRAZY OLD BASTARD!

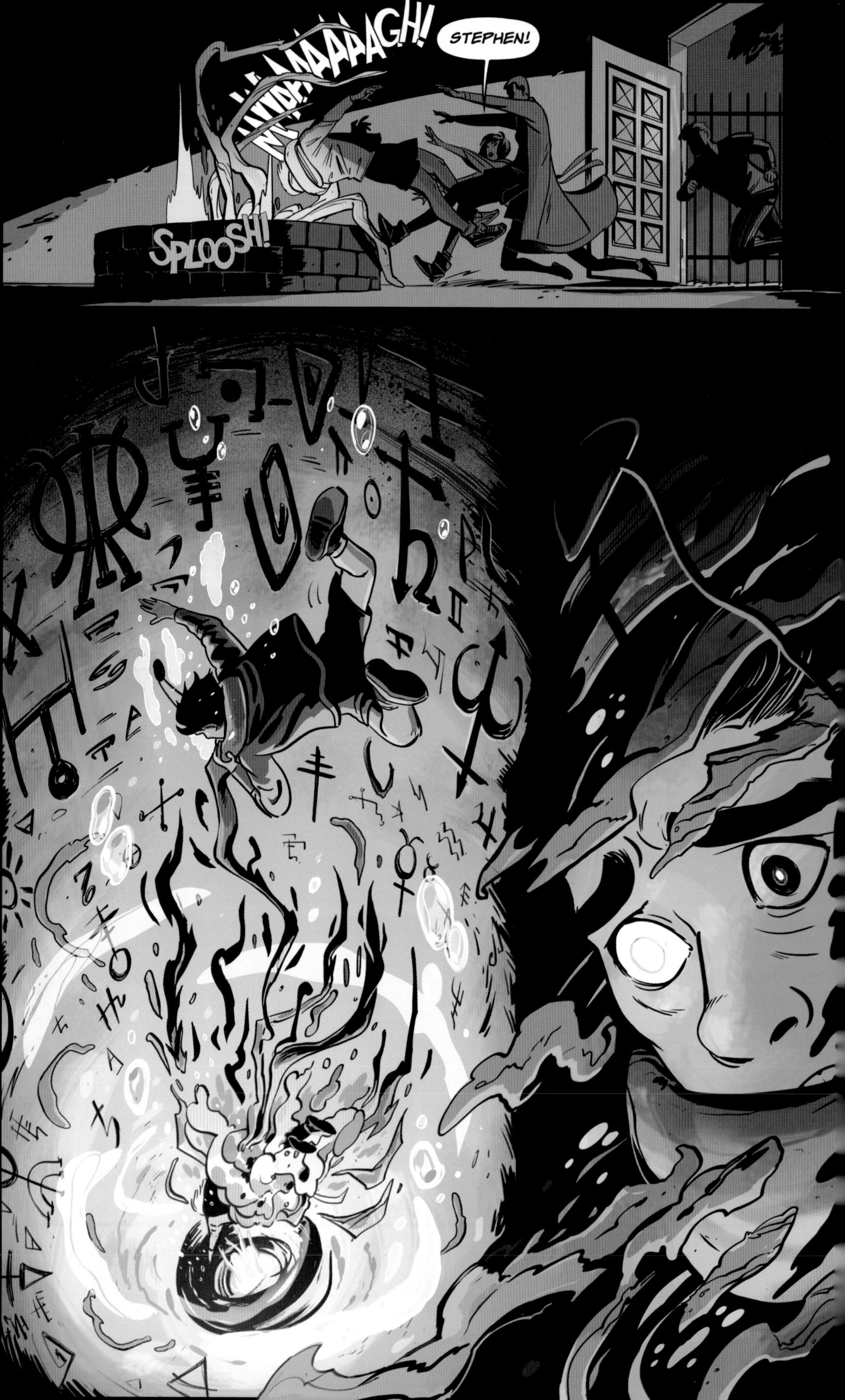
AAAAGH!
STEPHEN!
SPLOOSH!

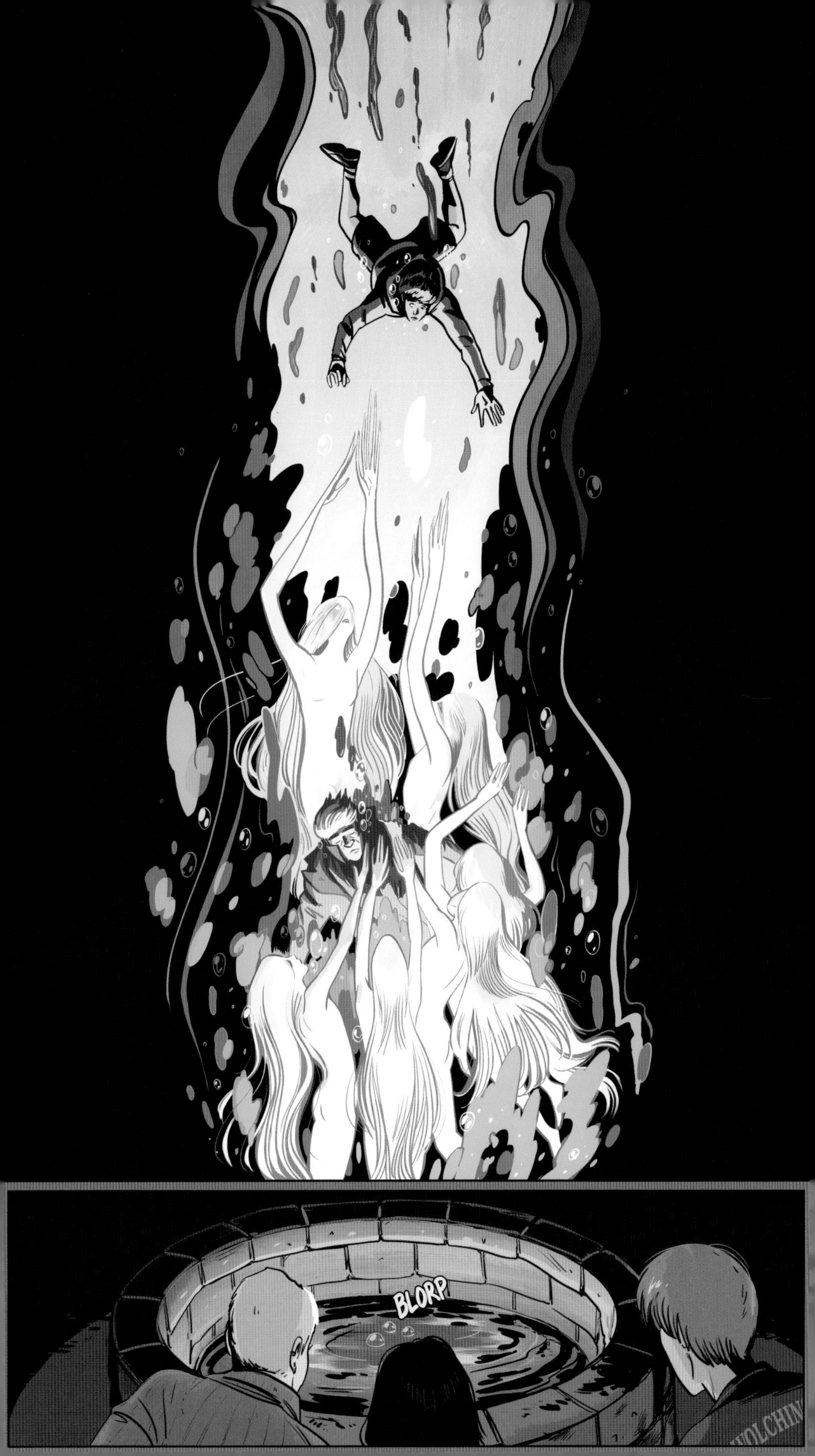
BLORP

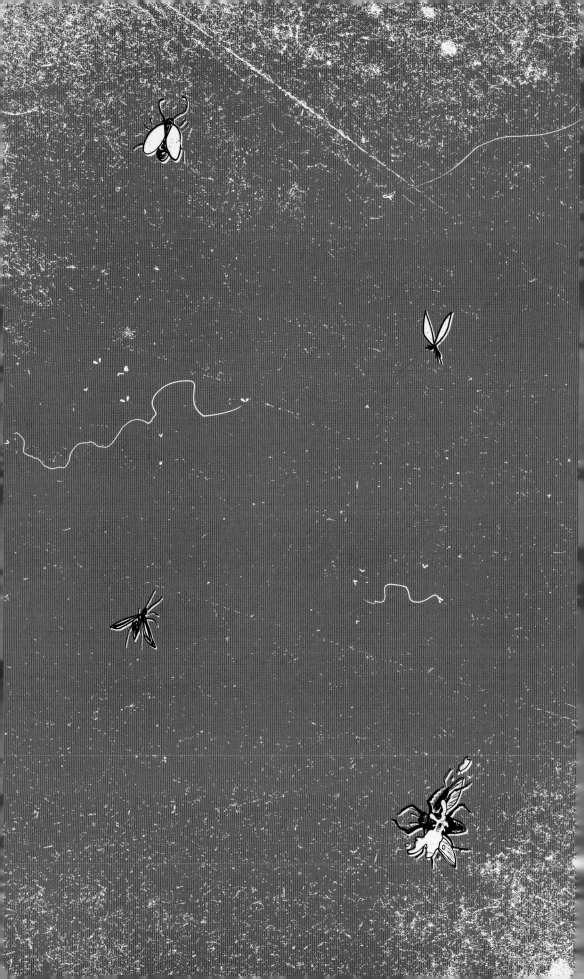

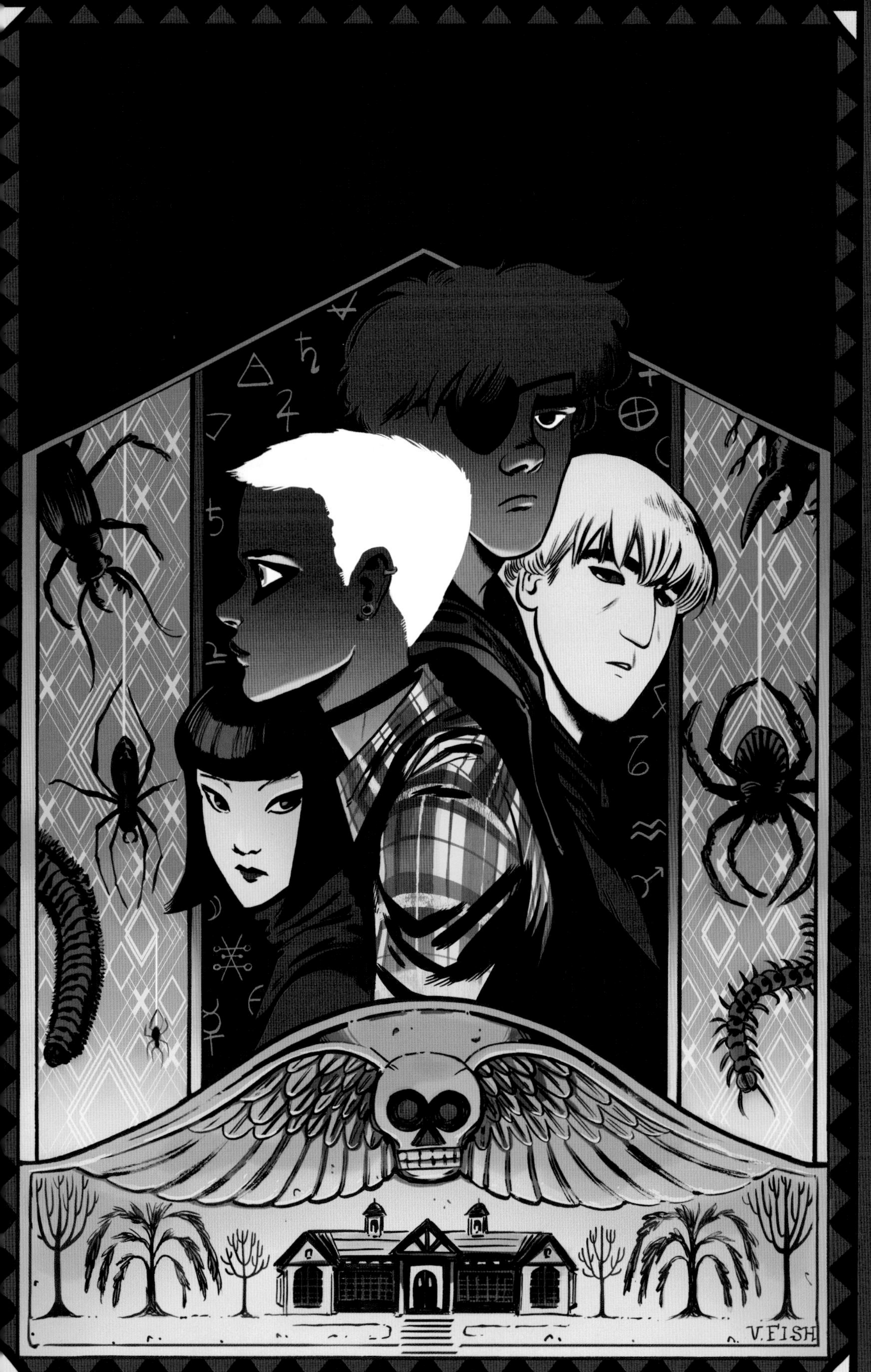
V. FISH

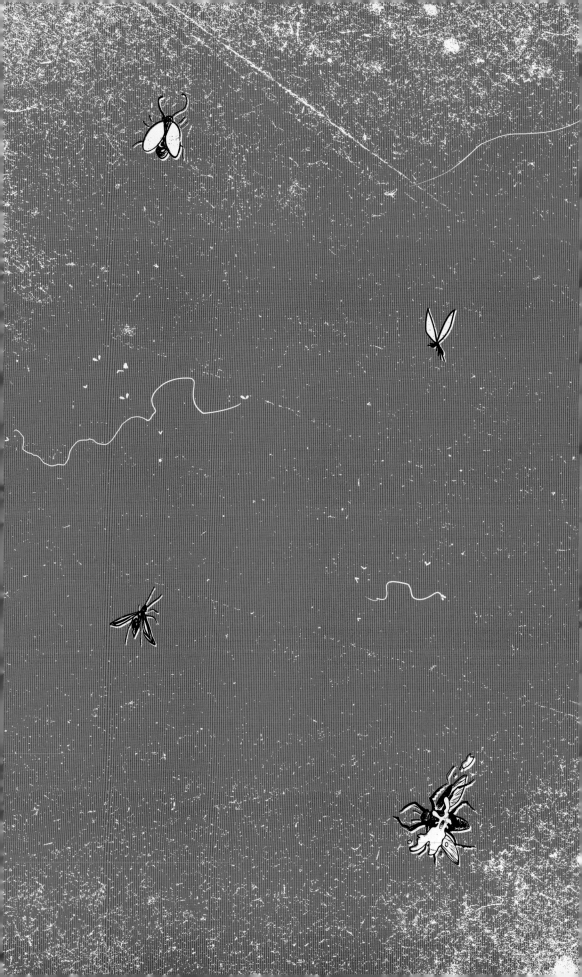

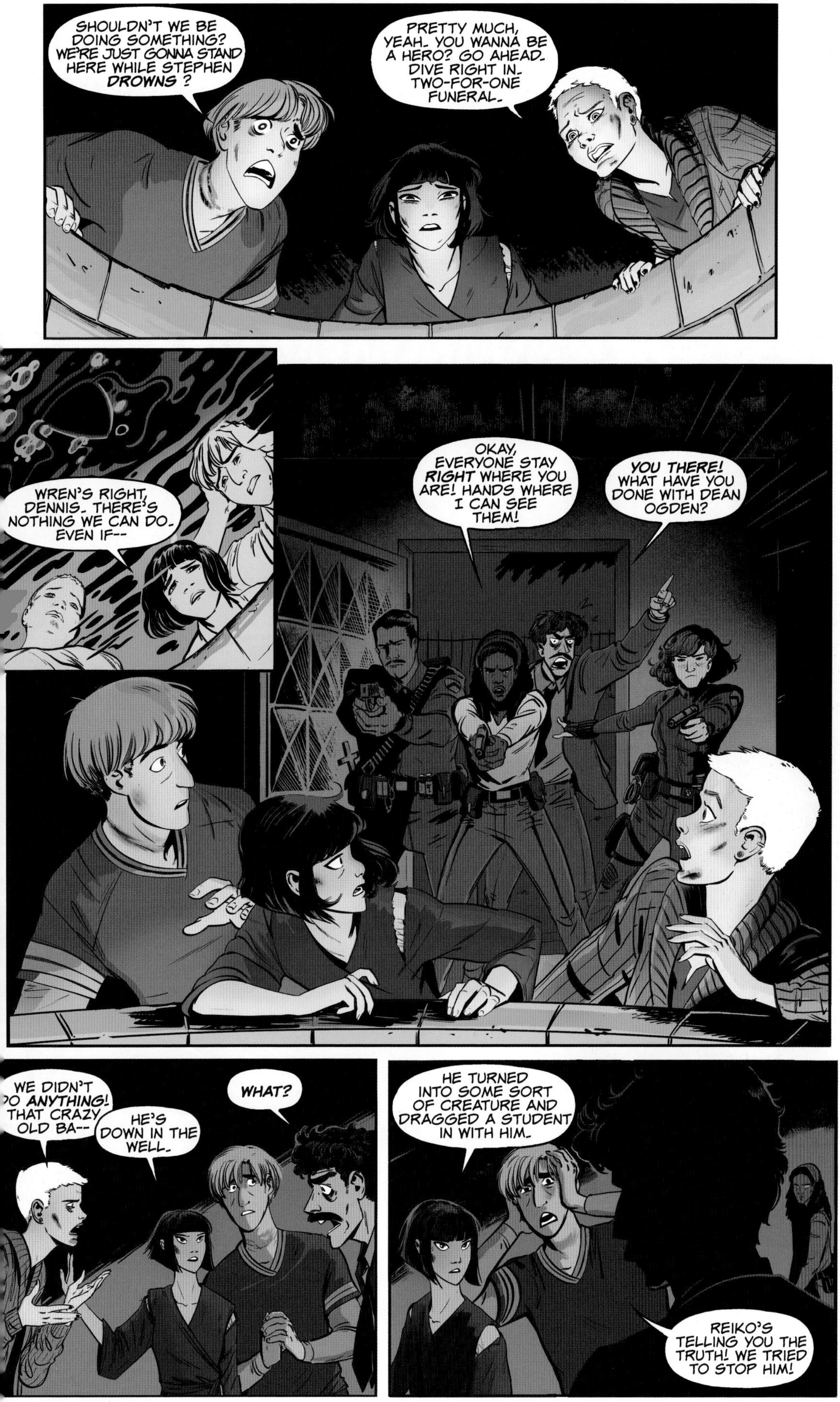
SHOULDN'T WE BE DOING SOMETHING? WE'RE JUST GONNA STAND HERE WHILE STEPHEN DROWNS ?
PRETTY MUCH, YEAH. YOU WANNA BE A HERO? GO AHEAD. DIVE RIGHT IN. TWO-FOR-ONE FUNERAL.
WREN'S RIGHT, DENNIS. THERE'S NOTHING WE CAN DO. EVEN IF--
OKAY, EVERYONE STAY RIGHT WHERE YOU ARE! HANDS WHERE I CAN SEE THEM!
YOU THERE! WHAT HAVE YOU DONE WITH DEAN OGDEN?
WE DIDN'T DO ANYTHING! THAT CRAZY OLD BA--
HE'S DOWN IN THE WELL.
WHAT?
HE TURNED INTO SOME SORT OF CREATURE AND DRAGGED A STUDENT IN WITH HIM.
REIKO'S TELLING YOU THE TRUTH! WE TRIED TO STOP HIM!

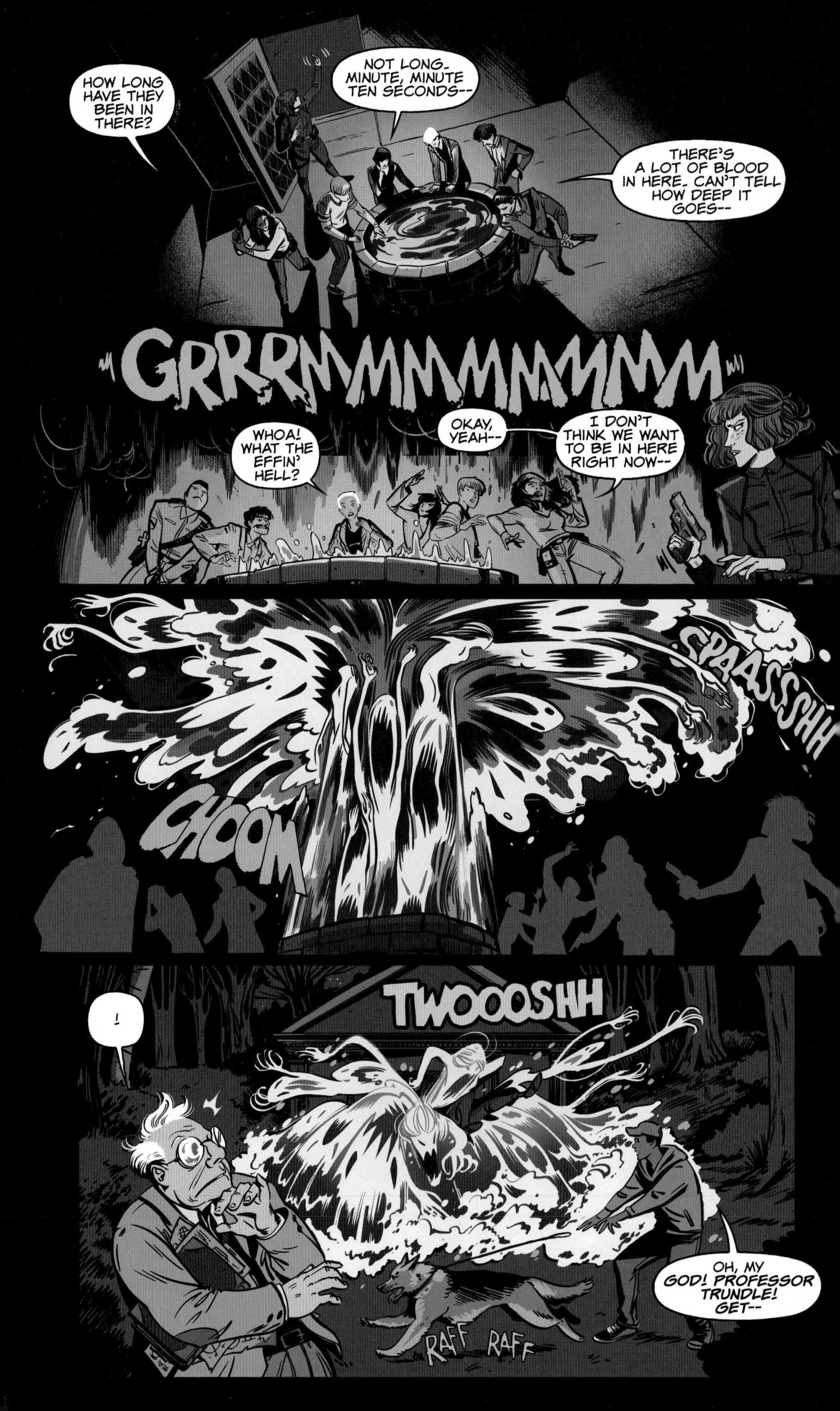
HOW LONG HAVE THEY BEEN IN THERE?
NOT LONG. MINUTE, MINUTE TEN SECONDS--
THERE'S A LOT OF BLOOD IN HERE. CAN'T TELL HOW DEEP IT GOES--
GRRRMMMMMMMMM
WHOA! WHAT THE EFFIN' HELL?
OKAY, YEAH--
I DON'T THINK WE WANT TO BE IN HERE RIGHT NOW--
SPAASSSHH
CHOOM
TWOOOSHH
!
OH, MY GOD! PROFESSOR TRUNDLE! GET--
RAFF RAFF

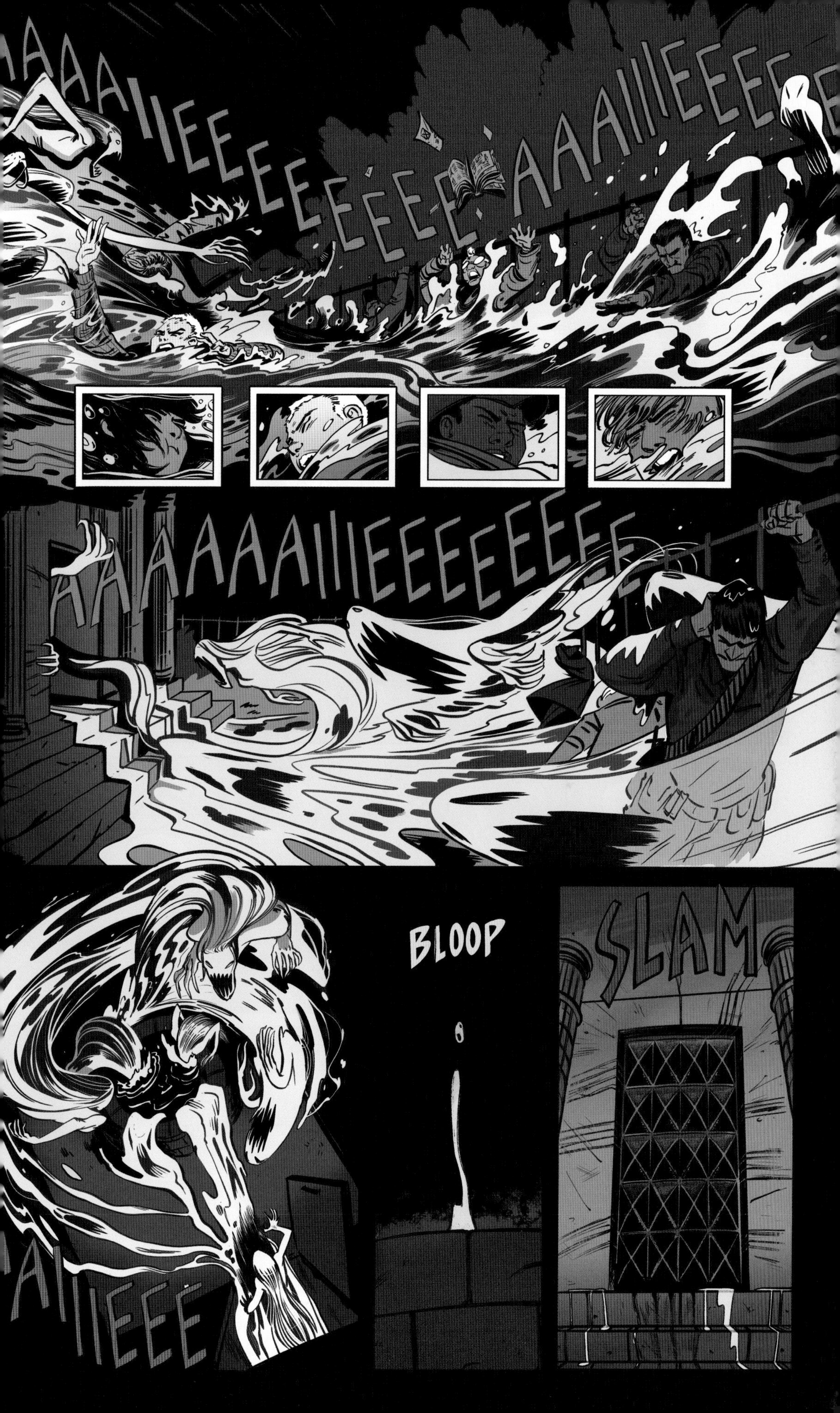
AAAAIIIEEEEEEEEE
AAAIIIEEEEE
AAAAAIIIEEEEEEEEE
AIIIEEEE
BLOOP
SLAM

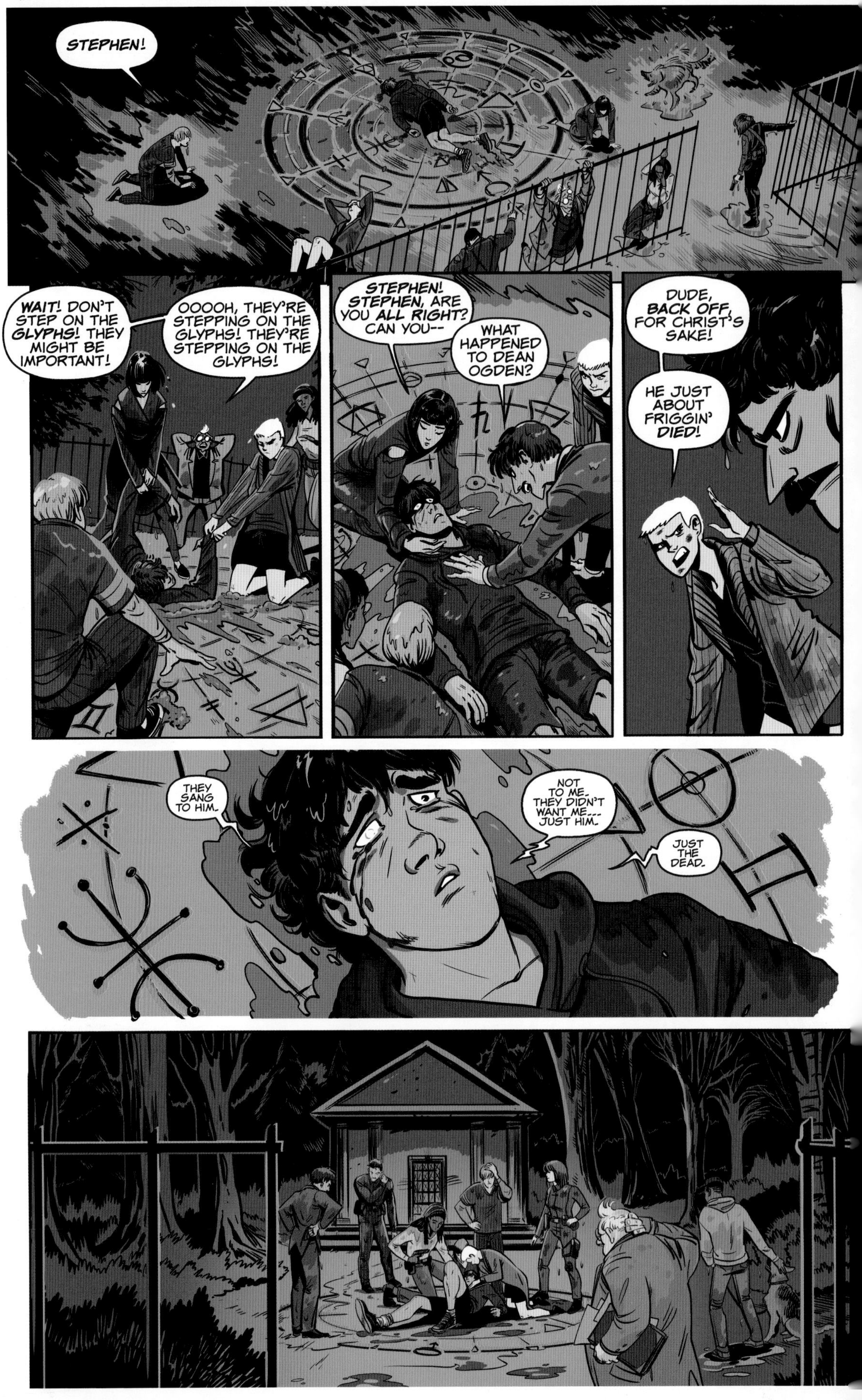
STEPHEN!
WAIT! DON'T STEP ON THE GLYPHS! THEY MIGHT BE IMPORTANT!
OOOOH, THEY'RE STEPPING ON THE GLYPHS! THEY'RE STEPPING ON THE GLYPHS!
STEPHEN! STEPHEN, ARE YOU ALL RIGHT? CAN YOU--
WHAT HAPPENED TO DEAN OGDEN?
DUDE, BACK OFF, FOR CHRIST'S SAKE!
HE JUST ABOUT FRIGGIN' DIED!
THEY SANG TO HIM.
NOT TO ME. THEY DIDN'T WANT ME... JUST HIM.
JUST THE DEAD.

IS THERE ANYTHING ELSE ANY OF YOU CAN REMEMBER? ANYTHING?

I CAN'T THINK OF ANYTHING.

I TOLD YOU EVERYTHING I KNOW... OR THINK I KNOW.

HEY, *I'VE* GOT A QUESTION... WHAT THE *HELL* IS GOING ON HERE?

YOU'LL EXCUSE ME, BUT I DON'T HAVE TIME FOR QUESTIONS RIGHT NOW.

LET ME REMIND YOU I JUST LOST MY CLOSEST FRIEND AND MENTOR.

AND UNTIL THINGS GET SORTED OUT OR I THROW MYSELF BENEATH A FAST-MOVING TRUCK, I AM--MUCH TO MY OWN INCREASING *HORROR*--THE ACTING DEAN OF THIS SCHOOL.

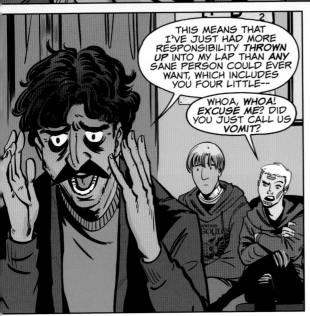

THIS MEANS THAT I'VE JUST HAD MORE RESPONSIBILITY *THROWN* UP INTO MY LAP THAN *ANY* SANE PERSON COULD EVER WANT, WHICH INCLUDES YOU FOUR LITTLE--

WHOA, WHOA! *EXCUSE ME?* DID YOU JUST CALL US VOMIT?

IT'S BEEN A LONG NIGHT, COLBY. EVERYONE'S KEYED UP. WHY DON'T YOU GIVE THESE KIDS A BREAK?

RIGHT.

DR. SORUM'S RIGHT. WE'LL FINISH THIS LATER. MY OFFICE, THREE O'CLOCK.

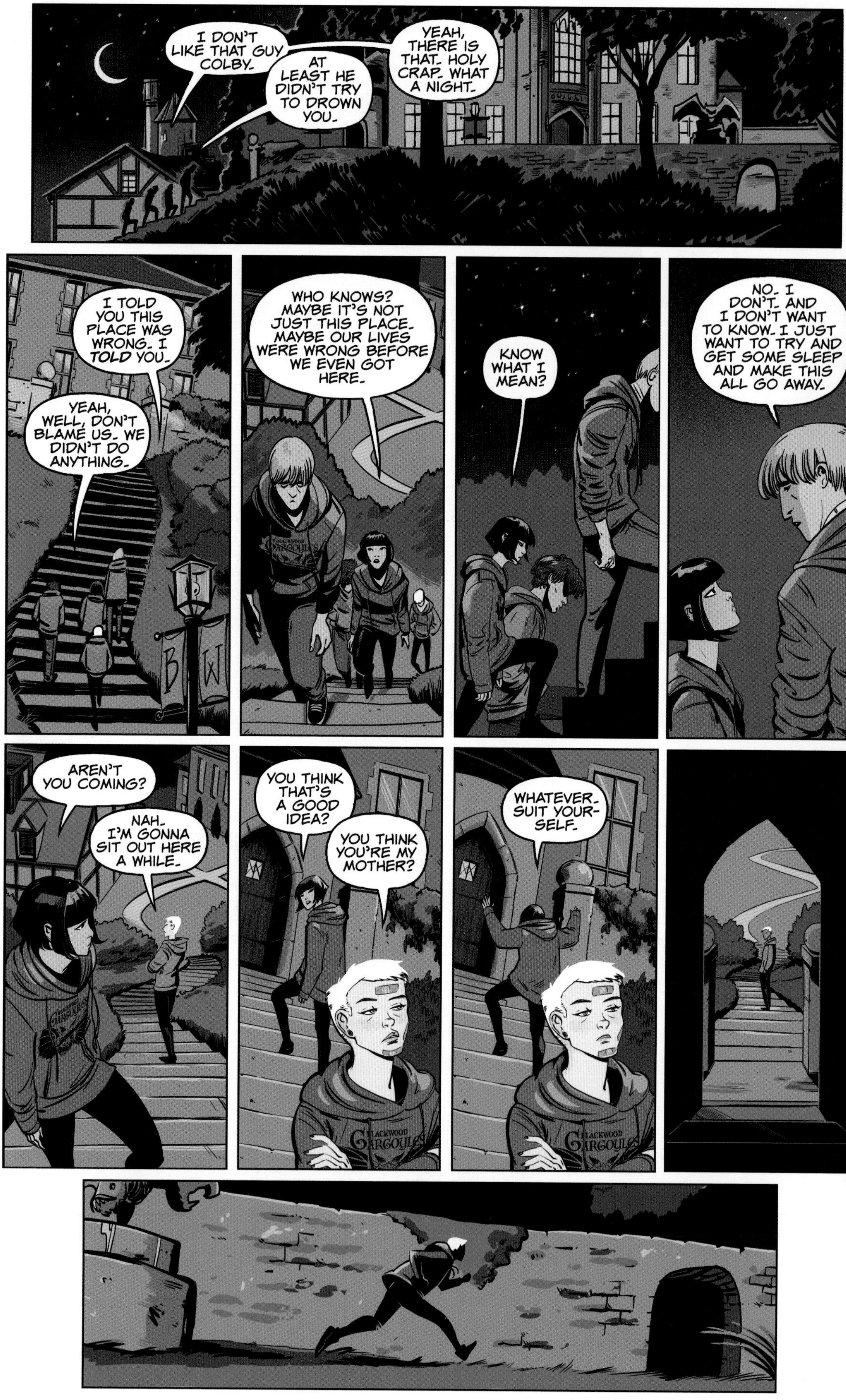
I DON'T LIKE THAT GUY COLBY.
AT LEAST HE DIDN'T TRY TO DROWN YOU.
YEAH, THERE IS THAT. HOLY CRAP. WHAT A NIGHT.
I TOLD YOU THIS PLACE WAS WRONG. I *TOLD* YOU.
YEAH, WELL, DON'T BLAME US. WE DIDN'T DO ANYTHING.
BLACKWOOD GARGOYLES
WHO KNOWS? MAYBE IT'S NOT JUST THIS PLACE. MAYBE OUR LIVES WERE WRONG BEFORE WE EVEN GOT HERE.
KNOW WHAT I MEAN?
NO. I DON'T. AND I DON'T WANT TO KNOW. I JUST WANT TO TRY AND GET SOME SLEEP AND MAKE THIS ALL GO AWAY.
AREN'T YOU COMING?
NAH. I'M GONNA SIT OUT HERE A WHILE.
YOU THINK THAT'S A GOOD IDEA?
YOU THINK YOU'RE MY MOTHER?
WHATEVER. SUIT YOURSELF.

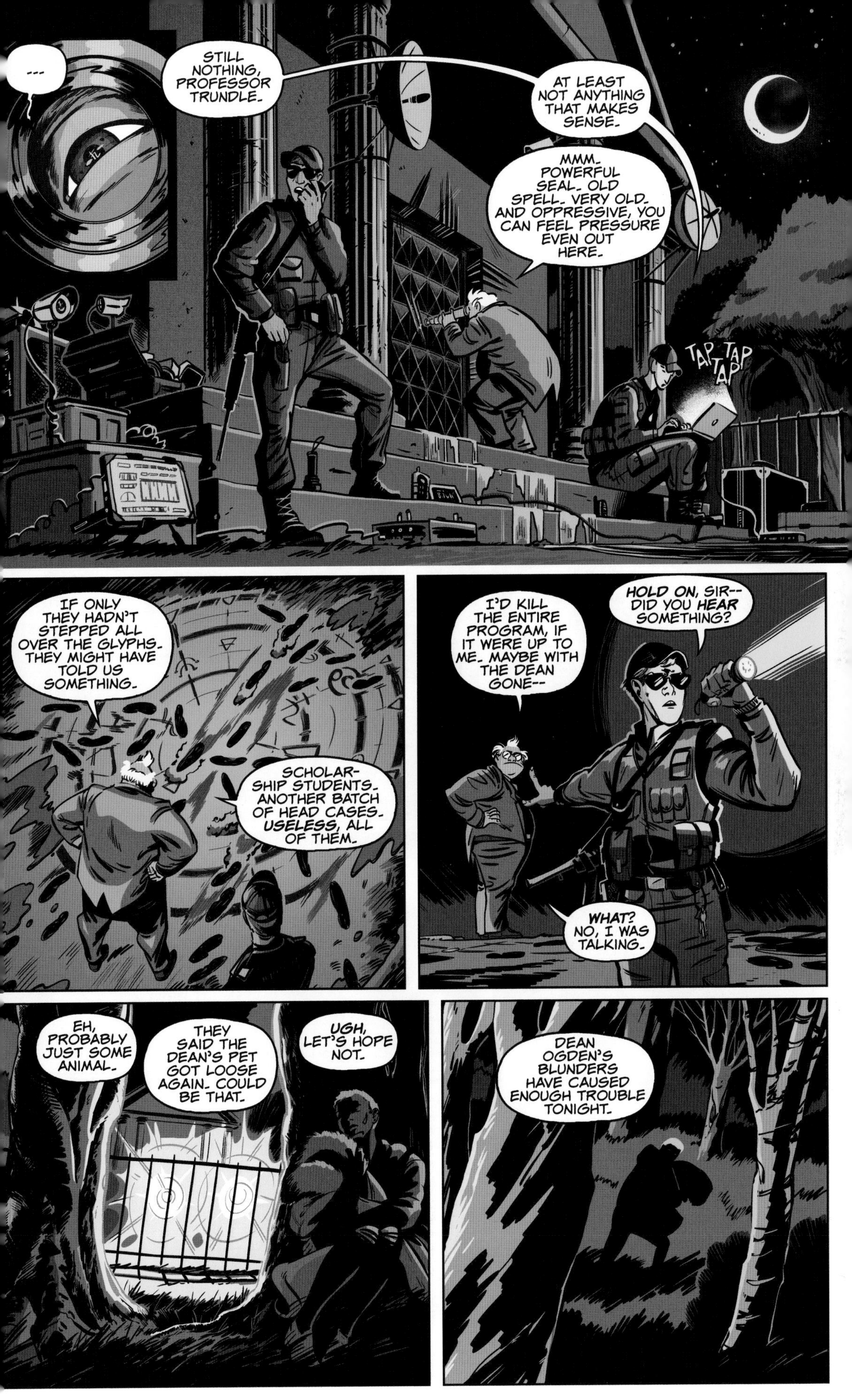
...
STILL NOTHING, PROFESSOR TRUNDLE.
AT LEAST NOT ANYTHING THAT MAKES SENSE.
MMM. POWERFUL SEAL. OLD SPELL. VERY OLD. AND OPPRESSIVE, YOU CAN FEEL PRESSURE EVEN OUT HERE.
TAP TAP TAP
IF ONLY THEY HADN'T STEPPED ALL OVER THE GLYPHS. THEY MIGHT HAVE TOLD US SOMETHING.
SCHOLAR-SHIP STUDENTS. ANOTHER BATCH OF HEAD CASES. USELESS, ALL OF THEM.
I'D KILL THE ENTIRE PROGRAM, IF IT WERE UP TO ME. MAYBE WITH THE DEAN GONE--
HOLD ON, SIR-- DID YOU HEAR SOMETHING?
WHAT? NO, I WAS TALKING.
EH, PROBABLY JUST SOME ANIMAL.
THEY SAID THE DEAN'S PET GOT LOOSE AGAIN. COULD BE THAT.
UGH, LET'S HOPE NOT.
DEAN OGDEN'S BLUNDERS HAVE CAUSED ENOUGH TROUBLE TONIGHT.

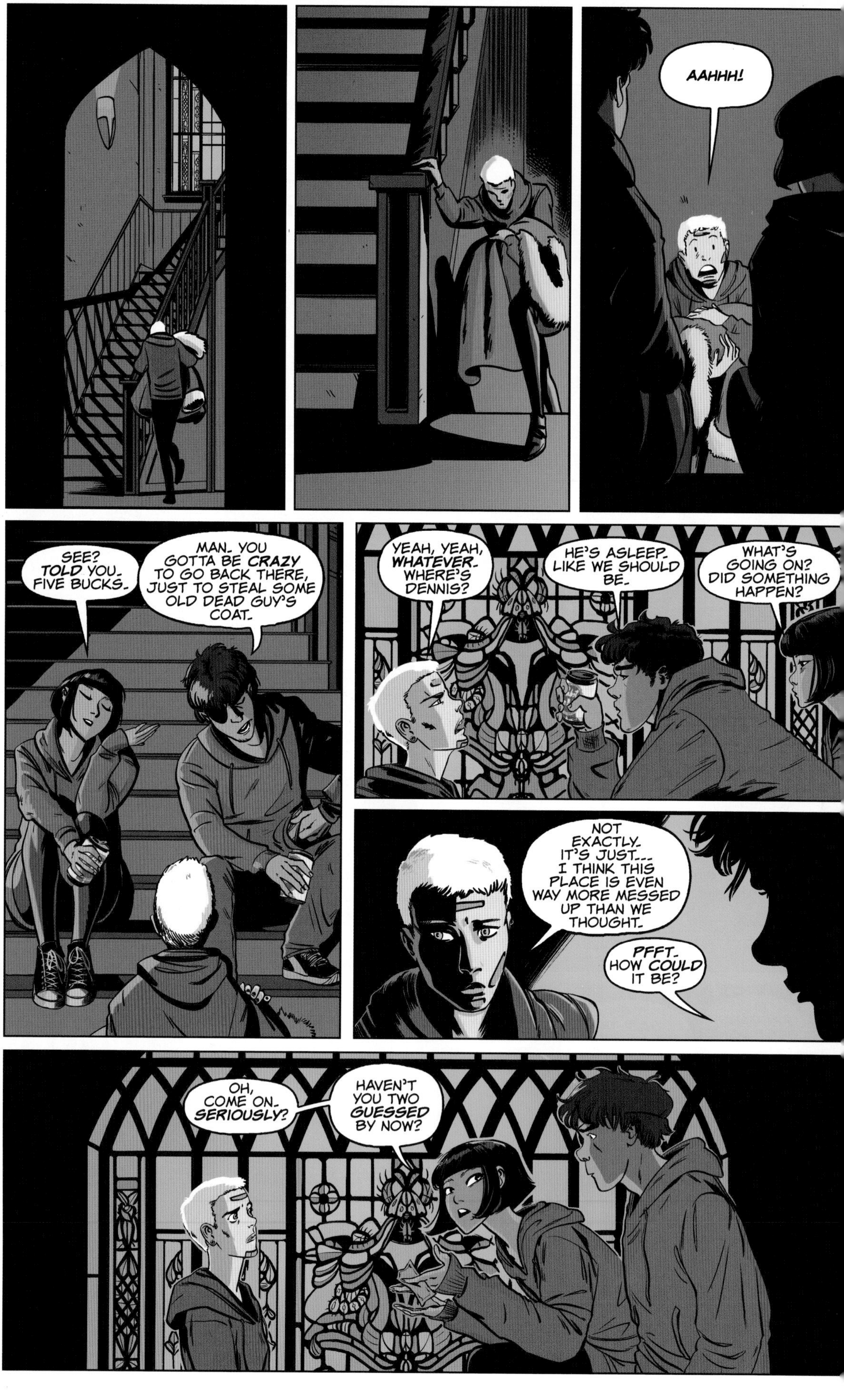
AAHHH!
SEE? TOLD YOU. FIVE BUCKS.
MAN. YOU GOTTA BE CRAZY TO GO BACK THERE, JUST TO STEAL SOME OLD DEAD GUY'S COAT.
YEAH, YEAH, WHATEVER. WHERE'S DENNIS?
HE'S ASLEEP. LIKE WE SHOULD BE.
WHAT'S GOING ON? DID SOMETHING HAPPEN?
NOT EXACTLY. IT'S JUST... I THINK THIS PLACE IS EVEN WAY MORE MESSED UP THAN WE THOUGHT.
PFFT. HOW COULD IT BE?
OH, COME ON. SERIOUSLY?
HAVEN'T YOU TWO GUESSED BY NOW?

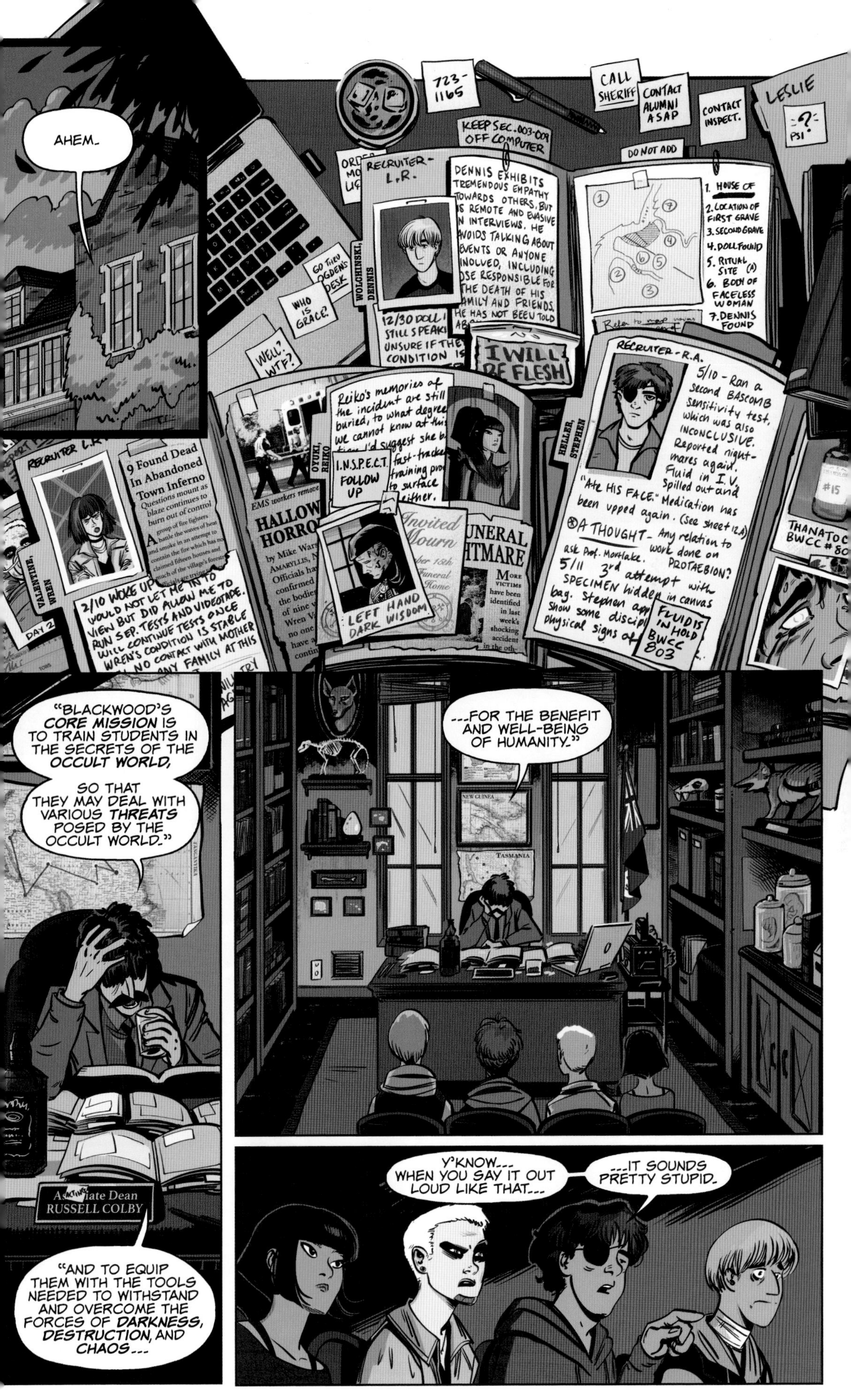
AHEM.
"BLACKWOOD'S CORE MISSION IS TO TRAIN STUDENTS IN THE SECRETS OF THE OCCULT WORLD,
SO THAT THEY MAY DEAL WITH VARIOUS THREATS POSED BY THE OCCULT WORLD."
...FOR THE BENEFIT AND WELL-BEING OF HUMANITY."
"AND TO EQUIP THEM WITH THE TOOLS NEEDED TO WITHSTAND AND OVERCOME THE FORCES OF DARKNESS, DESTRUCTION, AND CHAOS...
Y'KNOW... WHEN YOU SAY IT OUT LOUD LIKE THAT...
...IT SOUNDS PRETTY STUPID.

WHAT CAN I TELL YOU? IT'S AN OUTDATED MANUAL.

SHOULD BE A NEWER ONE AROUND HERE SOMEWHERE....

SHUFF CLUNK

RUSSE

SO IT'S *TRUE* THEN? LIKE REIKO SAID? YOU'RE RUNNING AN OCCULT SCHOOL. AN *ACTUAL* OCCULT SCHOOL.

MAGIC AND GHOSTS AND ALL THAT STUFF.

WELL, IF YOU WANT TO PUT IT IN STRICTLY MORONIC TERMS....

YEAH, I *DO*, ACTUALLY.

OKAY. *GREAT.* MAKES THINGS EASIER FOR ME.

NOW, THEN-- THERE ARE *TWO* SCHOOLS HERE AT BLACKWOOD. GOT THAT?

THERE'S THE ONE WE LET *EVERYONE* SEE, THE LOOPY ONE THAT TEACHES THE HISTORY OF FUNNY OLD BELIEFS AND PRACTICES AND WHAT HAVE YOU.

AND THEN THERE'S THE *OTHER* SCHOOL, HIDDEN INSIDE THAT ONE, A SECRET EVEN TO MANY OF OUR STUDENTS.

WHERE IT'S ALL *REAL.* AN ALWAYS H. BEEN.

Drink Me

NGK

--COUGH--

HANGOVER CURE.

WORKS LIKE A CHARM, FORTY PERCENT OF THE TIME. HERE'S TO HOPING.

--COUGH--

TAK

TAXONOMY

OYUKI, R

OH, HEY. FOUND A NEWER MANUAL.

BLACKWOOD COLLEGE
Policies & Practices
1988 Edition

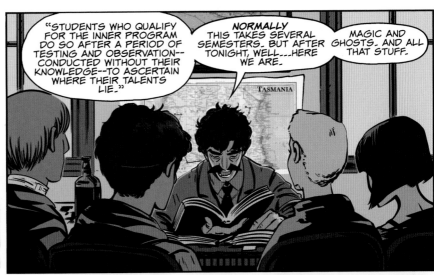

"STUDENTS WHO QUALIFY FOR THE INNER PROGRAM DO SO AFTER A PERIOD OF TESTING AND OBSERVATION-- CONDUCTED WITHOUT THEIR KNOWLEDGE--TO ASCERTAIN WHERE THEIR TALENTS LIE."

NORMALLY THIS TAKES SEVERAL SEMESTERS. BUT AFTER TONIGHT, WELL...HERE WE ARE.

MAGIC AND GHOSTS. AND ALL THAT STUFF.

TASMANIA

SERIOUSLY? YOU GIVE OUT SCHOLARSHIPS TO A SCHOOL THAT'S ALL *MESSED UP* LIKE THIS?

THAT'S *WRONG,* MAN. THAT'S JUST *EFFING* WRONG.

MAYBE. MAYBE NOT. SEE, I'VE READ YOUR RECRUITMENT FILES. SO I KNOW LAST NIGHT WASN'T THE FIRST TIME YOU FOUR HAVE EXPERIENCED SOMETHING "ALL MESSED UP."

EACH OF YOU HAS BEEN THROUGH SOME VERY TRYING--AND VERY *TRAGIC*-- EVENTS OF A CERTAIN NATURE.

THAT'S HOW YOU CAME TO OUR ATTENTION. WE'VE FOUND THAT YOUNG PEOPLE WITH YOUR PARTICULAR BACKGROUNDS CAN BE PROMISING CANDIDATES FOR LEARNING...

...WELL, YOU KNOW.

THE SECRETS OF THE OCCULT WORLD.

FOR THE SOMETHING- SOMETHING OF HUMANITY.

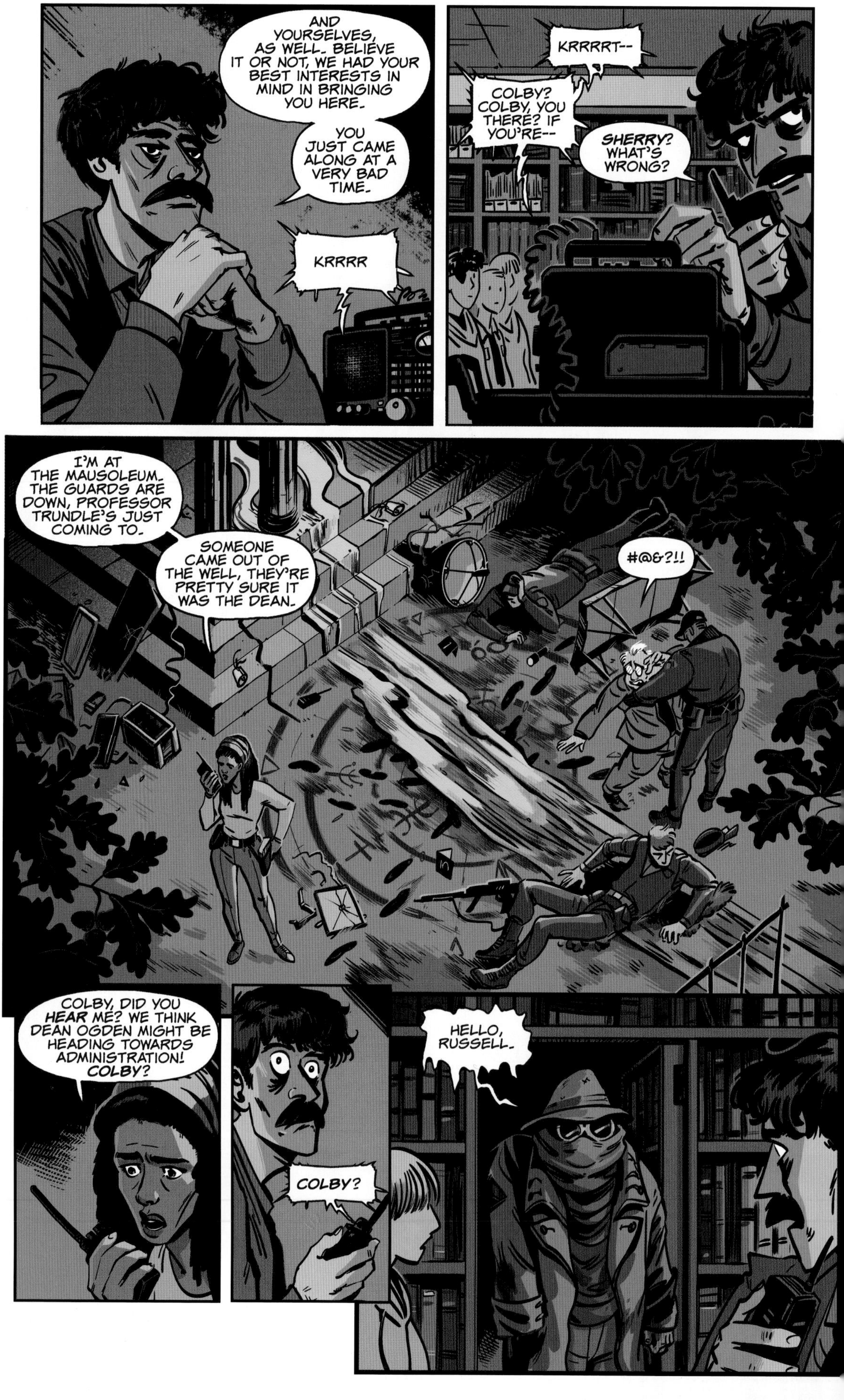
AND YOURSELVES, AS WELL. BELIEVE IT OR NOT, WE HAD YOUR BEST INTERESTS IN MIND IN BRINGING YOU HERE.
YOU JUST CAME ALONG AT A VERY BAD TIME.
KRRRR
KRRRRT--
COLBY? COLBY, YOU THERE? IF YOU'RE--
SHERRY? WHAT'S WRONG?
I'M AT THE MAUSOLEUM. THE GUARDS ARE DOWN, PROFESSOR TRUNDLE'S JUST COMING TO.
SOMEONE CAME OUT OF THE WELL, THEY'RE PRETTY SURE IT WAS THE DEAN.
#@&?!!
COLBY, DID YOU HEAR ME? WE THINK DEAN OGDEN MIGHT BE HEADING TOWARDS ADMINISTRATION! COLBY?
COLBY?
HELLO, RUSSELL.

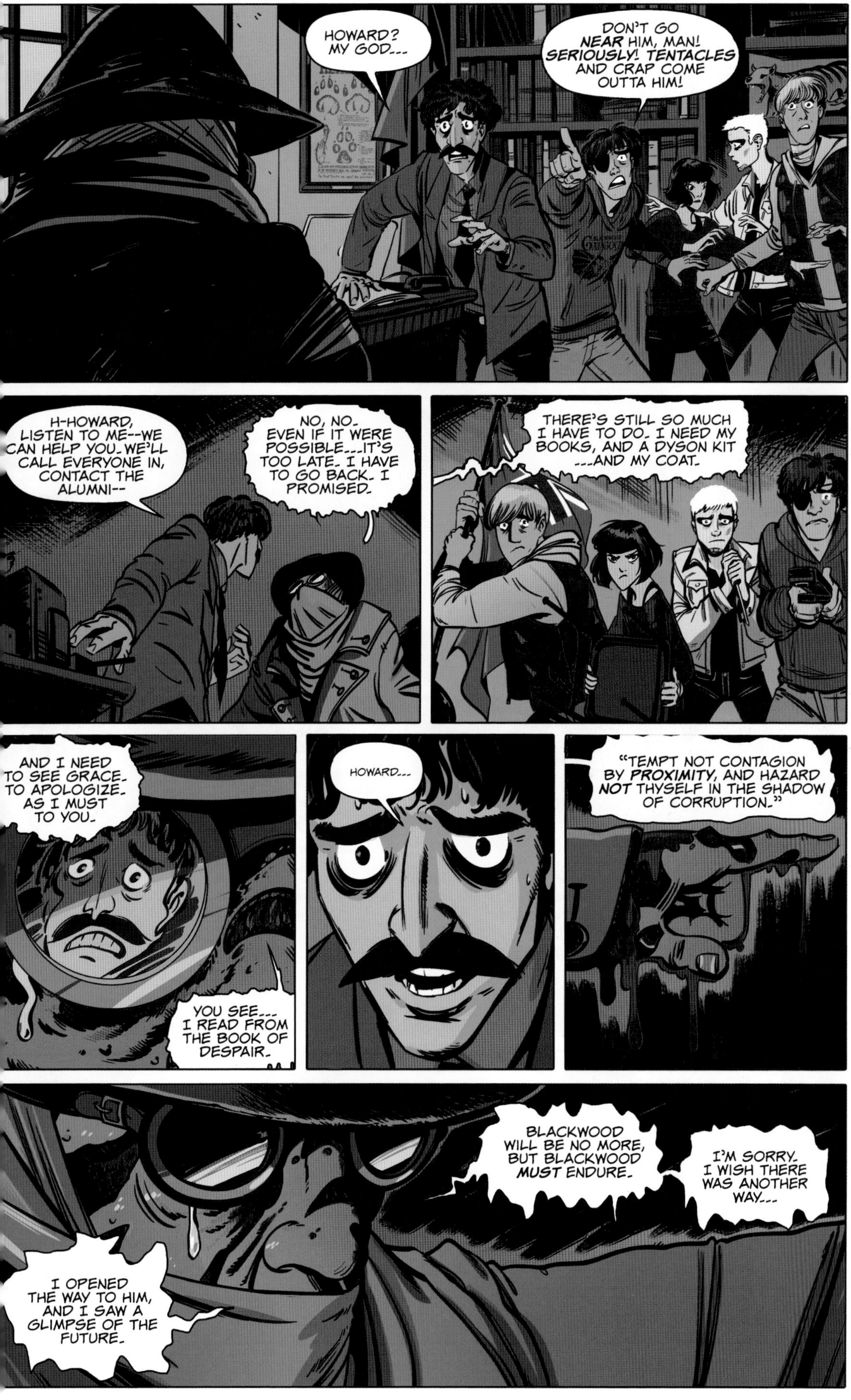
HOWARD? MY GOD...
DON'T GO NEAR HIM, MAN! SERIOUSLY! TENTACLES AND CRAP COME OUTTA HIM!
H-HOWARD, LISTEN TO ME--WE CAN HELP YOU. WE'LL CALL EVERYONE IN, CONTACT THE ALUMNI--
NO, NO. EVEN IF IT WERE POSSIBLE...IT'S TOO LATE. I HAVE TO GO BACK. I PROMISED.
THERE'S STILL SO MUCH I HAVE TO DO. I NEED MY BOOKS, AND A DYSON KIT ...AND MY COAT.
AND I NEED TO SEE GRACE. TO APOLOGIZE. AS I MUST TO YOU.
YOU SEE... I READ FROM THE BOOK OF DESPAIR.
HOWARD...
"TEMPT NOT CONTAGION BY PROXIMITY, AND HAZARD NOT THYSELF IN THE SHADOW OF CORRUPTION."
I OPENED THE WAY TO HIM, AND I SAW A GLIMPSE OF THE FUTURE.
BLACKWOOD WILL BE NO MORE, BUT BLACKWOOD MUST ENDURE.
I'M SORRY. I WISH THERE WAS ANOTHER WAY...

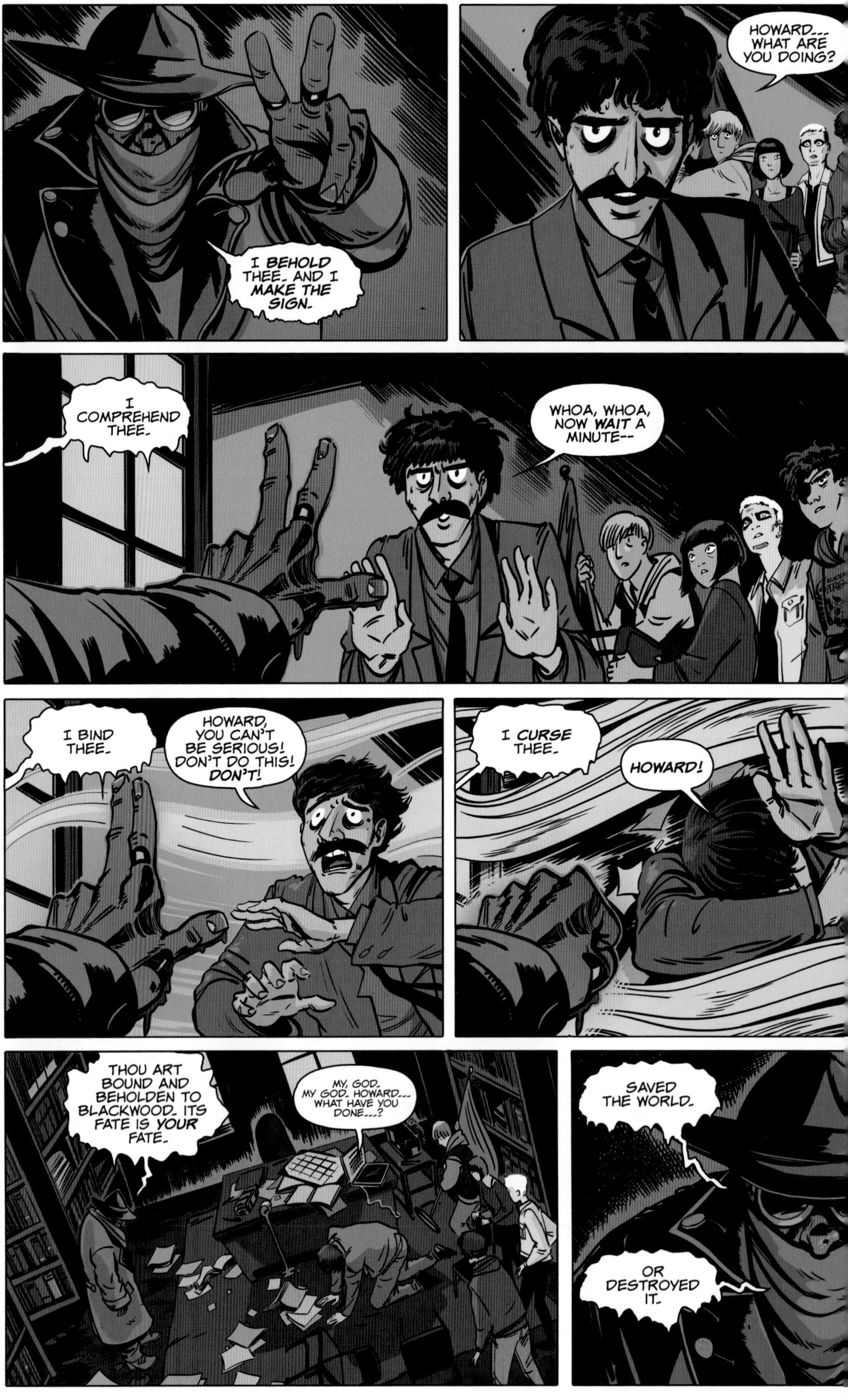
I BEHOLD THEE. AND I MAKE THE SIGN.
HOWARD... WHAT ARE YOU DOING?
I COMPREHEND THEE.
WHOA, WHOA, NOW WAIT A MINUTE--
I BIND THEE.
HOWARD, YOU CAN'T BE SERIOUS! DON'T DO THIS! DON'T!
I CURSE THEE.
HOWARD!
THOU ART BOUND AND BEHOLDEN TO BLACKWOOD. ITS FATE IS YOUR FATE.
MY, GOD. MY GOD. HOWARD... WHAT HAVE YOU DONE...?
SAVED THE WORLD.
OR DESTROYED IT.

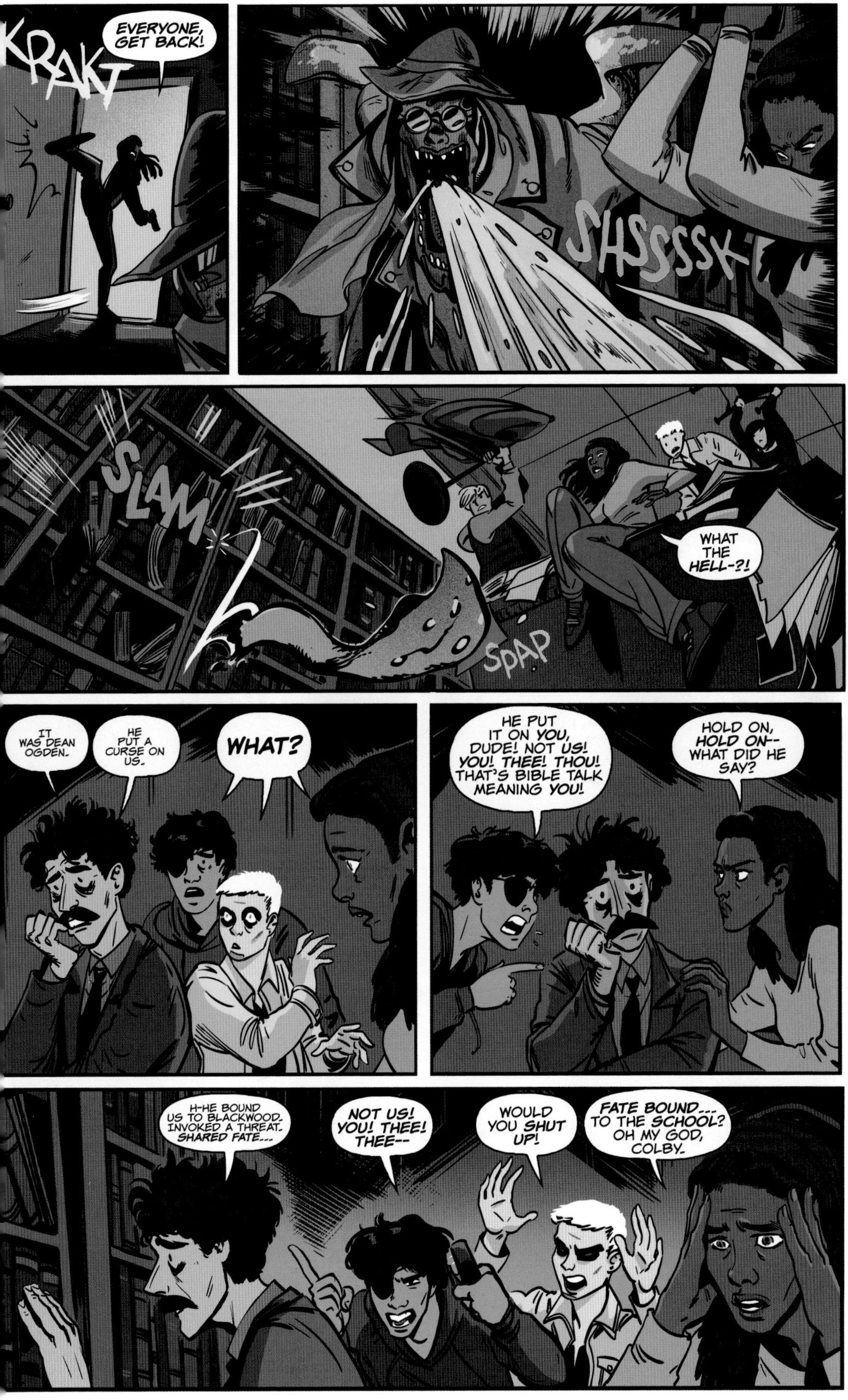
KRAKT
EVERYONE, GET BACK!
SHSSSK
SLAM
WHAT THE HELL--?!
SPAP
IT WAS DEAN OGDEN.
HE PUT A CURSE ON US.
WHAT?
HE PUT IT ON YOU, DUDE! NOT US! YOU! THEE! THOU! THAT'S BIBLE TALK MEANING YOU!
HOLD ON, HOLD ON-- WHAT DID HE SAY?
H-HE BOUND US TO BLACKWOOD. INVOKED A THREAT. SHARED FATE...
NOT US! YOU! THEE! THEE--
WOULD YOU SHUT UP!
FATE BOUND... TO THE SCHOOL? OH MY GOD, COLBY.

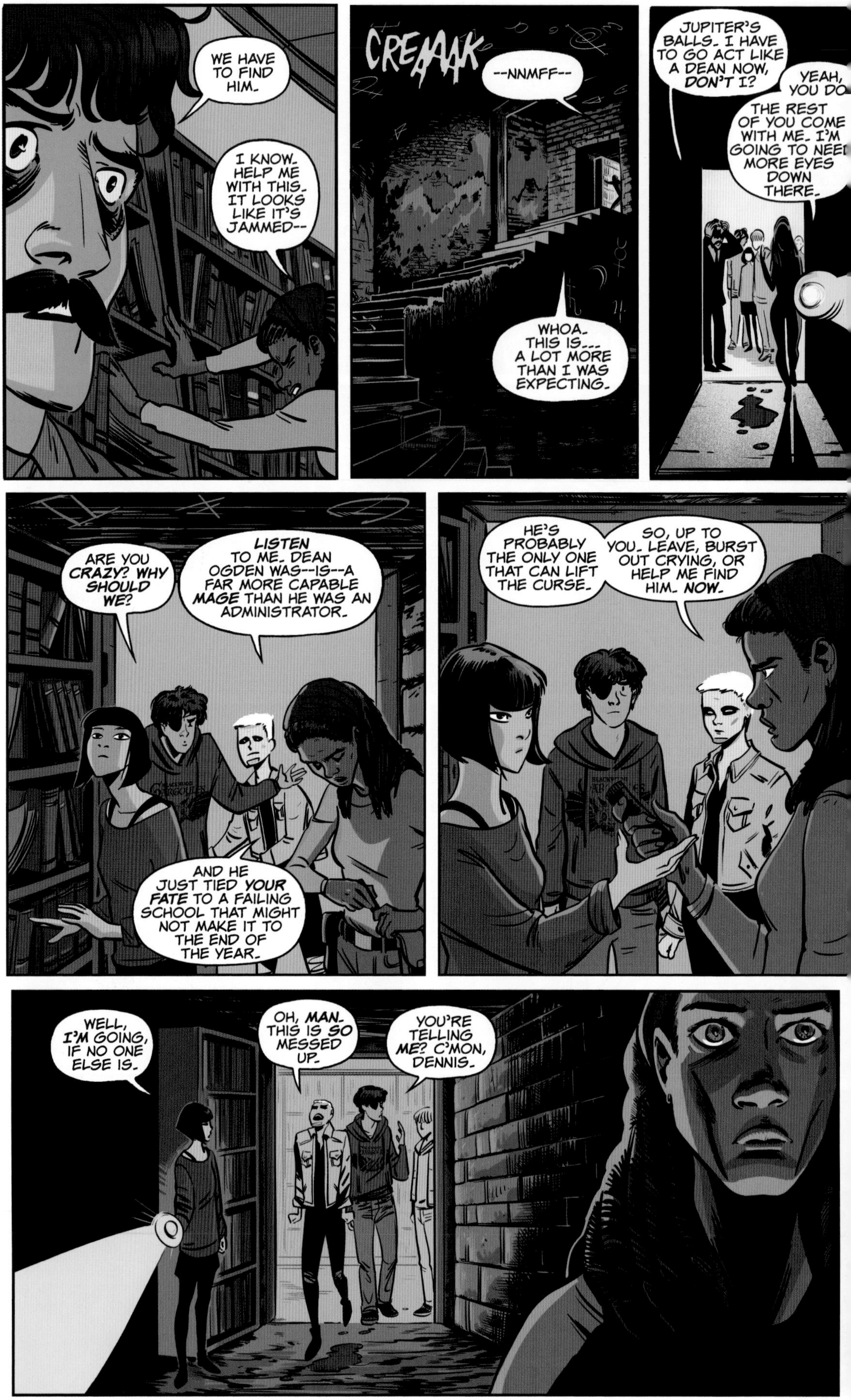

WE HAVE TO FIND HIM.
I KNOW. HELP ME WITH THIS. IT LOOKS LIKE IT'S JAMMED--
CREAAAK
--NNMFF--
WHOA. THIS IS... A LOT MORE THAN I WAS EXPECTING.
JUPITER'S BALLS. I HAVE TO GO ACT LIKE A DEAN NOW, DON'T I?
YEAH, YOU DO.
THE REST OF YOU COME WITH ME. I'M GOING TO NEED MORE EYES DOWN THERE.
ARE YOU CRAZY? WHY SHOULD WE?
LISTEN TO ME. DEAN OGDEN WAS--IS--A FAR MORE CAPABLE MAGE THAN HE WAS AN ADMINISTRATOR.
AND HE JUST TIED YOUR FATE TO A FAILING SCHOOL THAT MIGHT NOT MAKE IT TO THE END OF THE YEAR.
HE'S PROBABLY THE ONLY ONE THAT CAN LIFT THE CURSE.
SO, UP TO YOU. LEAVE, BURST OUT CRYING, OR HELP ME FIND HIM. NOW.
WELL, I'M GOING, IF NO ONE ELSE IS.
OH, MAN. THIS IS SO MESSED UP.
YOU'RE TELLING ME? C'MON, DENNIS.

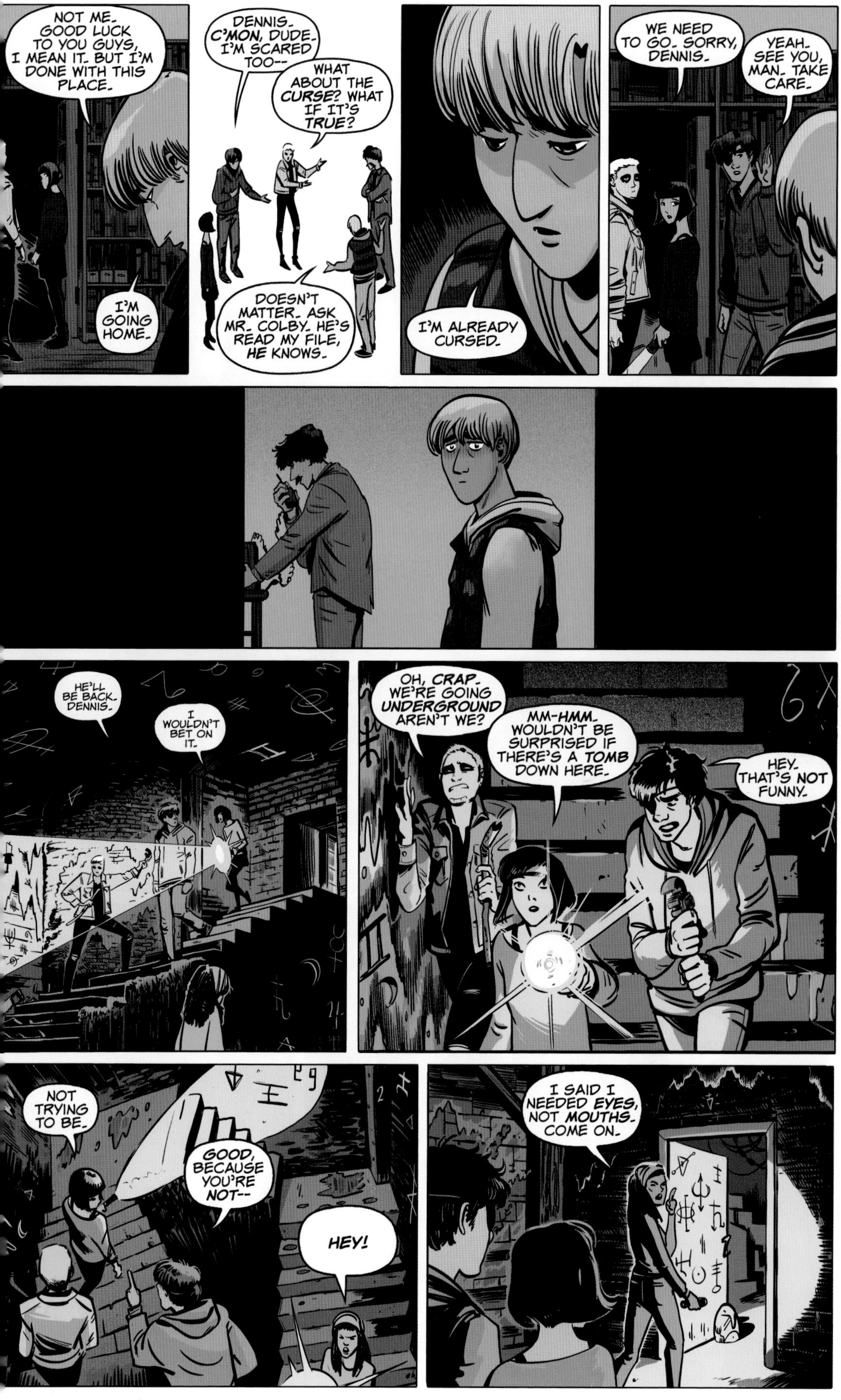
NOT ME. GOOD LUCK TO YOU GUYS, I MEAN IT. BUT I'M DONE WITH THIS PLACE.
I'M GOING HOME.
DENNIS. C'MON, DUDE. I'M SCARED TOO--
WHAT ABOUT THE CURSE? WHAT IF IT'S TRUE?
DOESN'T MATTER. ASK MR. COLBY. HE'S READ MY FILE, HE KNOWS.
I'M ALREADY CURSED.
WE NEED TO GO. SORRY, DENNIS.
YEAH. SEE YOU, MAN. TAKE CARE.
HE'LL BE BACK, DENNIS.
I WOULDN'T BET ON IT.
OH, CRAP. WE'RE GOING UNDERGROUND AREN'T WE?
MM-HMM. WOULDN'T BE SURPRISED IF THERE'S A TOMB DOWN HERE.
HEY. THAT'S NOT FUNNY.
NOT TRYING TO BE.
GOOD, BECAUSE YOU'RE NOT--
HEY!
I SAID I NEEDED EYES, NOT MOUTHS. COME ON.

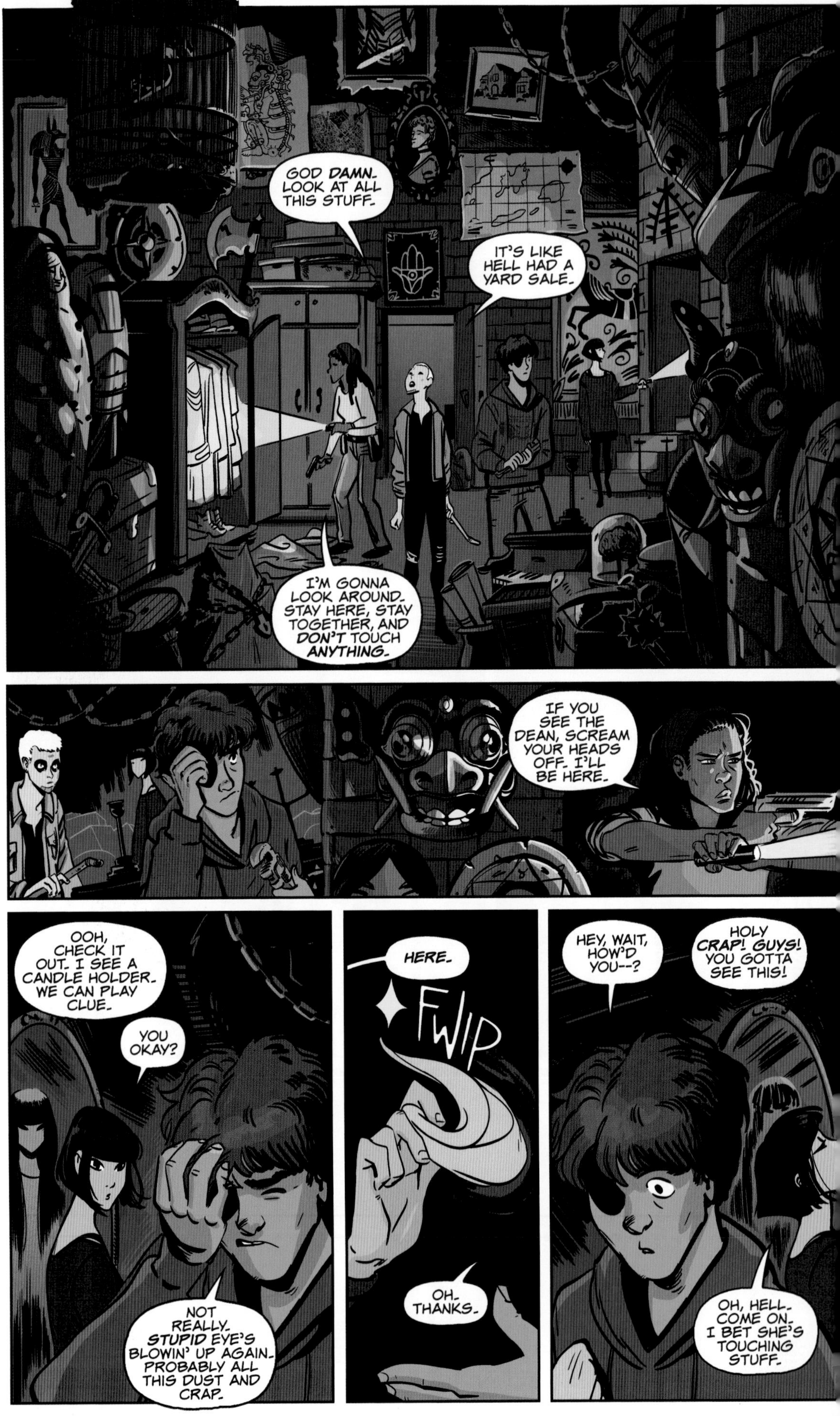
GOD DAMN. LOOK AT ALL THIS STUFF.
IT'S LIKE HELL HAD A YARD SALE.
I'M GONNA LOOK AROUND. STAY HERE, STAY TOGETHER, AND DON'T TOUCH ANYTHING.
IF YOU SEE THE DEAN, SCREAM YOUR HEADS OFF. I'LL BE HERE.
OOH, CHECK IT OUT. I SEE A CANDLE HOLDER. WE CAN PLAY CLUE.
YOU OKAY?
NOT REALLY. STUPID EYE'S BLOWIN' UP AGAIN. PROBABLY ALL THIS DUST AND CRAP.
HERE.
FWIP
OH. THANKS.
HEY, WAIT, HOW'D YOU--?
HOLY CRAP! GUYS! YOU GOTTA SEE THIS!
OH, HELL. COME ON. I BET SHE'S TOUCHING STUFF.

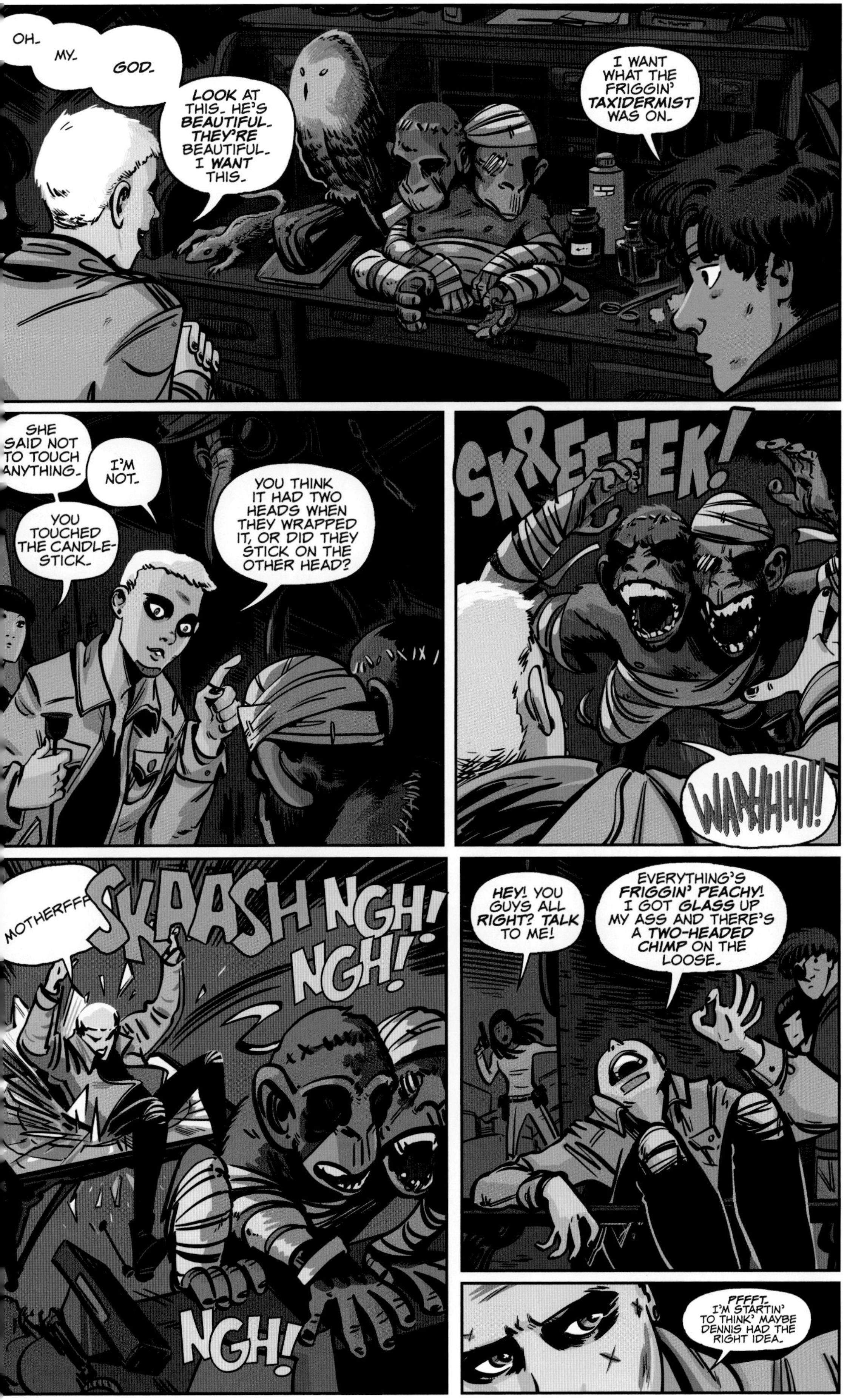
OH.
MY.
GOD.
LOOK AT THIS. HE'S BEAUTIFUL. THEY'RE BEAUTIFUL. I WANT THIS.
I WANT WHAT THE FRIGGIN' TAXIDERMIST WAS ON.
SHE SAID NOT TO TOUCH ANYTHING.
I'M NOT.
YOU TOUCHED THE CANDLE-STICK.
YOU THINK IT HAD TWO HEADS WHEN THEY WRAPPED IT, OR DID THEY STICK ON THE OTHER HEAD?
SKREEEEK!
WAHHHH!
MOTHERFFF
SKAASH
NGH!
NGH!
NGH!
HEY! YOU GUYS ALL RIGHT? TALK TO ME!
EVERYTHING'S FRIGGIN' PEACHY! I GOT GLASS UP MY ASS AND THERE'S A TWO-HEADED CHIMP ON THE LOOSE.
PFFFT. I'M STARTIN' TO THINK' MAYBE DENNIS HAD THE RIGHT IDEA.

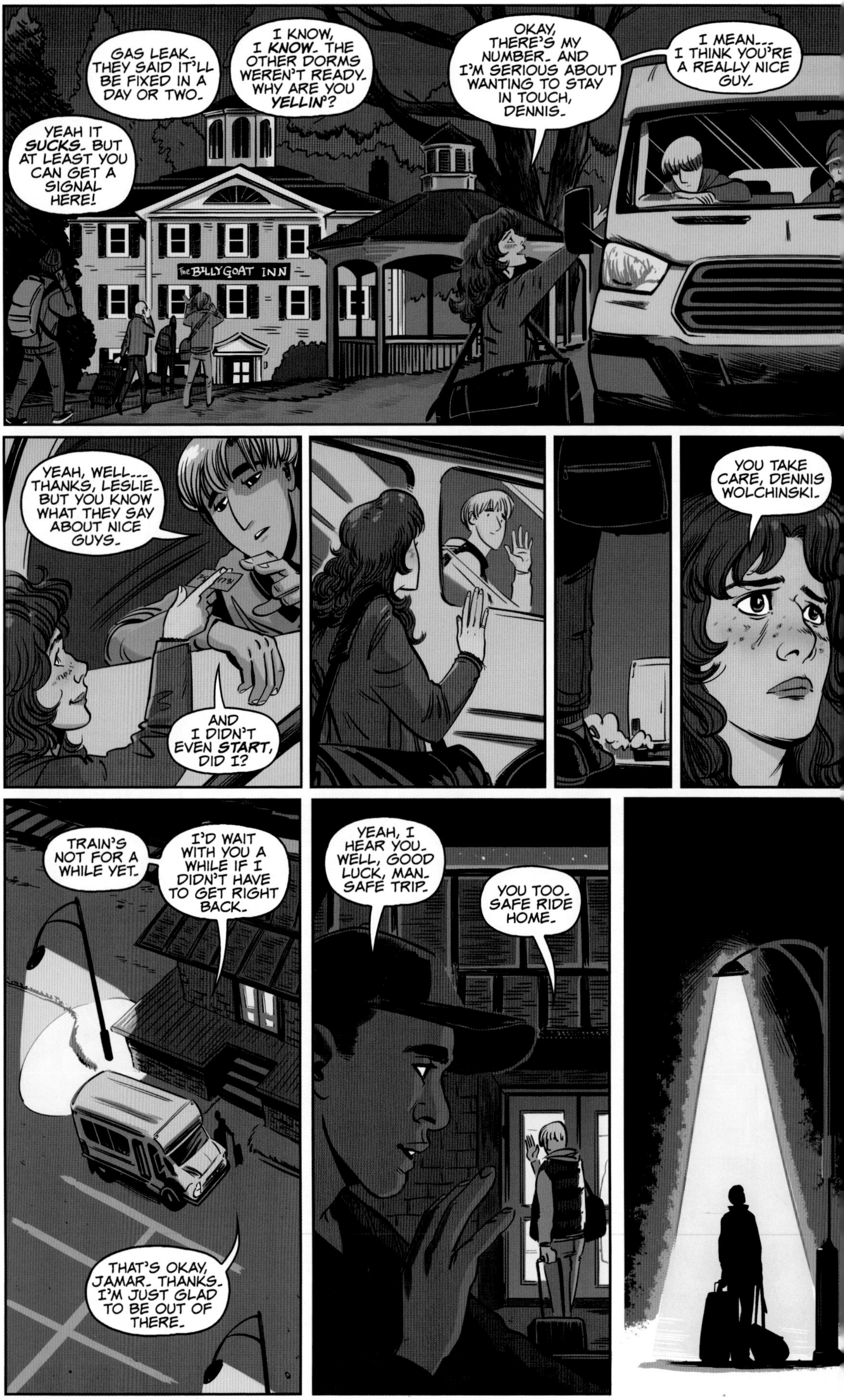
YEAH IT SUCKS. BUT AT LEAST YOU CAN GET A SIGNAL HERE!
GAS LEAK. THEY SAID IT'LL BE FIXED IN A DAY OR TWO.
I KNOW, I KNOW. THE OTHER DORMS WEREN'T READY. WHY ARE YOU YELLIN'?
The BILLYGOAT INN
OKAY, THERE'S MY NUMBER. AND I'M SERIOUS ABOUT WANTING TO STAY IN TOUCH, DENNIS.
I MEAN... I THINK YOU'RE A REALLY NICE GUY.
YEAH, WELL... THANKS, LESLIE. BUT YOU KNOW WHAT THEY SAY ABOUT NICE GUYS.
AND I DIDN'T EVEN START, DID I?
YOU TAKE CARE, DENNIS WOLCHINSKI.
TRAIN'S NOT FOR A WHILE YET.
I'D WAIT WITH YOU A WHILE IF I DIDN'T HAVE TO GET RIGHT BACK.
THAT'S OKAY, JAMAR. THANKS. I'M JUST GLAD TO BE OUT OF THERE.
YEAH, I HEAR YOU. WELL, GOOD LUCK, MAN. SAFE TRIP.
YOU TOO. SAFE RIDE HOME.

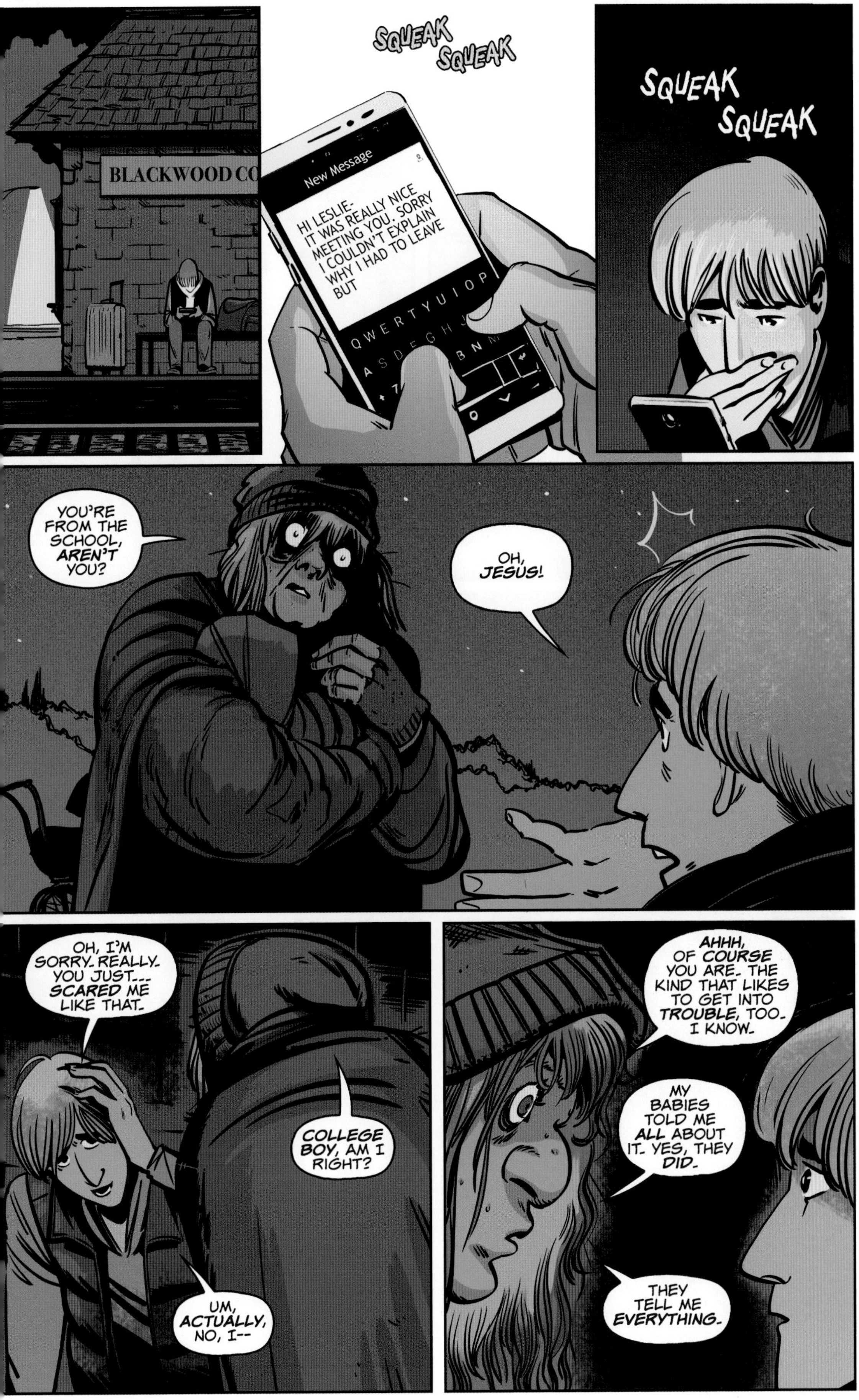
BLACKWOOD CO
SQUEAK SQUEAK
New Message
HI LESLIE- IT WAS REALLY NICE MEETING YOU. SORRY I COULDN'T EXPLAIN WHY I HAD TO LEAVE BUT
SQUEAK SQUEAK
YOU'RE FROM THE SCHOOL, AREN'T YOU?
OH, JESUS!
OH, I'M SORRY. REALLY. YOU JUST... SCARED ME LIKE THAT.
COLLEGE BOY, AM I RIGHT?
UM, ACTUALLY, NO, I--
AHHH, OF COURSE YOU ARE. THE KIND THAT LIKES TO GET INTO TROUBLE, TOO. I KNOW.
MY BABIES TOLD ME ALL ABOUT IT. YES, THEY DID.
THEY TELL ME EVERYTHING.

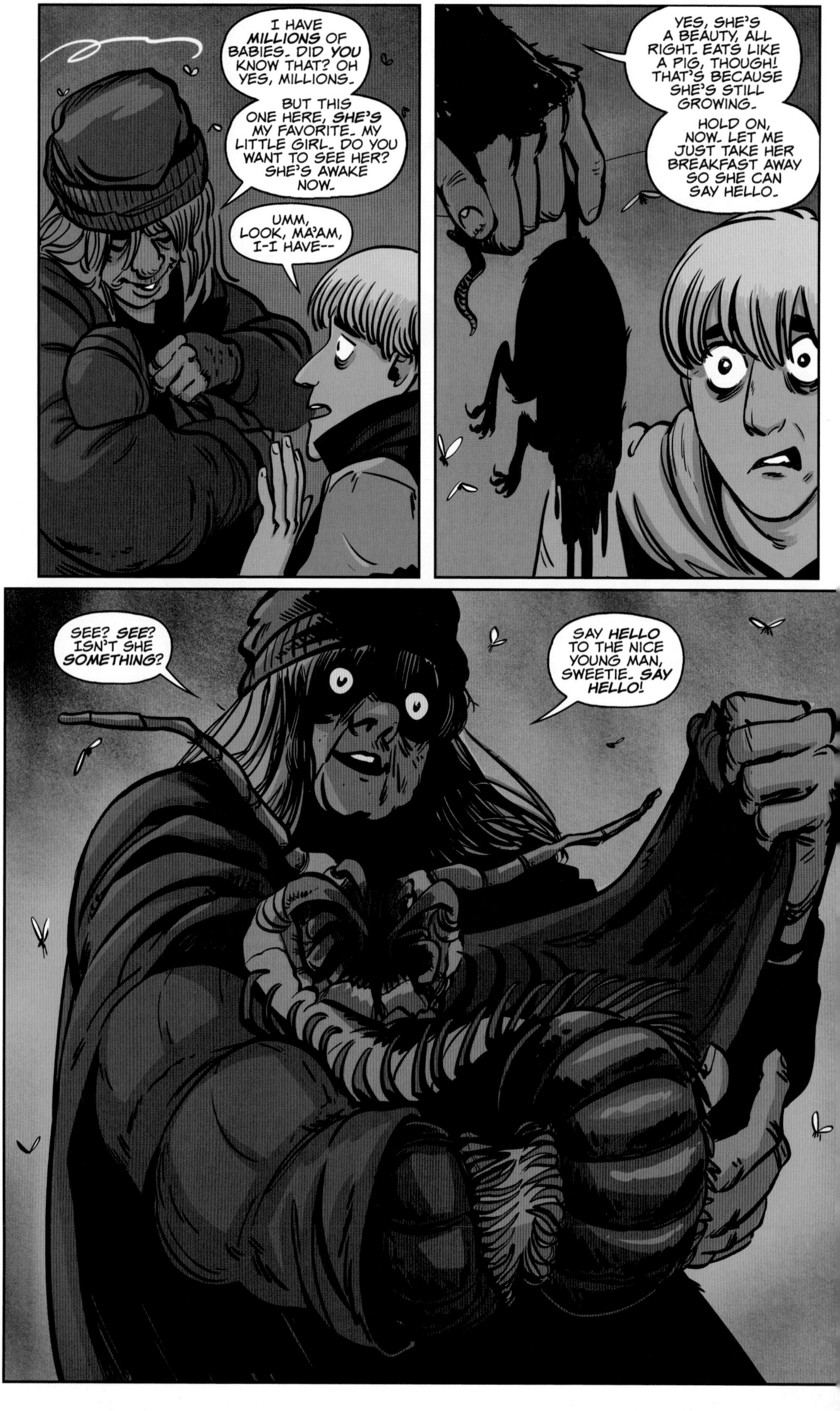

I HAVE **MILLIONS** OF BABIES. DID **YOU** KNOW THAT? OH YES, MILLIONS.
BUT THIS ONE HERE, **SHE'S** MY FAVORITE. MY LITTLE GIRL. DO YOU WANT TO SEE HER? SHE'S AWAKE NOW.
UMM, LOOK, MA'AM, I-I HAVE--
YES, SHE'S A BEAUTY, ALL RIGHT. EATS LIKE A PIG, THOUGH! THAT'S BECAUSE SHE'S STILL GROWING.
HOLD ON, NOW. LET ME JUST TAKE HER BREAKFAST AWAY SO SHE CAN SAY HELLO.
SEE? **SEE?** ISN'T SHE **SOMETHING?**
SAY **HELLO** TO THE NICE YOUNG MAN, SWEETIE. **SAY HELLO!**

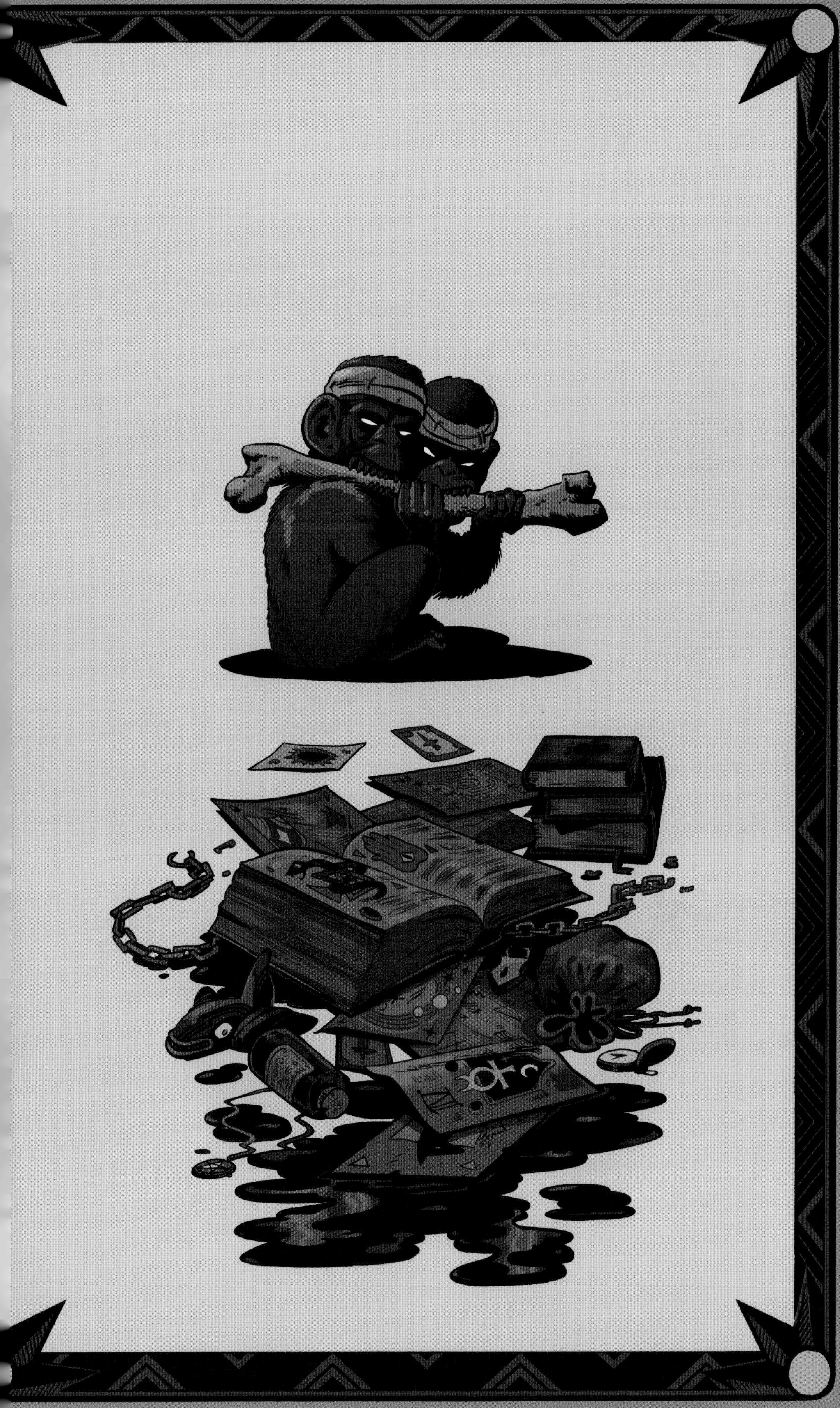

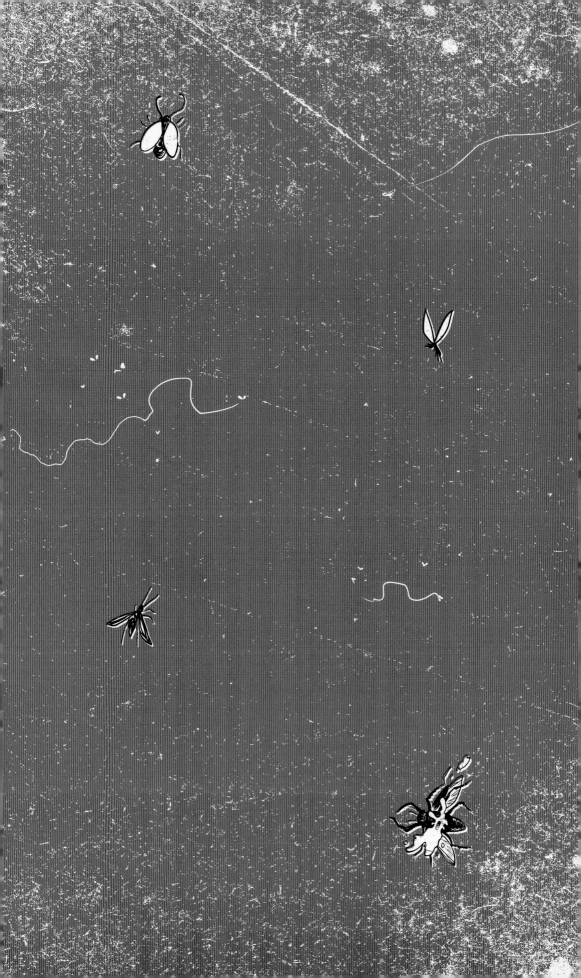

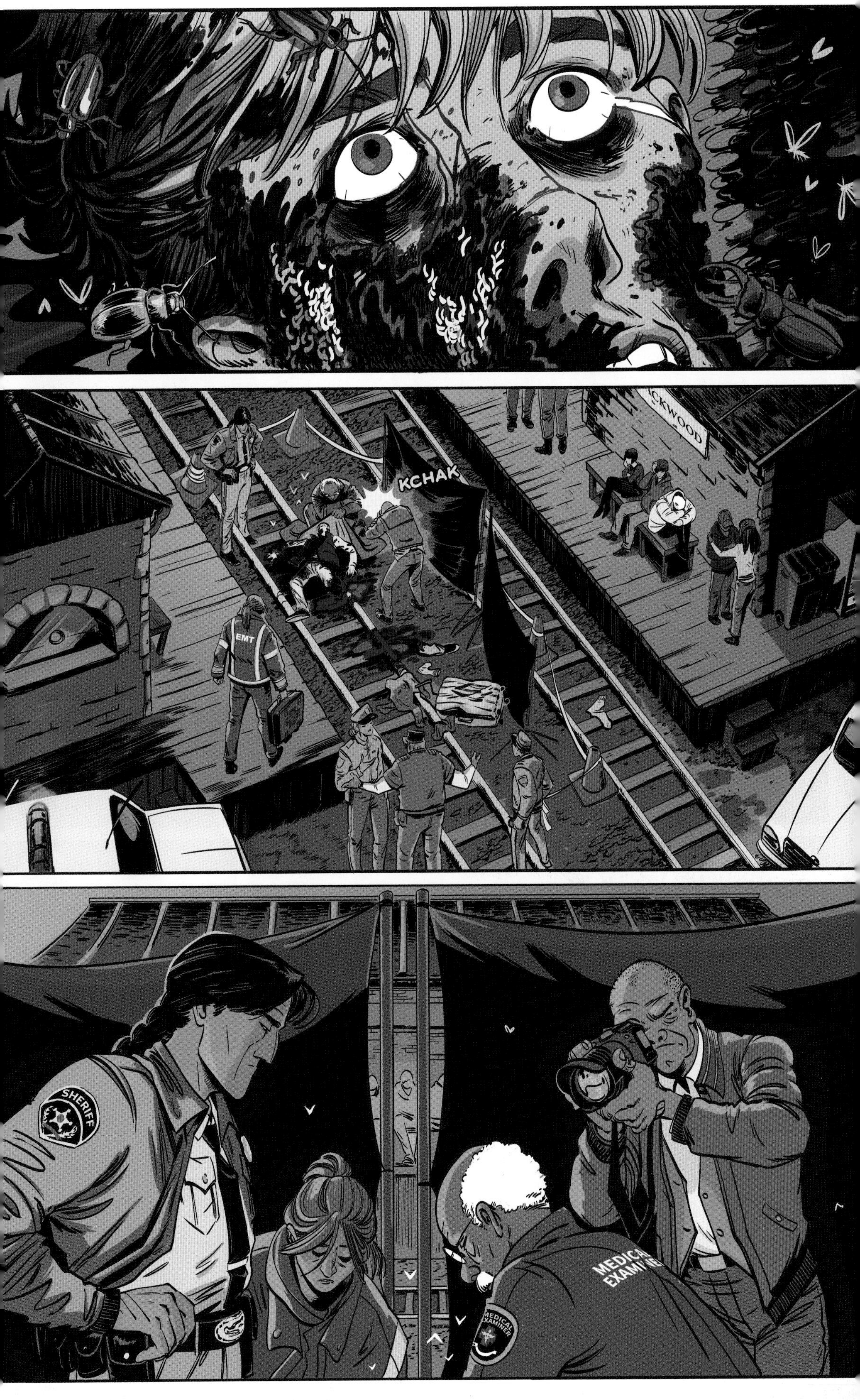
KCHAK
EMT
SHERIFF
MEDICAL EXAMINER

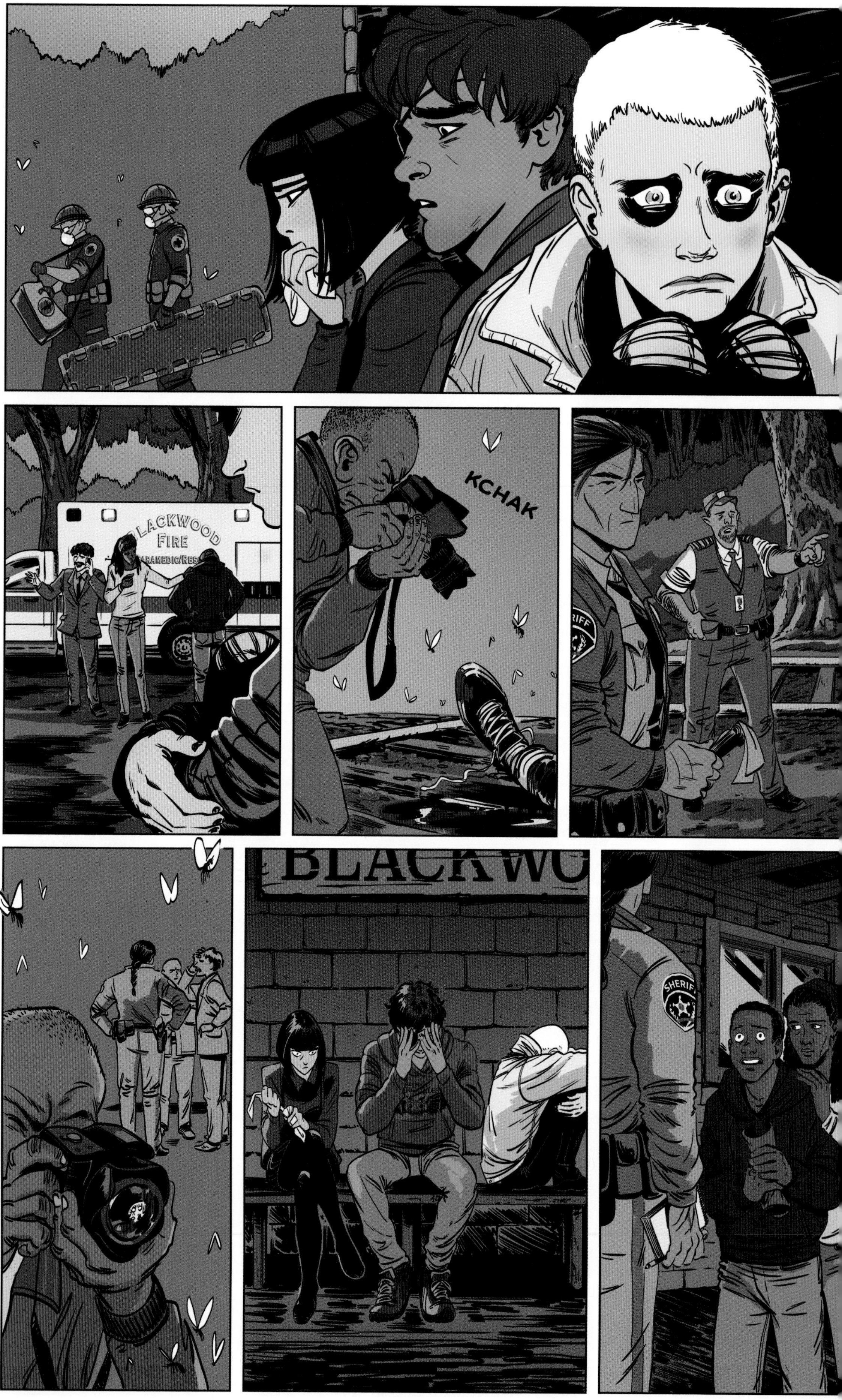
BLACKWOOD
FIRE
PARAMEDIC/RES
KCHAK
SHERIFF
BLACKWO

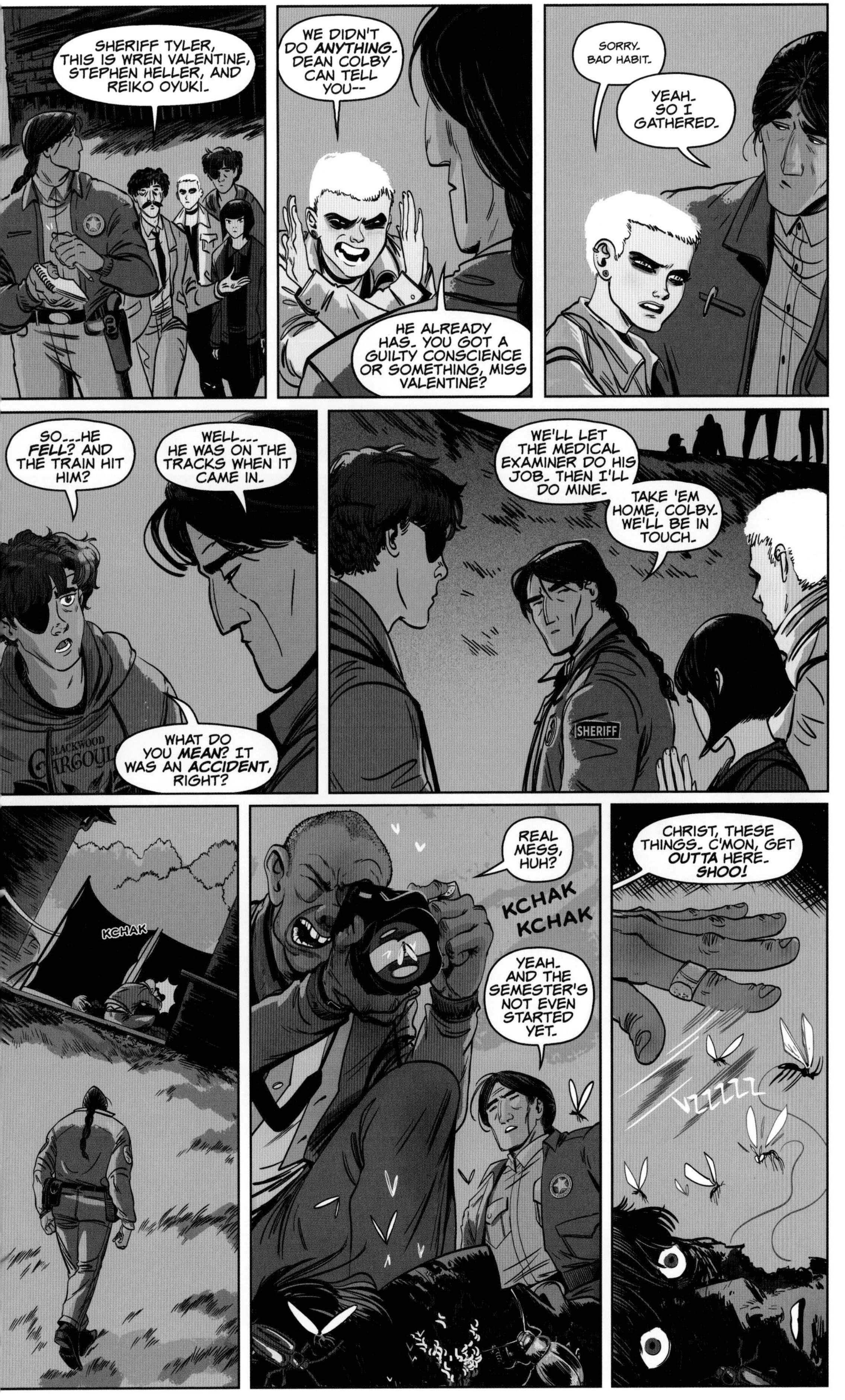

SHERIFF TYLER, THIS IS WREN VALENTINE, STEPHEN HELLER, AND REIKO OYUKI.
WE DIDN'T DO ANYTHING. DEAN COLBY CAN TELL YOU--
HE ALREADY HAS. YOU GOT A GUILTY CONSCIENCE OR SOMETHING, MISS VALENTINE?
SORRY. BAD HABIT.
YEAH. SO I GATHERED.
SO...HE FELL? AND THE TRAIN HIT HIM?
WELL... HE WAS ON THE TRACKS WHEN IT CAME IN.
WHAT DO YOU MEAN? IT WAS AN ACCIDENT, RIGHT?
BLACKWOOD GARGOYL
WE'LL LET THE MEDICAL EXAMINER DO HIS JOB. THEN I'LL DO MINE.
TAKE 'EM HOME, COLBY. WE'LL BE IN TOUCH.
SHERIFF
KCHAK
REAL MESS, HUH?
KCHAK
KCHAK
YEAH. AND THE SEMESTER'S NOT EVEN STARTED YET.
CHRIST, THESE THINGS. C'MON, GET OUTTA HERE. SHOO!
VZZZZZ

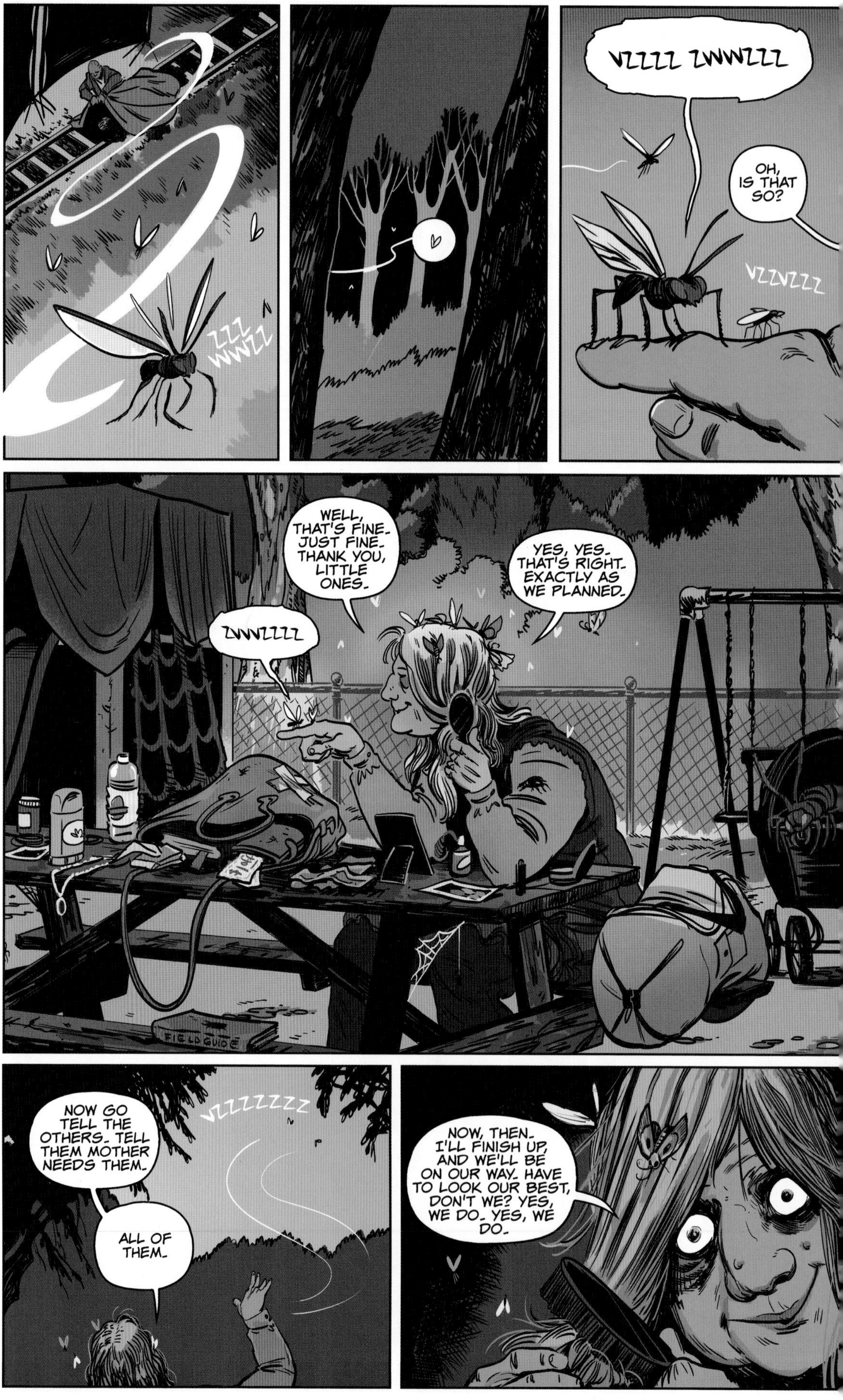
ZZZ WWZZ
VZZZZ ZWWZZZ
OH, IS THAT SO?
VZZVZZZ
ZWWZZZZ
WELL, THAT'S FINE. JUST FINE. THANK YOU, LITTLE ONES.
YES, YES. THAT'S RIGHT. EXACTLY AS WE PLANNED.
FIELD GUIDE
NOW GO TELL THE OTHERS. TELL THEM MOTHER NEEDS THEM.
VZZZZZZZ
ALL OF THEM.
NOW, THEN. I'LL FINISH UP, AND WE'LL BE ON OUR WAY. HAVE TO LOOK OUR BEST, DON'T WE? YES, WE DO. YES, WE DO.

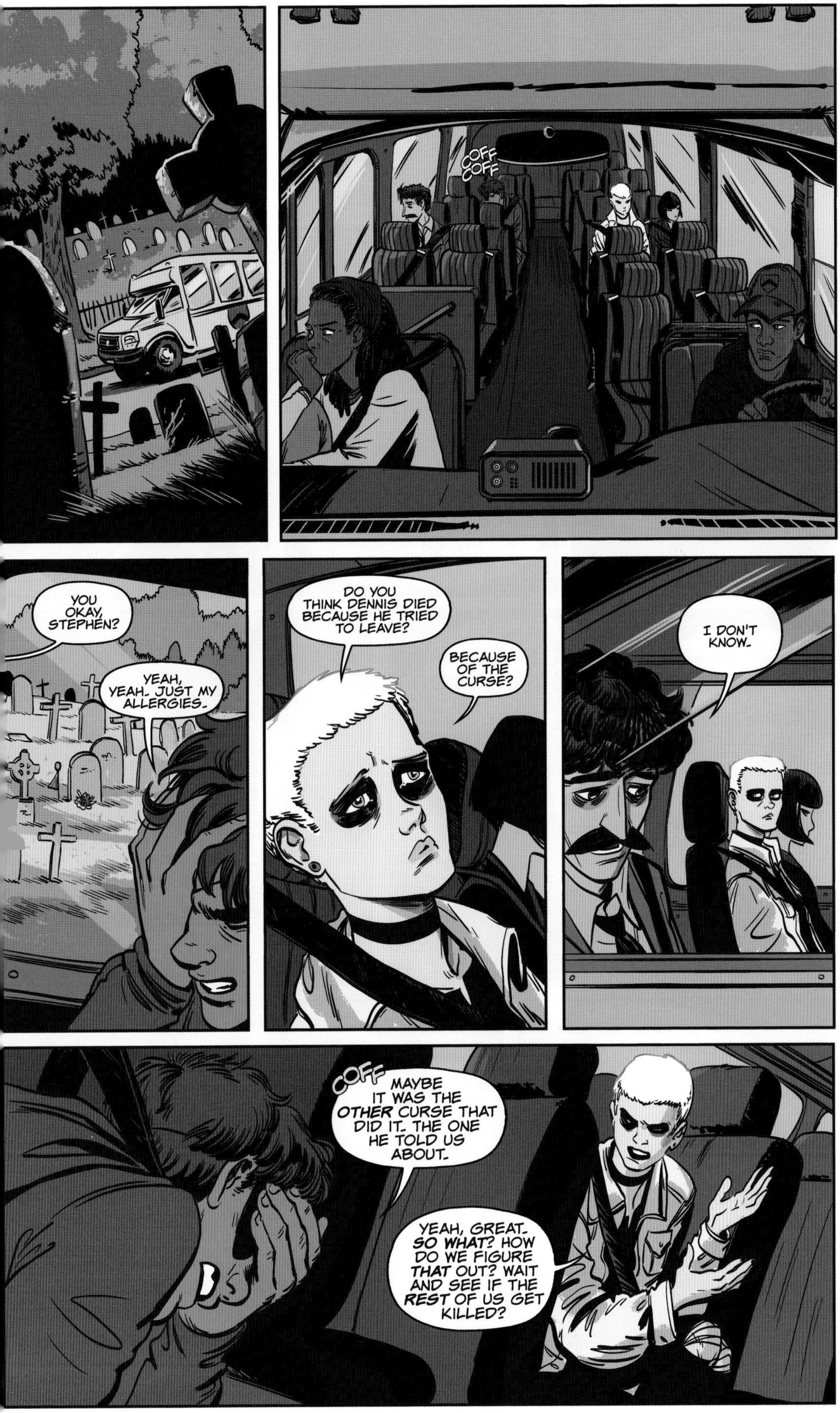
COFF COFF
YOU OKAY, STEPHEN?
YEAH, YEAH. JUST MY ALLERGIES.
DO YOU THINK DENNIS DIED BECAUSE HE TRIED TO LEAVE?
BECAUSE OF THE CURSE?
I DON'T KNOW.
COFF
MAYBE IT WAS THE **OTHER** CURSE THAT DID IT. THE ONE HE TOLD US ABOUT.
YEAH, GREAT. **SO WHAT?** HOW DO WE FIGURE **THAT** OUT? WAIT AND SEE IF THE **REST** OF US GET KILLED?

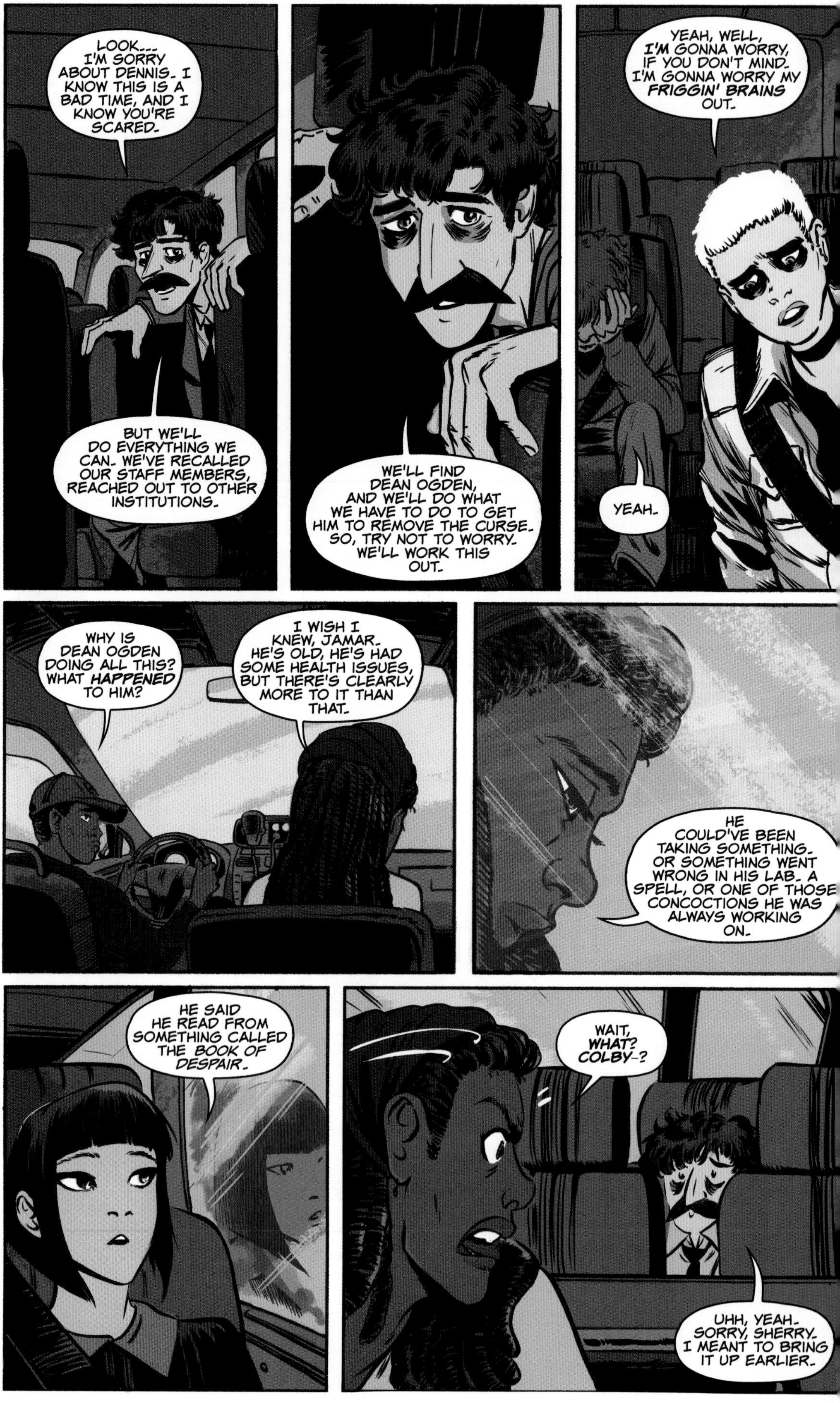
LOOK... I'M SORRY ABOUT DENNIS. I KNOW THIS IS A BAD TIME, AND I KNOW YOU'RE SCARED.
BUT WE'LL DO EVERYTHING WE CAN. WE'VE RECALLED OUR STAFF MEMBERS, REACHED OUT TO OTHER INSTITUTIONS.
WE'LL FIND DEAN OGDEN, AND WE'LL DO WHAT WE HAVE TO DO TO GET HIM TO REMOVE THE CURSE. SO, TRY NOT TO WORRY. WE'LL WORK THIS OUT.
YEAH.
YEAH, WELL, *I'M* GONNA WORRY, IF YOU DON'T MIND. I'M GONNA WORRY MY *FRIGGIN' BRAINS* OUT.
WHY IS DEAN OGDEN DOING ALL THIS? WHAT *HAPPENED* TO HIM?
I WISH I KNEW, JAMAR. HE'S OLD, HE'S HAD SOME HEALTH ISSUES, BUT THERE'S CLEARLY MORE TO IT THAN THAT.
HE COULD'VE BEEN TAKING SOMETHING. OR SOMETHING WENT WRONG IN HIS LAB. A SPELL, OR ONE OF THOSE CONCOCTIONS HE WAS ALWAYS WORKING ON.
HE SAID HE READ FROM SOMETHING CALLED THE *BOOK OF DESPAIR*.
WAIT, *WHAT? COLBY*-?
UHH, YEAH. SORRY, SHERRY. I MEANT TO BRING IT UP EARLIER.

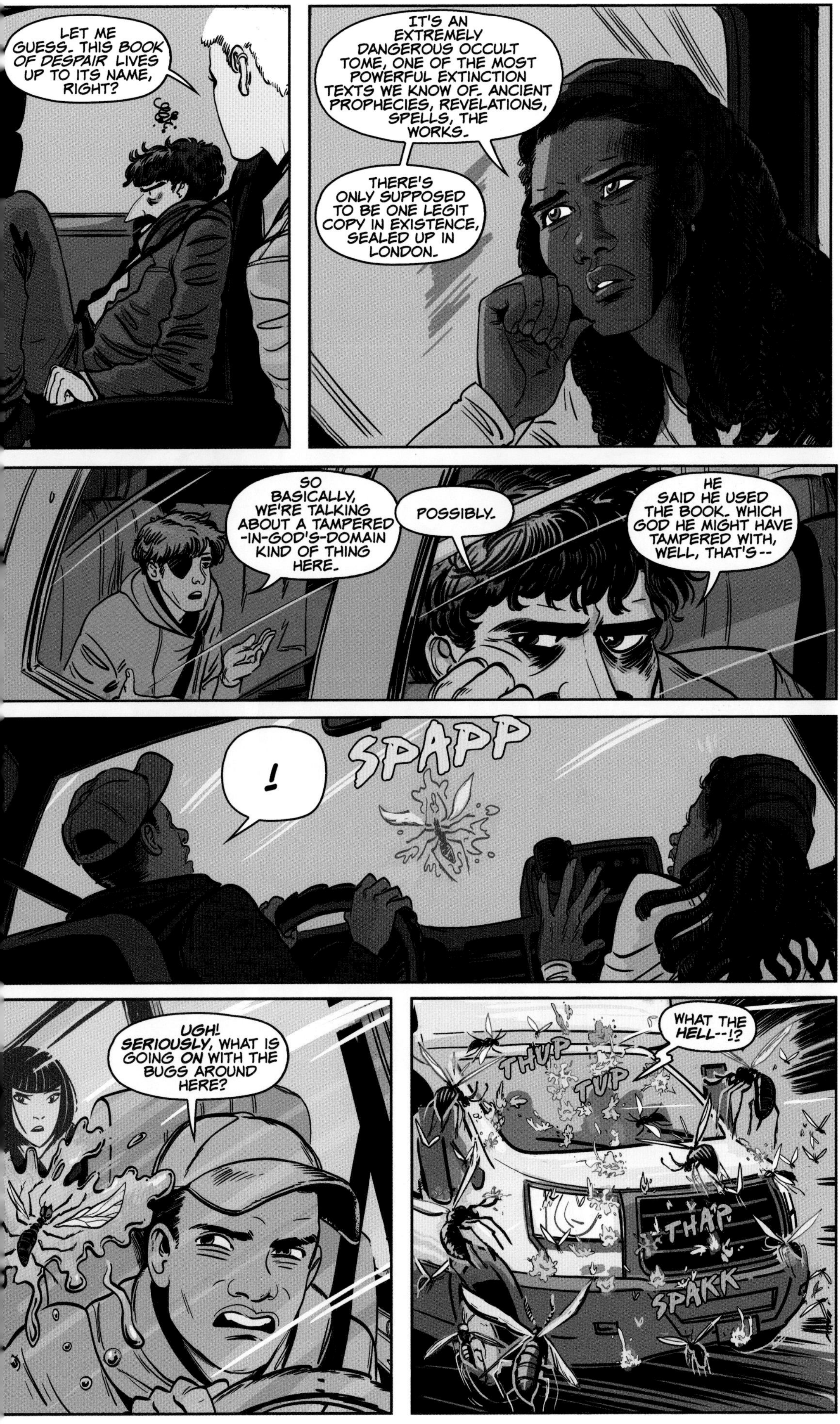
LET ME GUESS. THIS BOOK OF DESPAIR LIVES UP TO ITS NAME, RIGHT?
IT'S AN EXTREMELY DANGEROUS OCCULT TOME, ONE OF THE MOST POWERFUL EXTINCTION TEXTS WE KNOW OF. ANCIENT PROPHECIES, REVELATIONS, SPELLS, THE WORKS.
THERE'S ONLY SUPPOSED TO BE ONE LEGIT COPY IN EXISTENCE, SEALED UP IN LONDON.
SO BASICALLY, WE'RE TALKING ABOUT A TAMPERED-IN-GOD'S-DOMAIN KIND OF THING HERE.
POSSIBLY.
HE SAID HE USED THE BOOK. WHICH GOD HE MIGHT HAVE TAMPERED WITH, WELL, THAT'S--
!
SPAPP
UGH! SERIOUSLY, WHAT IS GOING ON WITH THE BUGS AROUND HERE?
WHAT THE HELL--!?
THUP
TUP
THAP
SPAKK

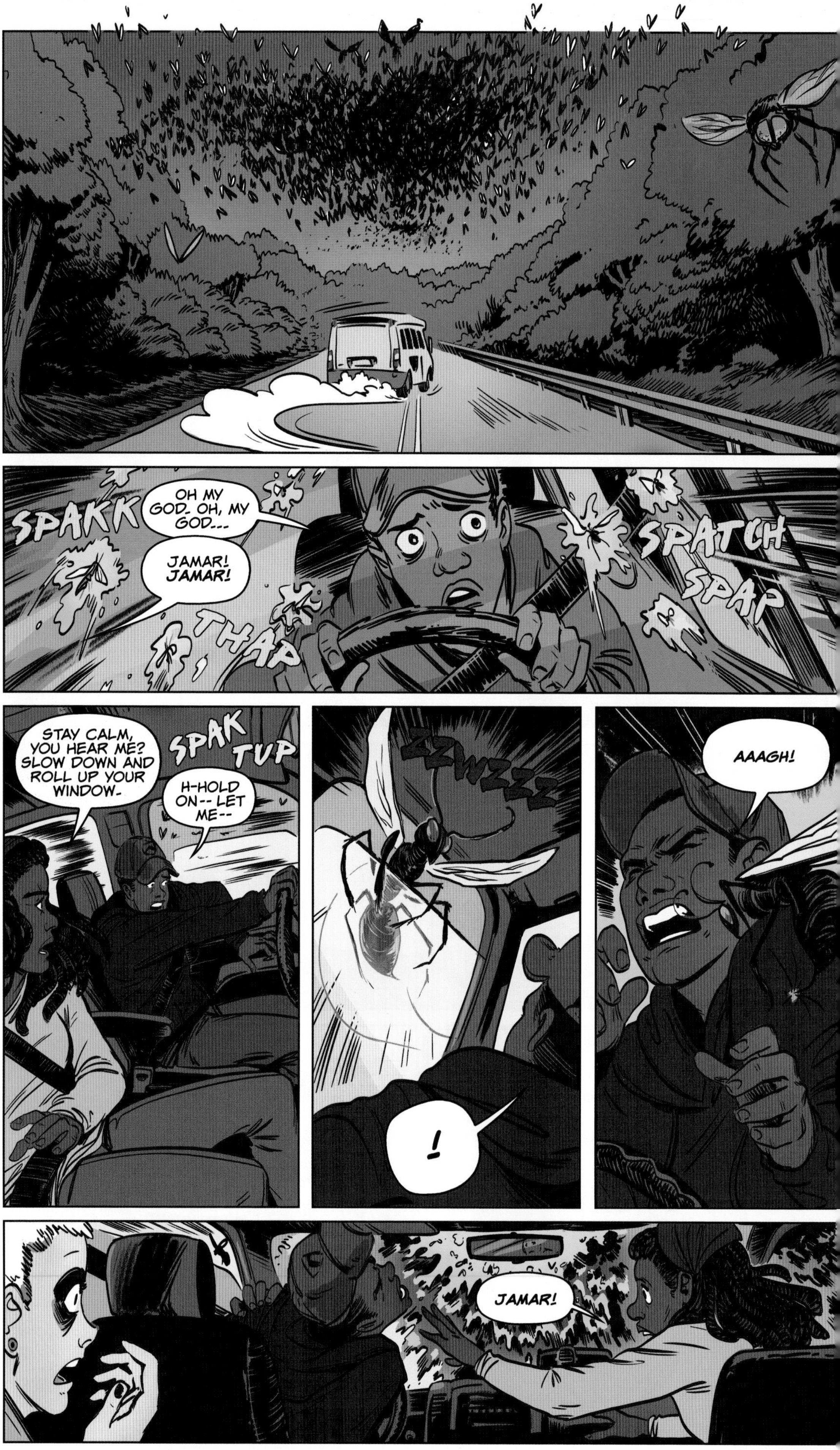
SPAKK
OH MY GOD. OH, MY GOD...
JAMAR! JAMAR!
SPATCH
SPAP
THAP
STAY CALM, YOU HEAR ME? SLOW DOWN AND ROLL UP YOUR WINDOW.
SPAK
TUP
H-HOLD ON-- LET ME--
ZZWZZZ
!
AAAGH!
JAMAR!

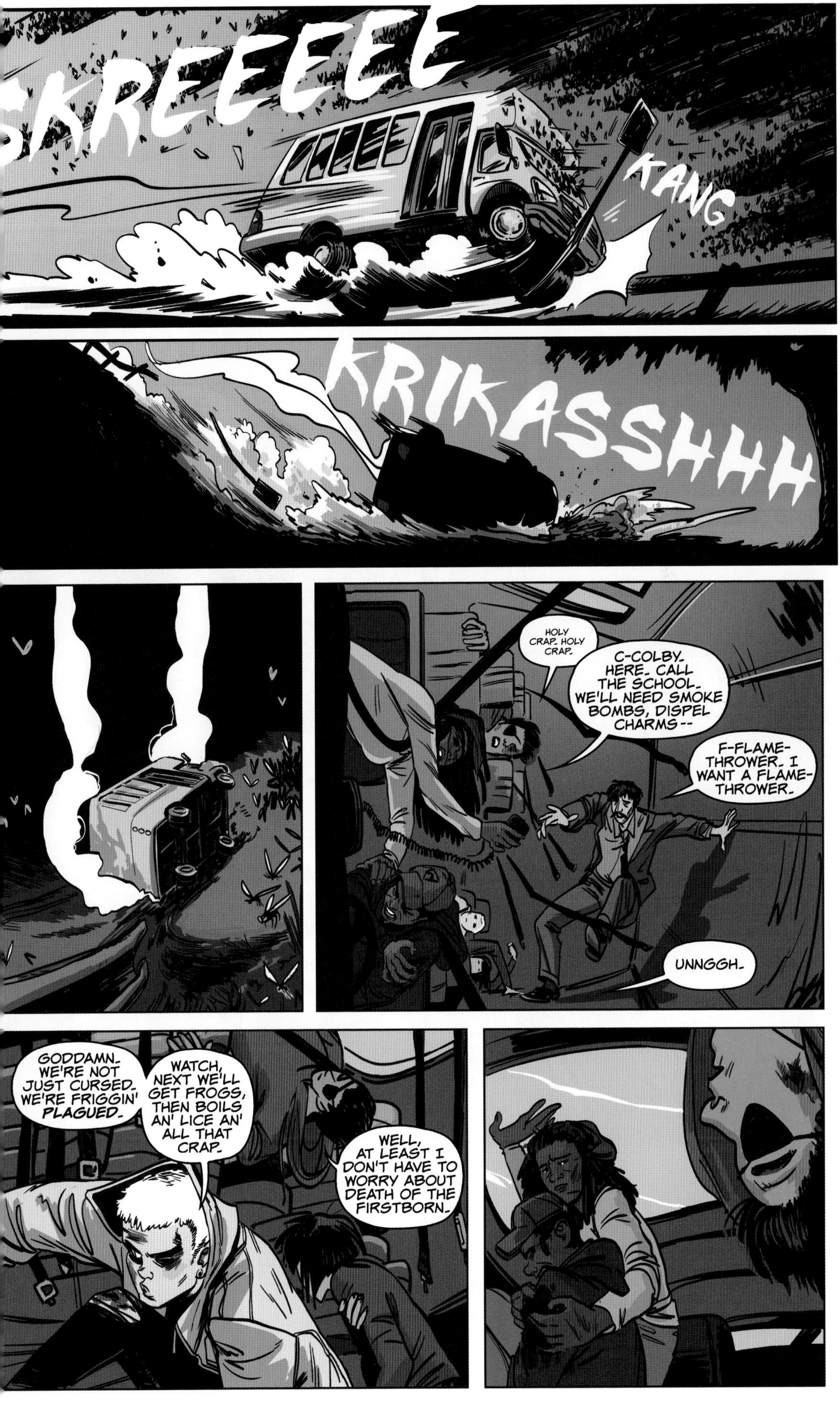
SKREEEEEE
KANG
KRIKASSHHH
HOLY CRAP. HOLY CRAP.
C-COLBY. HERE. CALL THE SCHOOL. WE'LL NEED SMOKE BOMBS, DISPEL CHARMS --
F-FLAME-THROWER. I WANT A FLAME-THROWER.
UNNGGH.
GODDAMN. WE'RE NOT JUST CURSED. WE'RE FRIGGIN' *PLAGUED*.
WATCH, NEXT WE'LL GET FROGS, THEN BOILS AN' LICE AN' ALL THAT CRAP.
WELL, AT LEAST I DON'T HAVE TO WORRY ABOUT DEATH OF THE FIRSTBORN.

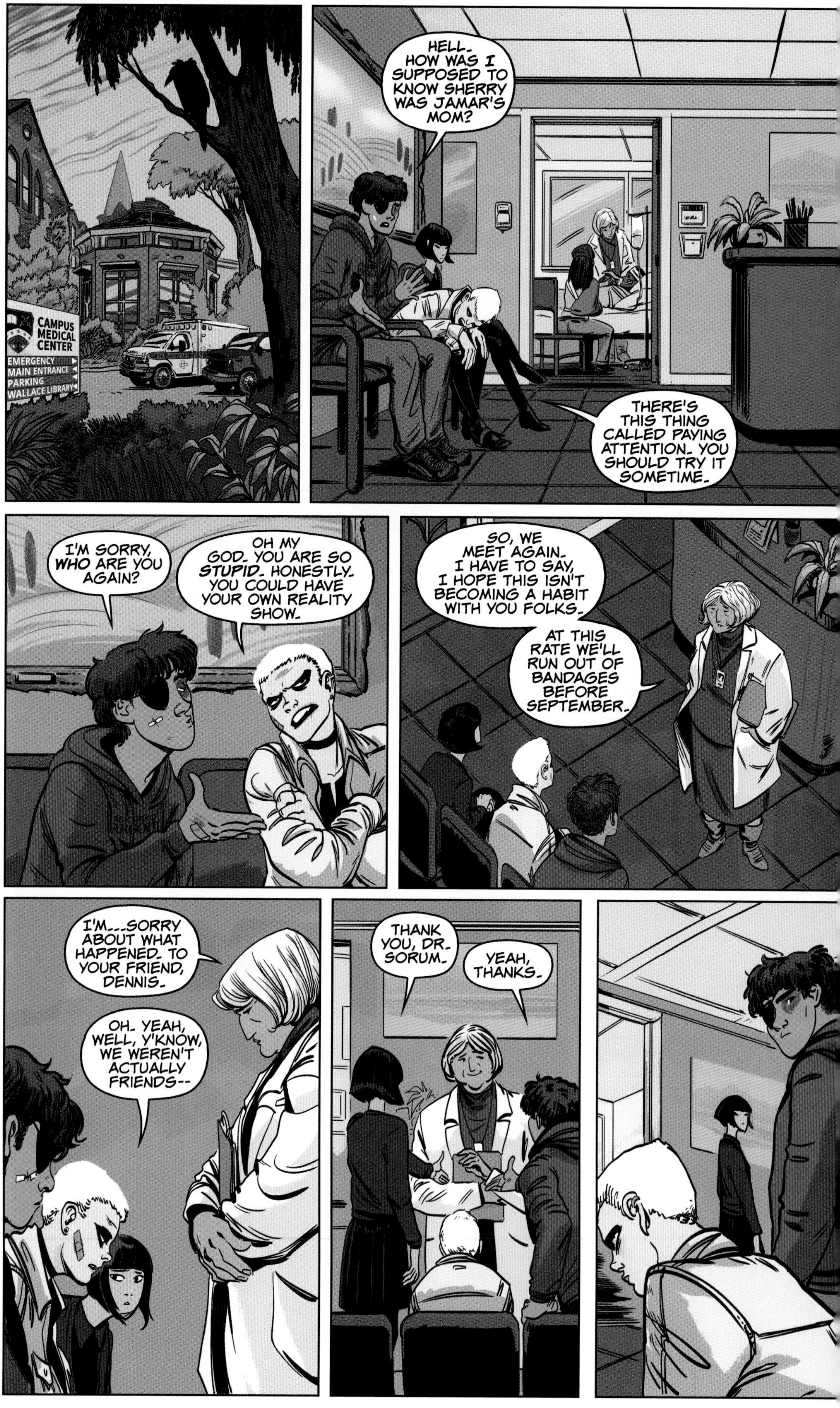
CAMPUS MEDICAL CENTER
EMERGENCY
MAIN ENTRANCE
PARKING
WALLACE LIBRARY
HELL. HOW WAS I SUPPOSED TO KNOW SHERRY WAS JAMAR'S MOM?
THERE'S THIS THING CALLED PAYING ATTENTION. YOU SHOULD TRY IT SOMETIME.
I'M SORRY, WHO ARE YOU AGAIN?
OH MY GOD. YOU ARE SO STUPID. HONESTLY. YOU COULD HAVE YOUR OWN REALITY SHOW.
SO, WE MEET AGAIN. I HAVE TO SAY, I HOPE THIS ISN'T BECOMING A HABIT WITH YOU FOLKS.
AT THIS RATE WE'LL RUN OUT OF BANDAGES BEFORE SEPTEMBER.
I'M...SORRY ABOUT WHAT HAPPENED. TO YOUR FRIEND, DENNIS.
OH. YEAH, WELL, Y'KNOW, WE WEREN'T ACTUALLY FRIENDS--
THANK YOU, DR. SORUM.
YEAH, THANKS.

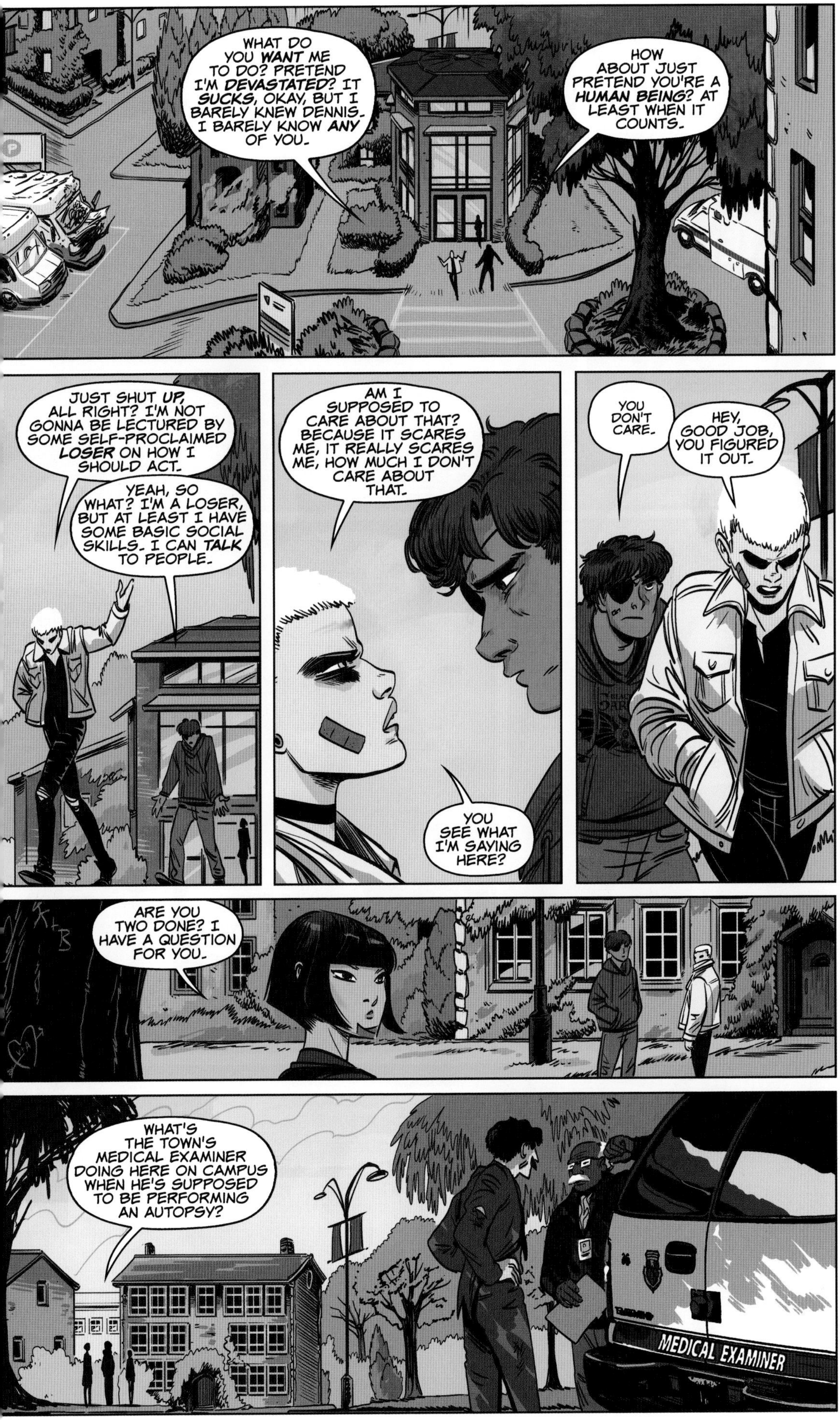
WHAT DO YOU WANT ME TO DO? PRETEND I'M DEVASTATED? IT SUCKS, OKAY, BUT I BARELY KNEW DENNIS. I BARELY KNOW ANY OF YOU.
HOW ABOUT JUST PRETEND YOU'RE A HUMAN BEING? AT LEAST WHEN IT COUNTS.
JUST SHUT UP, ALL RIGHT? I'M NOT GONNA BE LECTURED BY SOME SELF-PROCLAIMED LOSER ON HOW I SHOULD ACT.
YEAH, SO WHAT? I'M A LOSER, BUT AT LEAST I HAVE SOME BASIC SOCIAL SKILLS. I CAN TALK TO PEOPLE.
AM I SUPPOSED TO CARE ABOUT THAT? BECAUSE IT SCARES ME, IT REALLY SCARES ME, HOW MUCH I DON'T CARE ABOUT THAT.
YOU SEE WHAT I'M SAYING HERE?
YOU DON'T CARE.
HEY, GOOD JOB, YOU FIGURED IT OUT.
ARE YOU TWO DONE? I HAVE A QUESTION FOR YOU.
WHAT'S THE TOWN'S MEDICAL EXAMINER DOING HERE ON CAMPUS WHEN HE'S SUPPOSED TO BE PERFORMING AN AUTOPSY?
MEDICAL EXAMINER

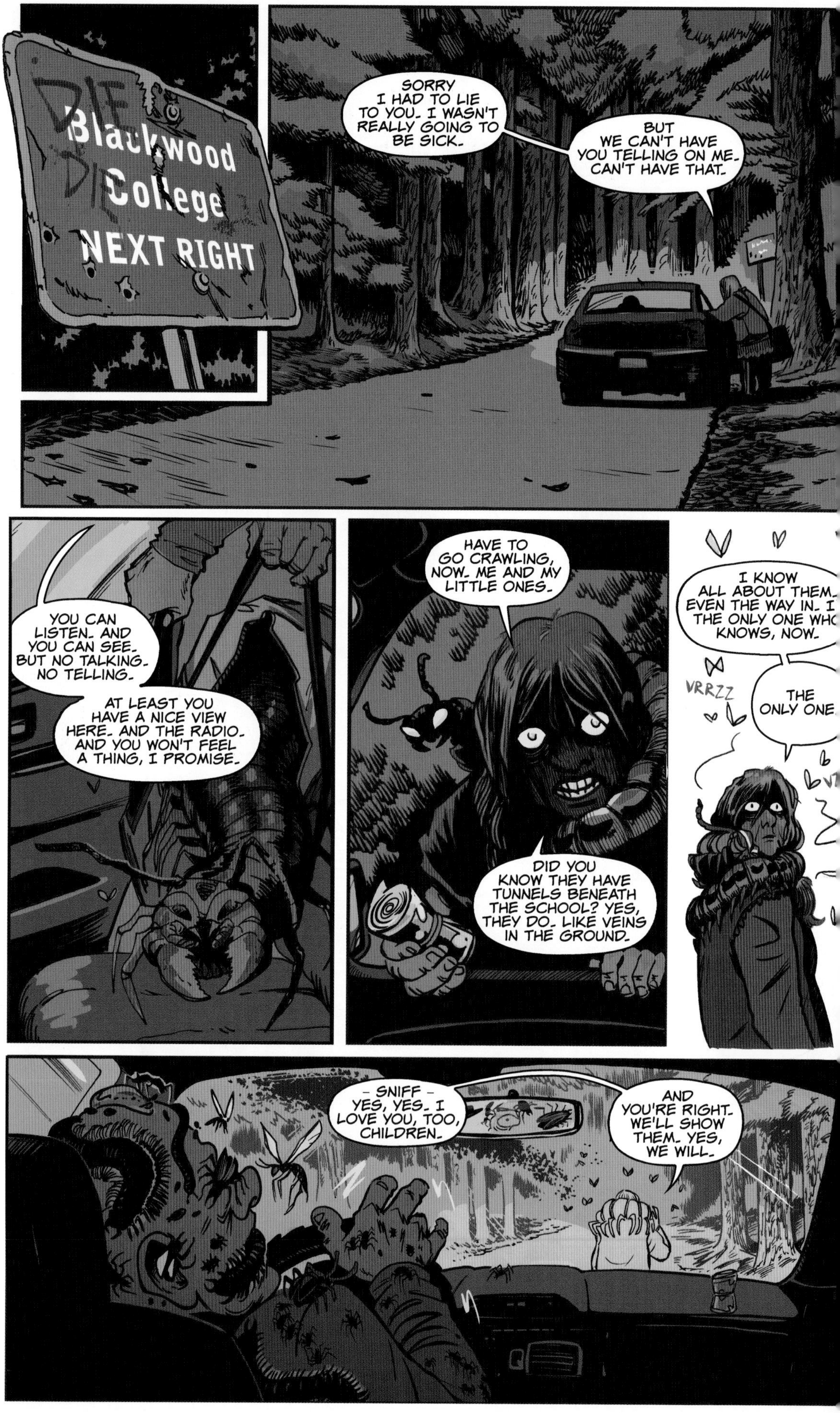

DIE
DIE
Blackwood College NEXT RIGHT
SORRY I HAD TO LIE TO YOU. I WASN'T REALLY GOING TO BE SICK.
BUT WE CAN'T HAVE YOU TELLING ON ME. CAN'T HAVE THAT.
YOU CAN LISTEN. AND YOU CAN SEE. BUT NO TALKING. NO TELLING.
AT LEAST YOU HAVE A NICE VIEW HERE. AND THE RADIO. AND YOU WON'T FEEL A THING, I PROMISE.
HAVE TO GO CRAWLING, NOW. ME AND MY LITTLE ONES.
DID YOU KNOW THEY HAVE TUNNELS BENEATH THE SCHOOL? YES, THEY DO. LIKE VEINS IN THE GROUND.
VRRZZ
- SNIFF - YES, YES. I LOVE YOU, TOO, CHILDREN.
AND YOU'RE RIGHT. WE'LL SHOW THEM. YES, WE WILL.

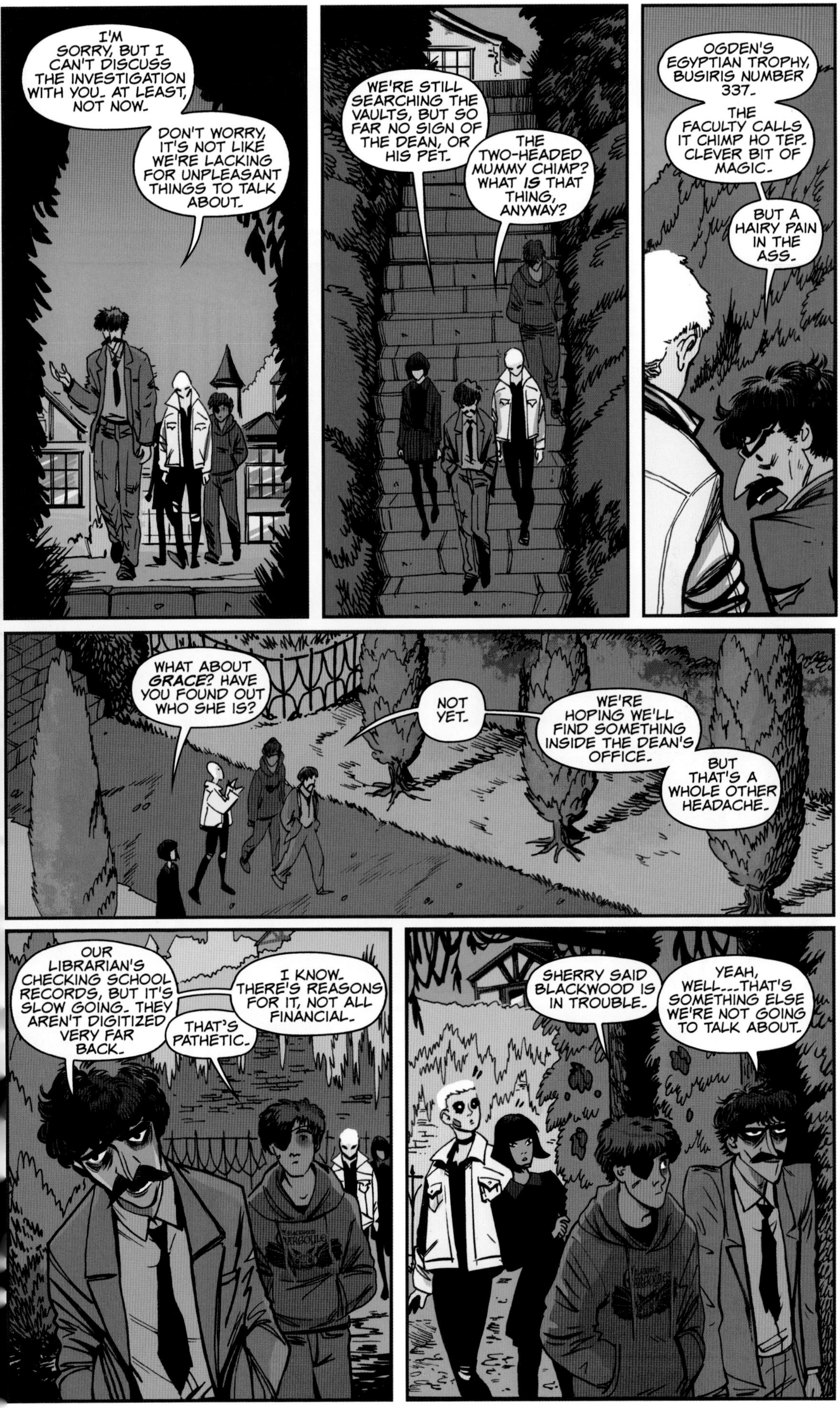
I'M SORRY, BUT I CAN'T DISCUSS THE INVESTIGATION WITH YOU. AT LEAST, NOT NOW.
DON'T WORRY, IT'S NOT LIKE WE'RE LACKING FOR UNPLEASANT THINGS TO TALK ABOUT.
WE'RE STILL SEARCHING THE VAULTS, BUT SO FAR NO SIGN OF THE DEAN, OR HIS PET.
THE TWO-HEADED MUMMY CHIMP? WHAT *IS* THAT THING, ANYWAY?
OGDEN'S EGYPTIAN TROPHY, BUSIRIS NUMBER 337.
THE FACULTY CALLS IT CHIMP HO TEP. CLEVER BIT OF MAGIC.
BUT A HAIRY PAIN IN THE ASS.
WHAT ABOUT ***GRACE***? HAVE YOU FOUND OUT WHO SHE IS?
NOT YET.
WE'RE HOPING WE'LL FIND SOMETHING INSIDE THE DEAN'S OFFICE.
BUT THAT'S A WHOLE OTHER HEADACHE.
OUR LIBRARIAN'S CHECKING SCHOOL RECORDS, BUT IT'S SLOW GOING. THEY AREN'T DIGITIZED VERY FAR BACK.
THAT'S PATHETIC.
I KNOW. THERE'S REASONS FOR IT, NOT ALL FINANCIAL.
SHERRY SAID BLACKWOOD IS IN TROUBLE.
YEAH, WELL... THAT'S SOMETHING ELSE WE'RE NOT GOING TO TALK ABOUT.

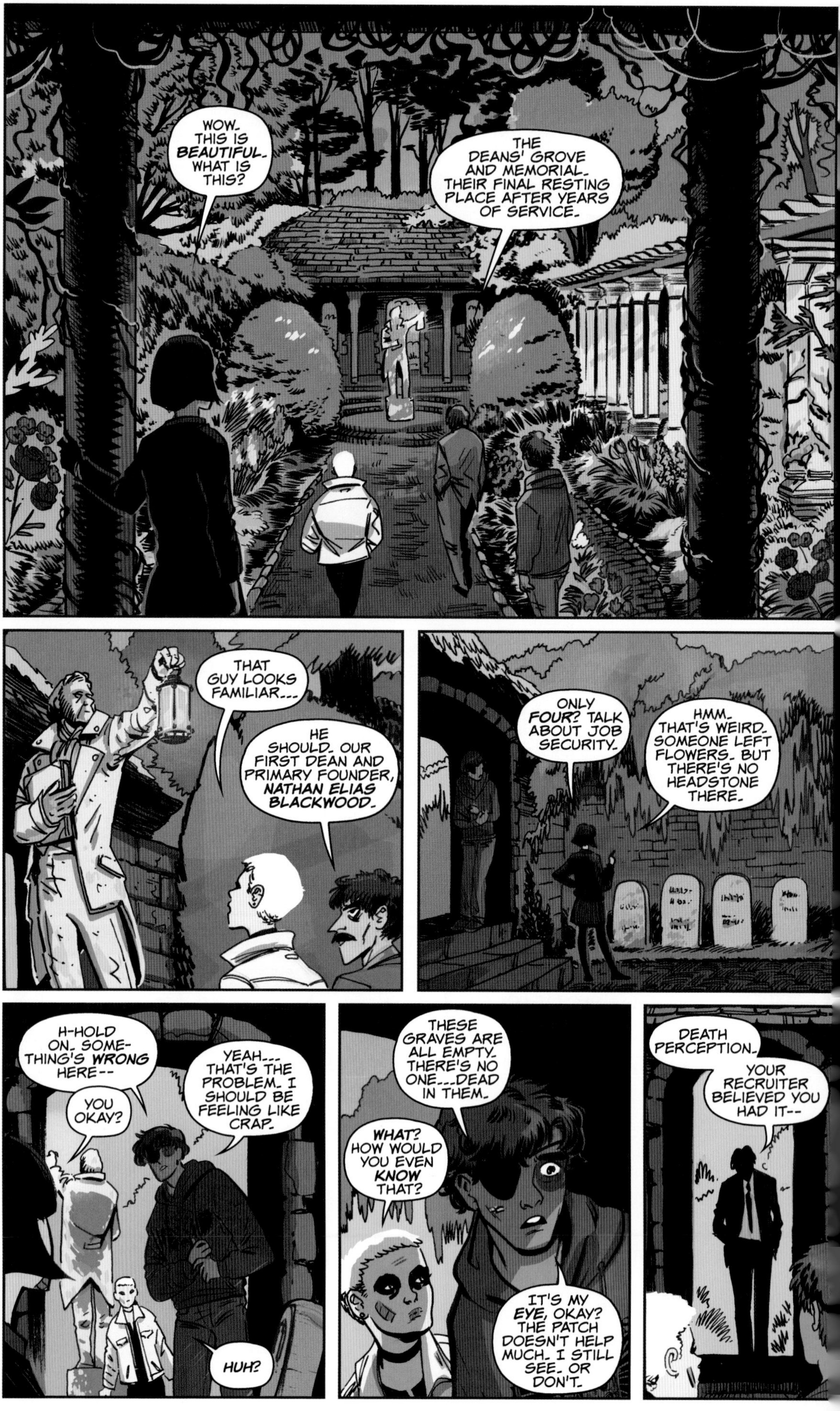
WOW. THIS IS BEAUTIFUL. WHAT IS THIS?
THE DEANS' GROVE AND MEMORIAL. THEIR FINAL RESTING PLACE AFTER YEARS OF SERVICE.
THAT GUY LOOKS FAMILIAR...
HE SHOULD. OUR FIRST DEAN AND PRIMARY FOUNDER, NATHAN ELIAS BLACKWOOD.
ONLY FOUR? TALK ABOUT JOB SECURITY.
HMM. THAT'S WEIRD. SOMEONE LEFT FLOWERS. BUT THERE'S NO HEADSTONE THERE.
H-HOLD ON. SOME-THING'S WRONG HERE--
YOU OKAY?
YEAH... THAT'S THE PROBLEM. I SHOULD BE FEELING LIKE CRAP.
HUH?
THESE GRAVES ARE ALL EMPTY. THERE'S NO ONE...DEAD IN THEM.
WHAT? HOW WOULD YOU EVEN KNOW THAT?
IT'S MY EYE, OKAY? THE PATCH DOESN'T HELP MUCH. I STILL SEE. OR DON'T.
DEATH PERCEPTION.
YOUR RECRUITER BELIEVED YOU HAD IT--

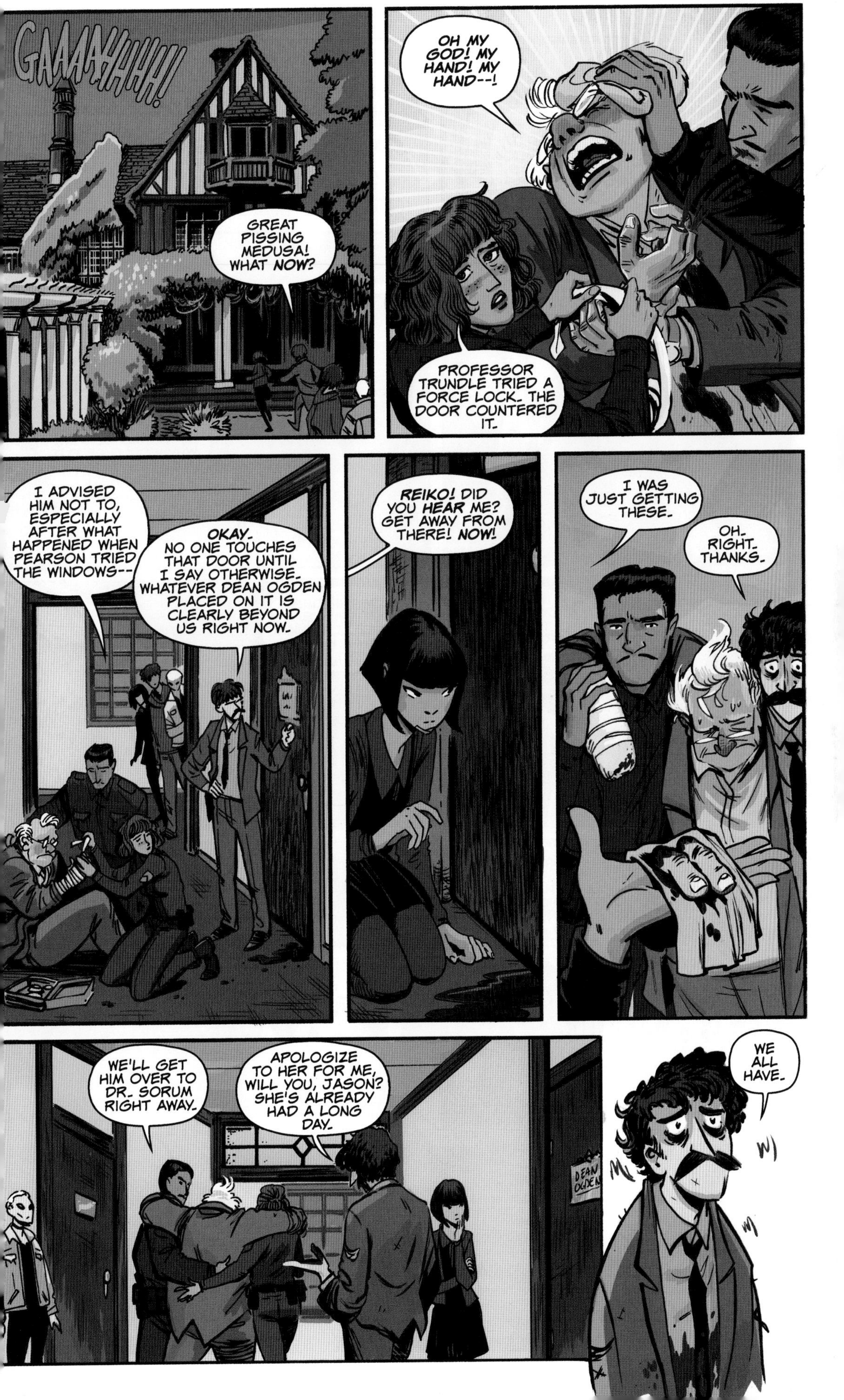
GAAAAHHHH!!
GREAT PISSING MEDUSA! WHAT NOW?
OH MY GOD! MY HAND! MY HAND--!
PROFESSOR TRUNDLE TRIED A FORCE LOCK. THE DOOR COUNTERED IT.
I ADVISED HIM NOT TO, ESPECIALLY AFTER WHAT HAPPENED WHEN PEARSON TRIED THE WINDOWS--
OKAY. NO ONE TOUCHES THAT DOOR UNTIL I SAY OTHERWISE. WHATEVER DEAN OGDEN PLACED ON IT IS CLEARLY BEYOND US RIGHT NOW.
REIKO! DID YOU HEAR ME? GET AWAY FROM THERE! NOW!
I WAS JUST GETTING THESE.
OH. RIGHT. THANKS.
WE'LL GET HIM OVER TO DR. SORUM RIGHT AWAY.
APOLOGIZE TO HER FOR ME, WILL YOU, JASON? SHE'S ALREADY HAD A LONG DAY.
DEAN OGDEN
WE ALL HAVE.

I DON'T CONTROL IT. IT JUST FLARES UP. AND I GET SICK, LIKE ALLERGIES. AND SOMETIMES I SEE THINGS.

LIKE WHAT? GHOSTS? DO YOU SEE--

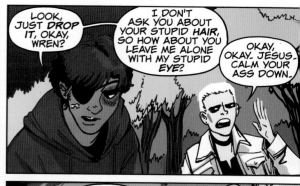

LOOK, JUST DROP IT, OKAY, WREN?

I DON'T ASK YOU ABOUT YOUR STUPID HAIR, SO HOW ABOUT YOU LEAVE ME ALONE WITH MY STUPID EYE?

OKAY, OKAY. JESUS. CALM YOUR ASS DOWN.

ANYWAY... IF THE GRAVES ARE EMPTY, SO WHAT? WHY WOULD IT HAVE ANYTHING TO DO WITH US?

I DUNNO. BUT THOSE FLOWERS BUG ME. IF IT WAS OGDEN, WHY WOULD HE PUT FLOWERS OVER HIS OWN GRAVE?

WHAT DO YOU THINK, REIKO?

I'M THINKING ABOUT THE DEAN'S OFFICE. I THINK I KNOW A WAY TO GET IN.

EXCUSE ME? ARE YOU HIGH? THAT CHUBBY OLD MAGIC DUDE GOT HIS FINGERS BLOWN OFF, AN' HE'S A FRIGGIN' PROFESSIONAL!

THERE IS A CURSE ON US, REMEMBER?! ARE YOU ACTUALLY TRYING TO KILL YOURSELF?

COULD YOU JUST, LIKE, SHUT UP AND LISTEN FOR ONE SECOND?

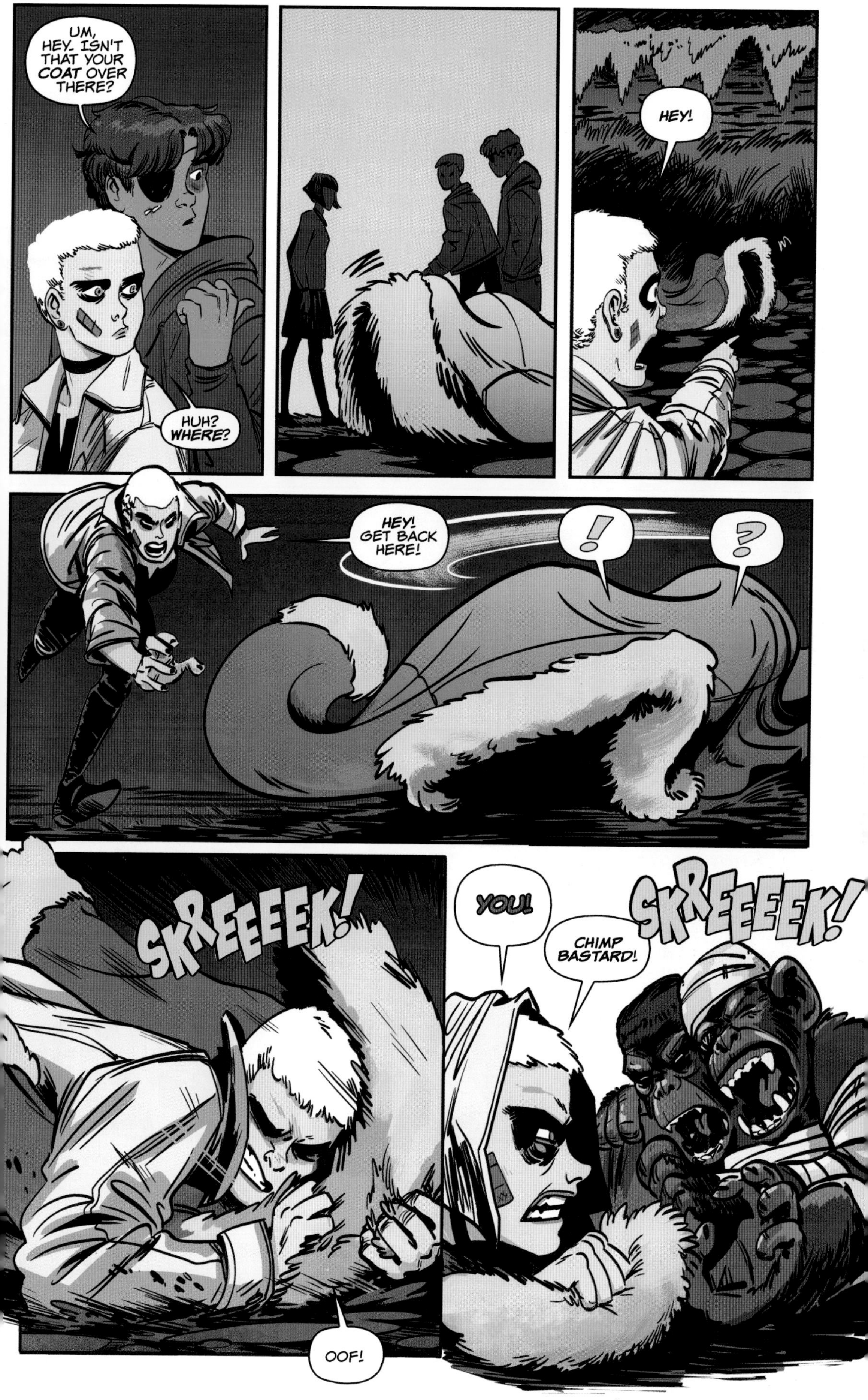
UM, HEY. ISN'T THAT YOUR COAT OVER THERE?
HUH? WHERE?
HEY!
HEY! GET BACK HERE!
!
?
SKREEEEK!
YOU!
CHIMP BASTARD!
SKREEEEK!
OOF!

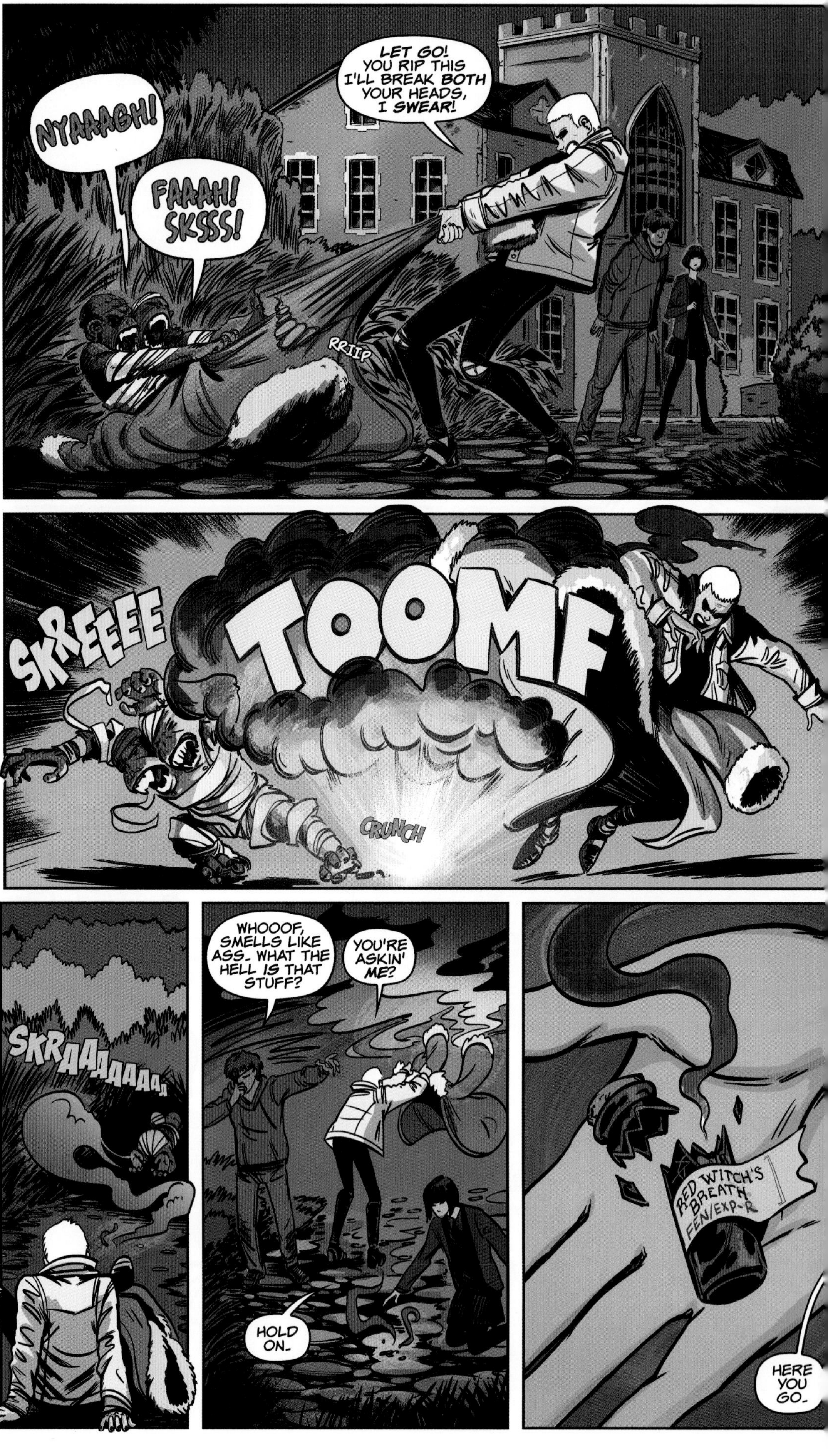

NYAAAGH!
FAAAH! SKSSS!
LET GO! YOU RIP THIS I'LL BREAK BOTH YOUR HEADS, I SWEAR!
RRIIP
SKREEEE
TOOMF
CRUNCH
SKRAAAAAAAA
WHOOOF, SMELLS LIKE ASS. WHAT THE HELL IS THAT STUFF?
YOU'RE ASKIN' ME?
HOLD ON.
RED WITCH'S BREATH
FEN/EXP-R
HERE YOU GO.

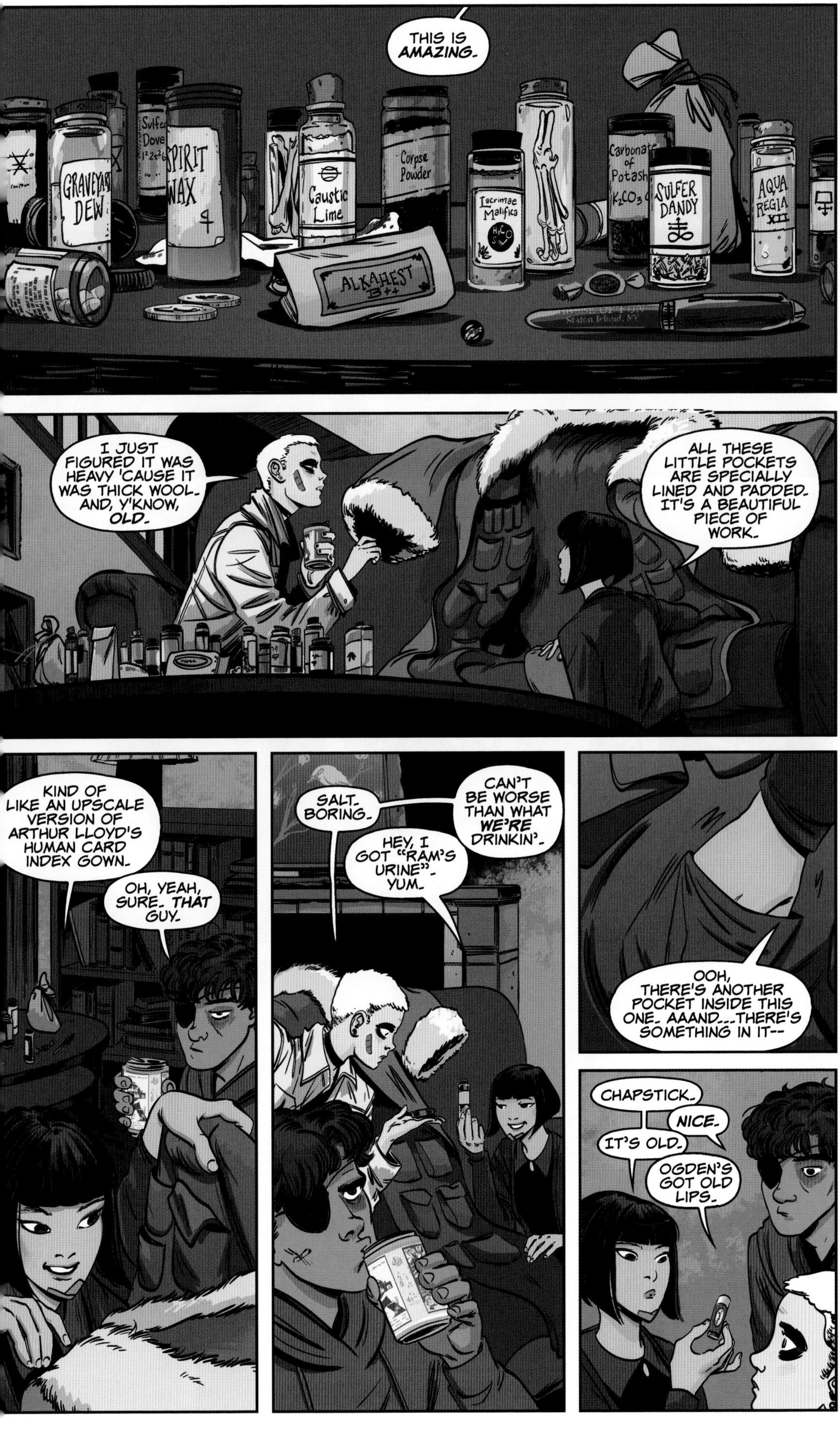
THIS IS AMAZING.
GRAVEYARD DEW
Sulfer Dove
SPIRIT WAX
Caustic Lime
Corpse Powder
Lacrimae Malifica
Carbonate of Potash
SULFER DANDY
AQUA REGIA XII
ALKAHEST
HOUSE OF FUN Staten Island, NY
I JUST FIGURED IT WAS HEAVY 'CAUSE IT WAS THICK WOOL. AND, Y'KNOW, OLD.
ALL THESE LITTLE POCKETS ARE SPECIALLY LINED AND PADDED. IT'S A BEAUTIFUL PIECE OF WORK.
KIND OF LIKE AN UPSCALE VERSION OF ARTHUR LLOYD'S HUMAN CARD INDEX GOWN.
OH, YEAH, SURE. THAT GUY.
SALT. BORING.
CAN'T BE WORSE THAN WHAT WE'RE DRINKIN'.
HEY, I GOT "RAM'S URINE". YUM.
OOH, THERE'S ANOTHER POCKET INSIDE THIS ONE. AAAND... THERE'S SOMETHING IN IT--
CHAPSTICK.
NICE.
IT'S OLD.
OGDEN'S GOT OLD LIPS.

WELL, I CAN SEE WHY OGDEN WANTED HIS COAT BACK. PRIVATE MAGIC STASH AN' ALL.

I DON'T KNOW. HE'D HAVE TO HAVE ALL THESE THINGS IN QUANTITY IN AN ALCHEMY LAB SOMEWHERE...

WHAT?

YOU KNOW ALL ABOUT THIS STUFF, DON'T YOU?

ALCHEMY? NOT REALLY--

NO, I MEAN ALL THIS STUFF. BLACKWOOD STUFF.

NOTHIN' FREAKS YOU OUT. NOTHIN' SURPRISES YOU. YOU PROBABLY KNEW ALL ABOUT THIS SCHOOL RIGHT FROM THE START--

HEY, ARE YOU EVEN LISTENIN' TO ME?

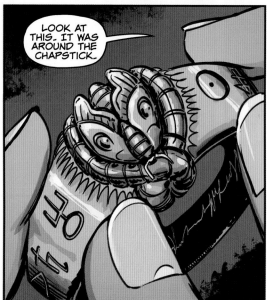

LOOK AT THIS. IT WAS AROUND THE CHAPSTICK.

THERE'S AN INSCRIPTION... "H.O. TO G.D. FOREVER MY QUEEN."

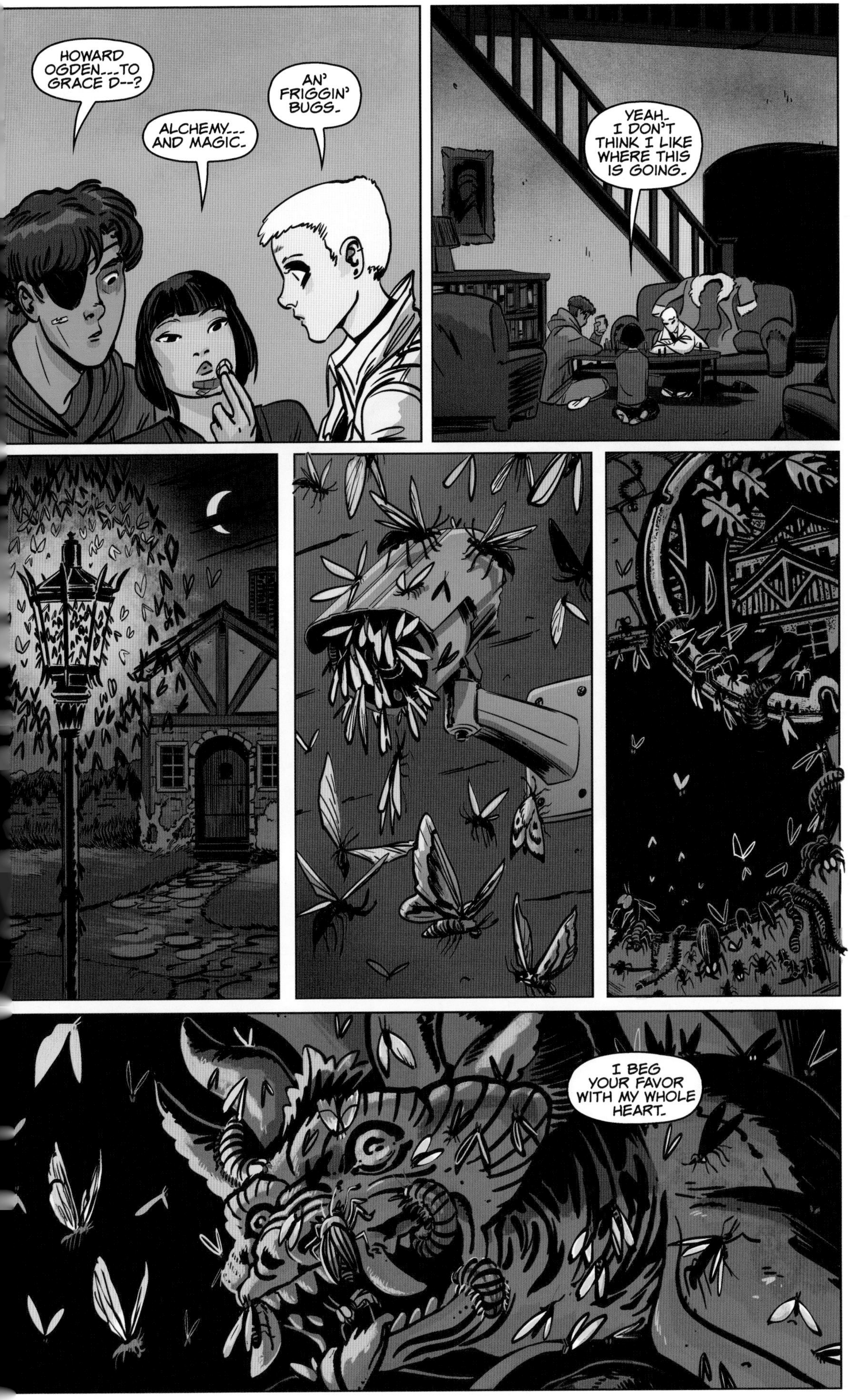
HOWARD OGDEN...TO GRACE D--?
ALCHEMY... AND MAGIC.
AN' FRIGGIN' BUGS.
YEAH. I DON'T THINK I LIKE WHERE THIS IS GOING.
I BEG YOUR FAVOR WITH MY WHOLE HEART.

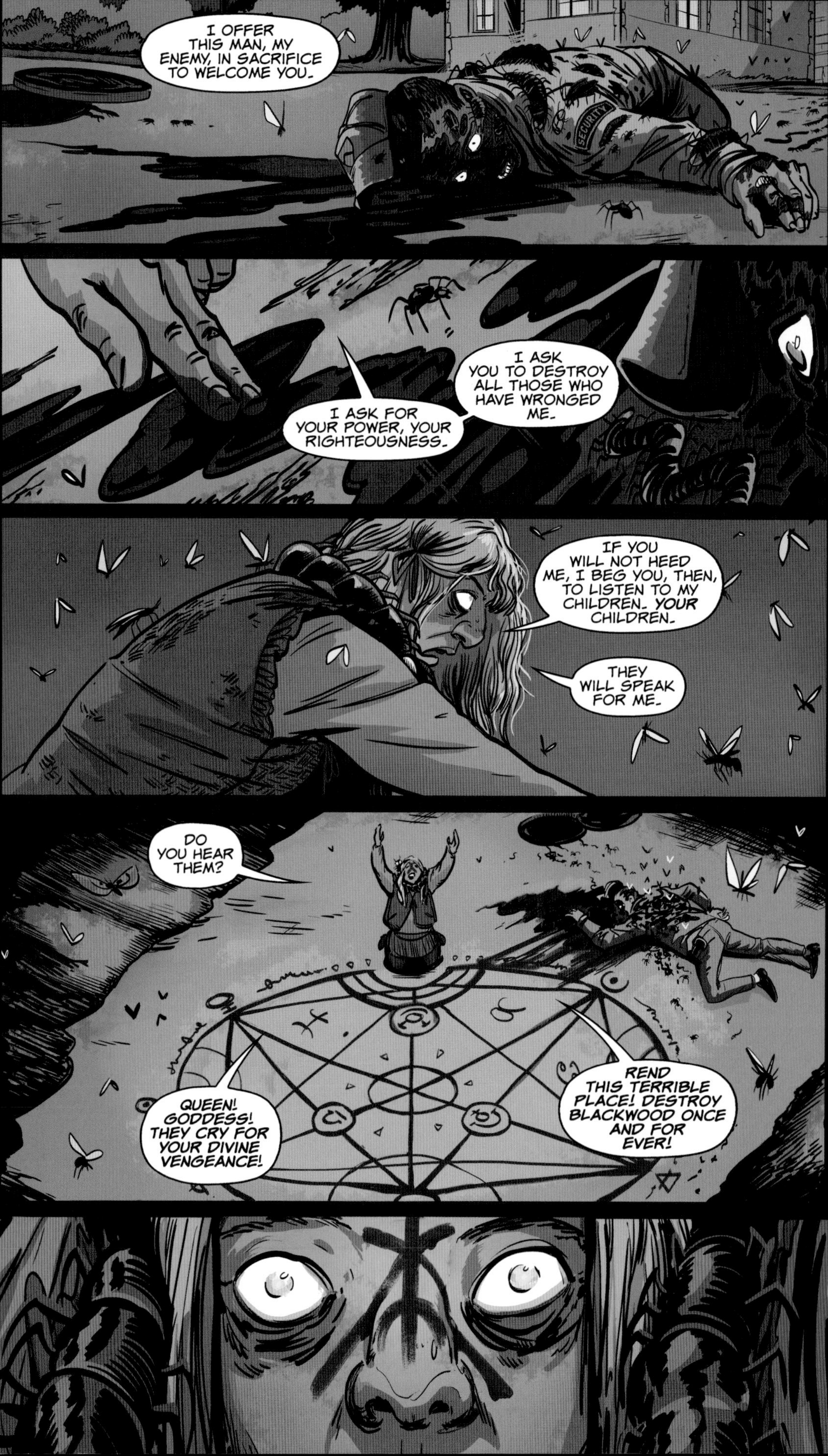
I OFFER THIS MAN, MY ENEMY, IN SACRIFICE TO WELCOME YOU.
SECURITY
I ASK FOR YOUR POWER, YOUR RIGHTEOUSNESS.
I ASK YOU TO DESTROY ALL THOSE WHO HAVE WRONGED ME.
IF YOU WILL NOT HEED ME, I BEG YOU, THEN, TO LISTEN TO MY CHILDREN. YOUR CHILDREN.
THEY WILL SPEAK FOR ME.
DO YOU HEAR THEM?
QUEEN! GODDESS! THEY CRY FOR YOUR DIVINE VENGEANCE!
REND THIS TERRIBLE PLACE! DESTROY BLACKWOOD ONCE AND FOR EVER!

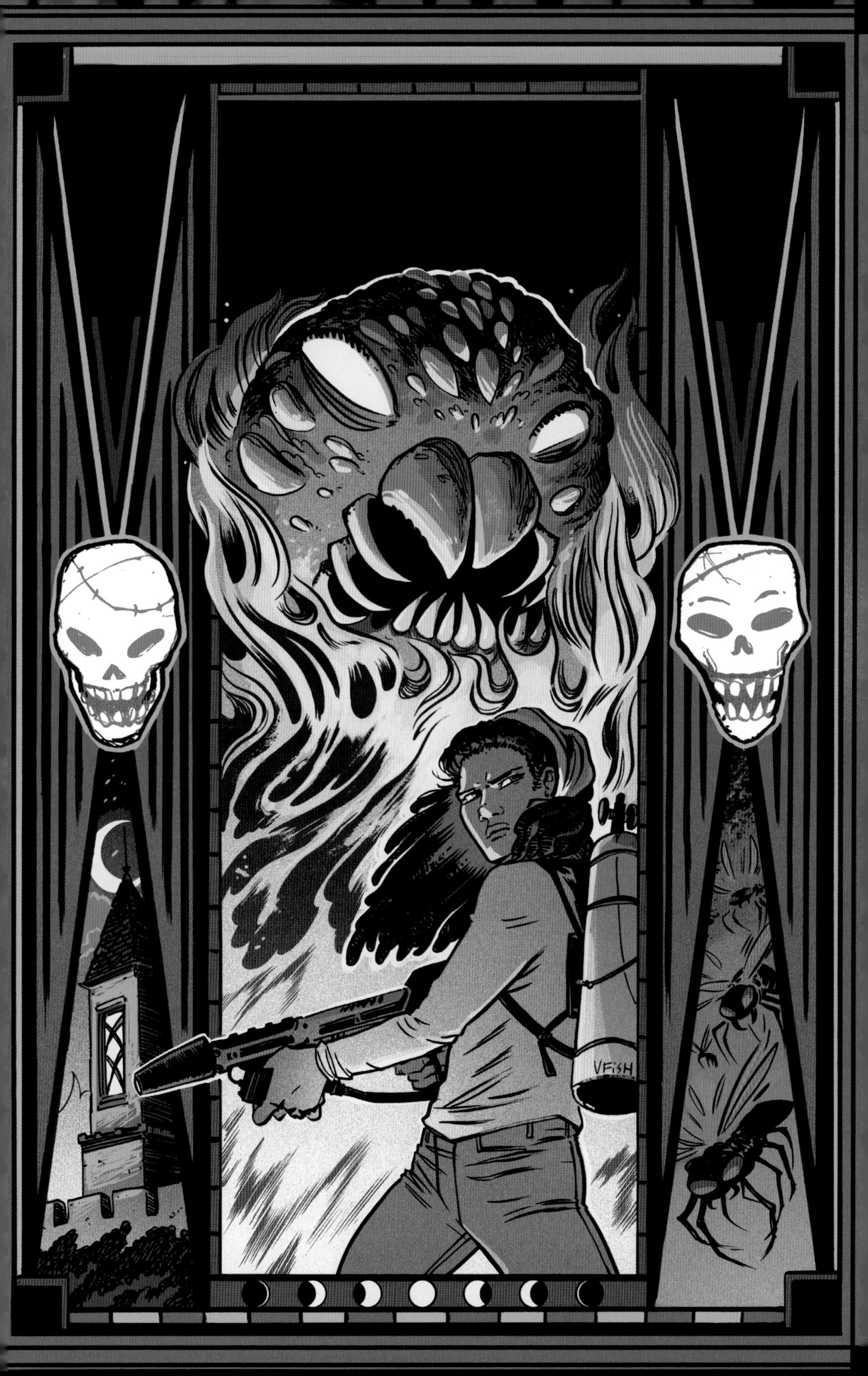
VFISH

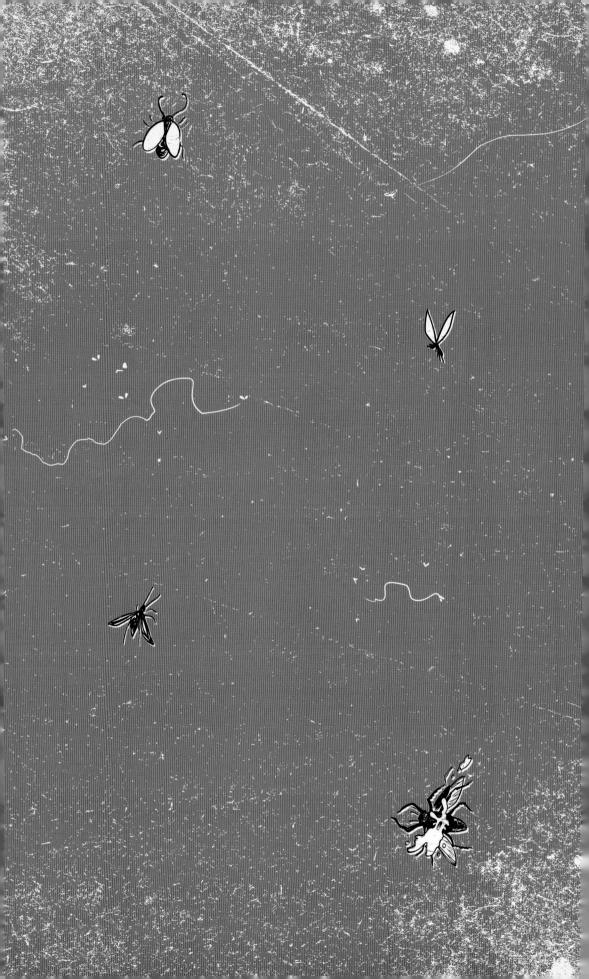

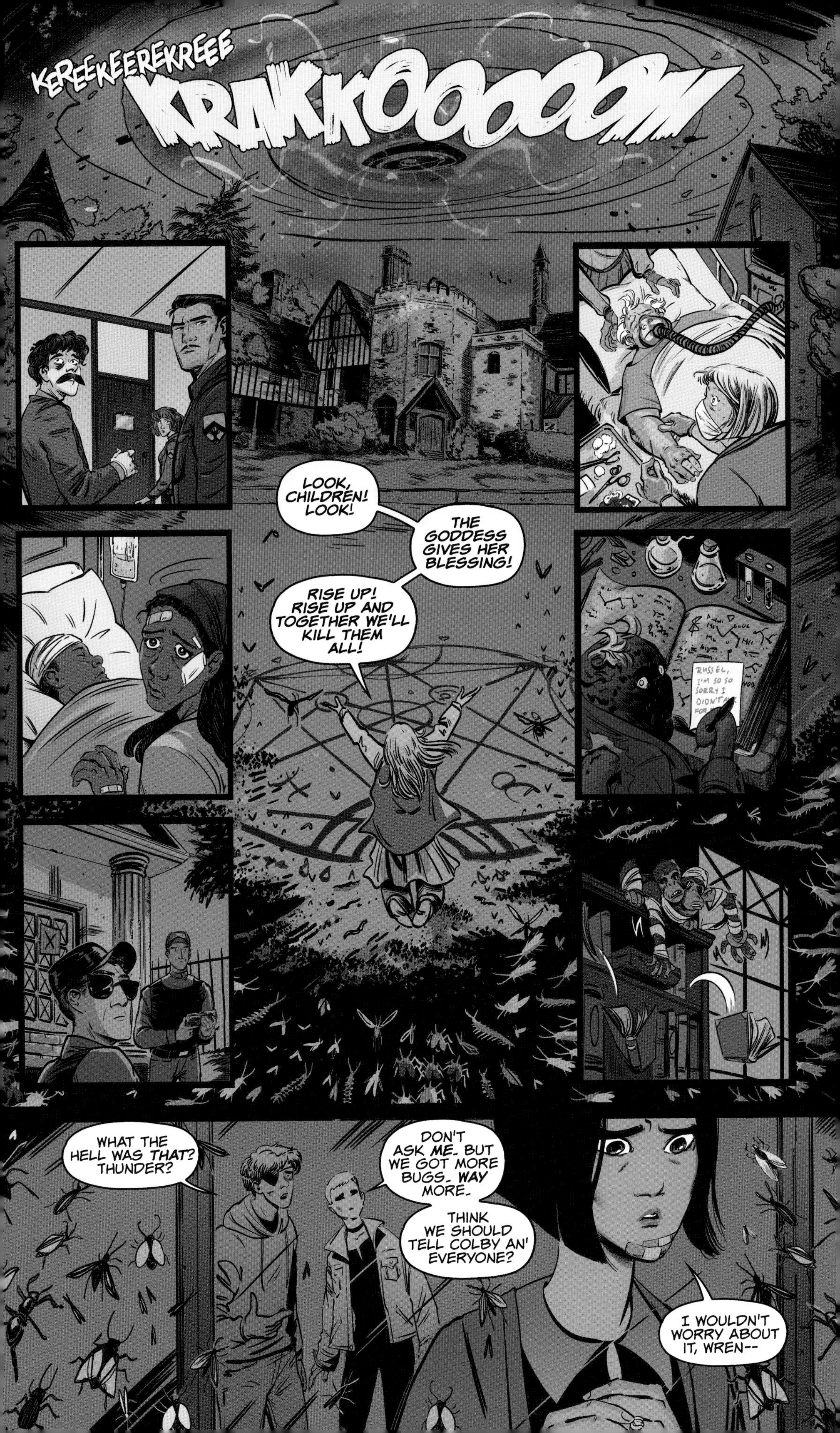
KEREEKEEREKREEE
KRAKKOOOOOM
LOOK, CHILDREN! LOOK!
THE GODDESS GIVES HER BLESSING!
RISE UP! RISE UP AND TOGETHER WE'LL KILL THEM ALL!
RUSSEL, I'M SO SO SORRY I DIDN'T
WHAT THE HELL WAS *THAT*? THUNDER?
DON'T ASK *ME*. BUT WE GOT MORE BUGS. *WAY* MORE.
THINK WE SHOULD TELL COLBY AN' EVERYONE?
I WOULDN'T WORRY ABOUT IT, WREN--

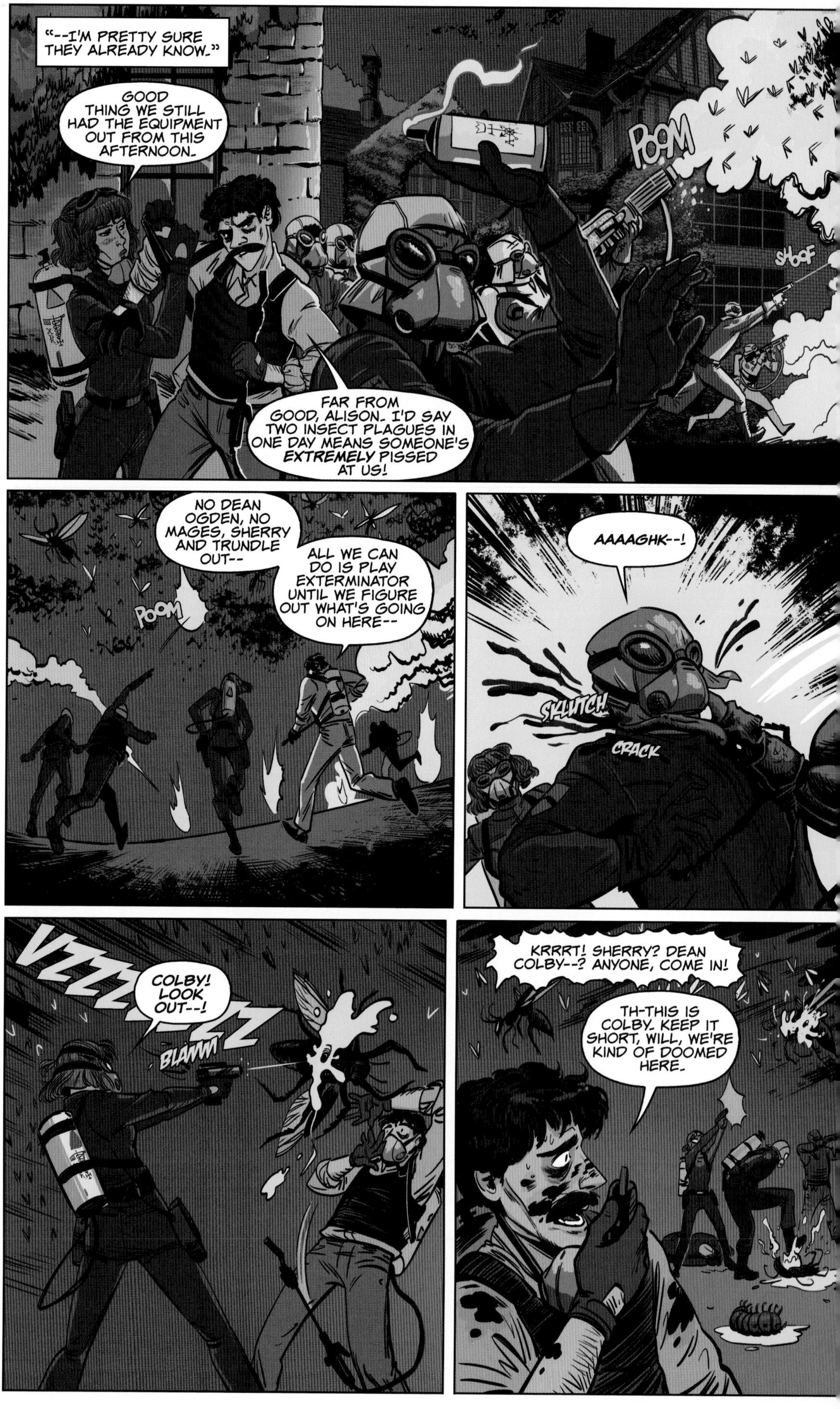
"--I'M PRETTY SURE THEY ALREADY KNOW."
GOOD THING WE STILL HAD THE EQUIPMENT OUT FROM THIS AFTERNOON.
POOM
SHOOF
FAR FROM GOOD, ALISON. I'D SAY TWO INSECT PLAGUES IN ONE DAY MEANS SOMEONE'S EXTREMELY PISSED AT US!
NO DEAN OGDEN, NO MAGES, SHERRY AND TRUNDLE OUT--
ALL WE CAN DO IS PLAY EXTERMINATOR UNTIL WE FIGURE OUT WHAT'S GOING ON HERE--
POOM
AAAAGHK--!
SKLUTCH
CRACK
VZZZZ-ZZ
COLBY! LOOK OUT--!
BLAMM
KRRRT! SHERRY? DEAN COLBY--? ANYONE, COME IN!
TH-THIS IS COLBY. KEEP IT SHORT, WILL, WE'RE KIND OF DOOMED HERE.

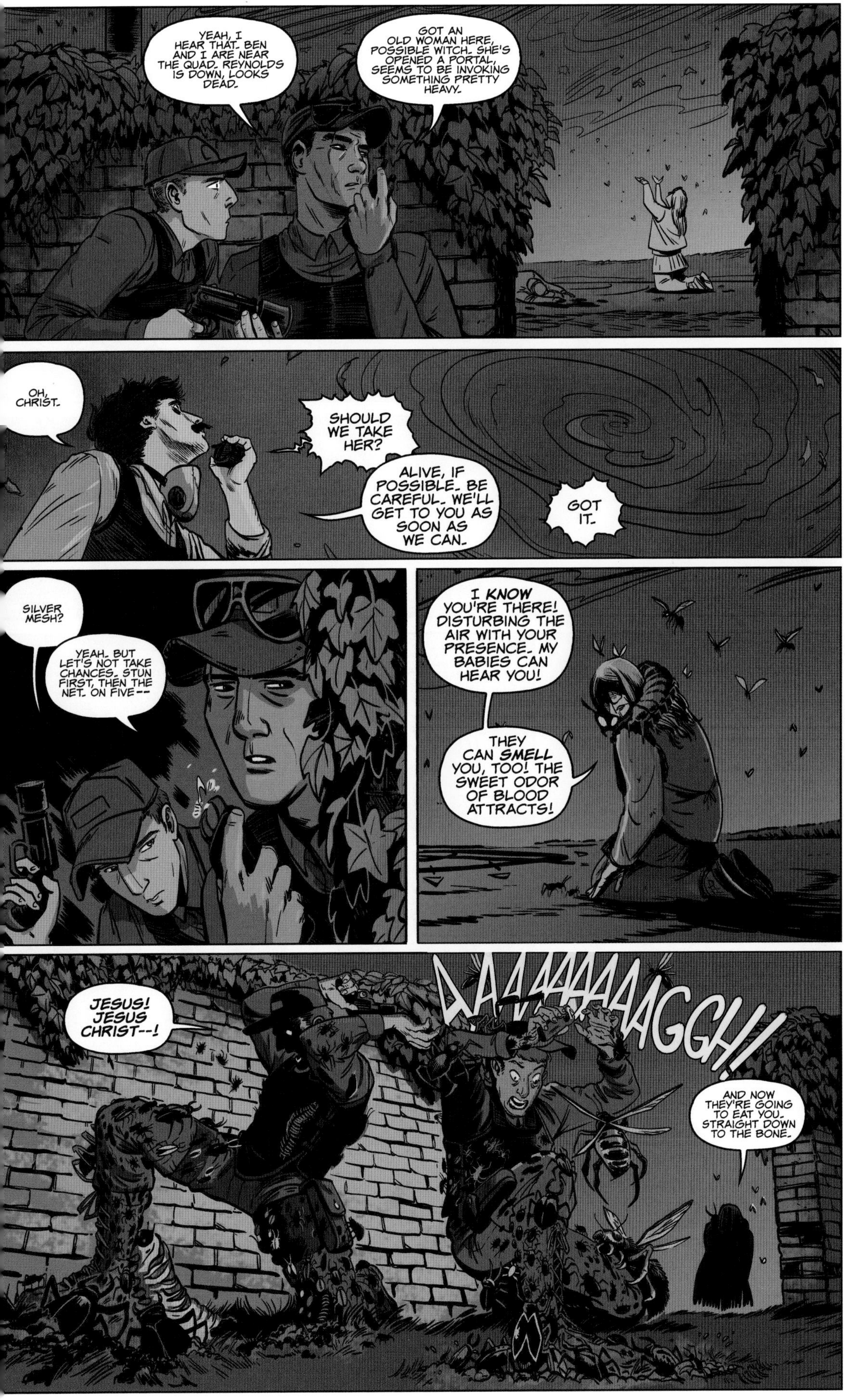
YEAH, I HEAR THAT. BEN AND I ARE NEAR THE QUAD. REYNOLDS IS DOWN, LOOKS DEAD.
GOT AN OLD WOMAN HERE, POSSIBLE WITCH. SHE'S OPENED A PORTAL, SEEMS TO BE INVOKING SOMETHING PRETTY HEAVY.
OH, CHRIST.
SHOULD WE TAKE HER?
ALIVE, IF POSSIBLE. BE CAREFUL. WE'LL GET TO YOU AS SOON AS WE CAN.
GOT IT.
SILVER MESH?
YEAH. BUT LET'S NOT TAKE CHANCES. STUN FIRST, THEN THE NET. ON FIVE--
I KNOW YOU'RE THERE! DISTURBING THE AIR WITH YOUR PRESENCE. MY BABIES CAN HEAR YOU!
THEY CAN SMELL YOU, TOO! THE SWEET ODOR OF BLOOD ATTRACTS!
JESUS! JESUS CHRIST--!
AAAAAAAAAGGH!!
AND NOW THEY'RE GOING TO EAT YOU. STRAIGHT DOWN TO THE BONE.

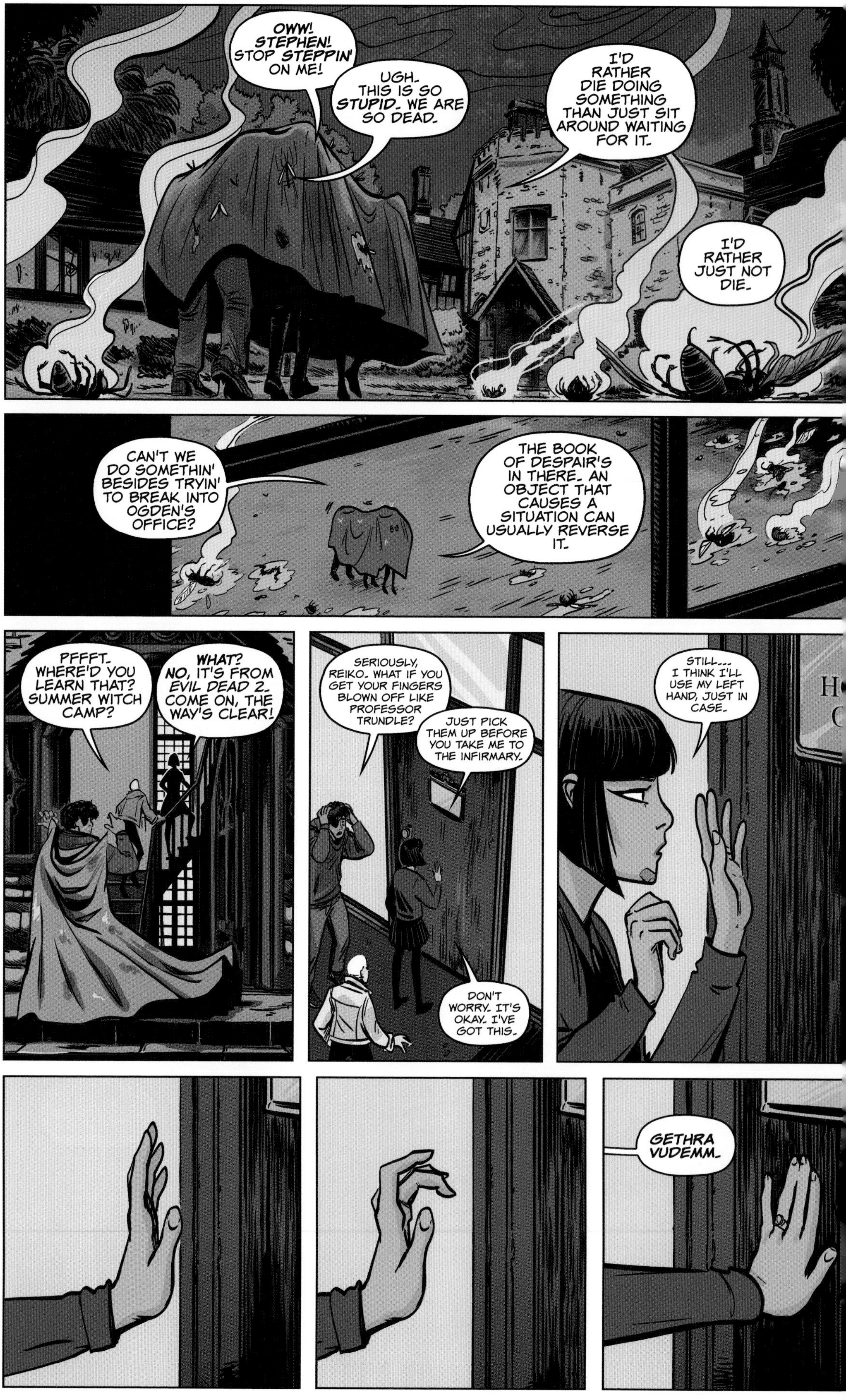
OWW! STEPHEN! STOP STEPPIN' ON ME!
UGH. THIS IS SO STUPID. WE ARE SO DEAD.
I'D RATHER DIE DOING SOMETHING THAN JUST SIT AROUND WAITING FOR IT.
I'D RATHER JUST NOT DIE.
CAN'T WE DO SOMETHIN' BESIDES TRYIN' TO BREAK INTO OGDEN'S OFFICE?
THE BOOK OF DESPAIR'S IN THERE. AN OBJECT THAT CAUSES A SITUATION CAN USUALLY REVERSE IT.
PFFFT. WHERE'D YOU LEARN THAT? SUMMER WITCH CAMP?
WHAT? NO, IT'S FROM EVIL DEAD 2. COME ON, THE WAY'S CLEAR!
SERIOUSLY, REIKO. WHAT IF YOU GET YOUR FINGERS BLOWN OFF LIKE PROFESSOR TRUNDLE?
JUST PICK THEM UP BEFORE YOU TAKE ME TO THE INFIRMARY.
DON'T WORRY. IT'S OKAY. I'VE GOT THIS.
STILL... I THINK I'LL USE MY LEFT HAND, JUST IN CASE.
GETHRA VUDEMM.

DEAN HOWARD OGDEN

CLICK
SHHHHK
KCHAK

CREEEEEEEEEEEEEEEEAAAK

HOLY CRAP. OKAY, SEE? YOU'RE A FRICKIN' WITCH. ADMIT IT.

PLEASE. THIS IS HOW OGDEN OPENED THE MAUSOLEUM DOOR. I FIGURED I'D TAKE A CHANCE HE USED THE SAME SPELL HERE.

YOU CAUGHT THAT? WHILE HE WAS TRYIN' TO KILL US?

I PAY ATTENTION. YOU SHOULD TRY IT SOMETIME.

MAN. EVEN IF THE BOOK'S HERE IT'LL TAKE US FOREVER TO FIND IT.

I'LL TAKE THE SHELVES. BE CAREFUL. STILL TIME TO LOSE SOME FINGERS.

GREAT. GUESS I'LL START WITH THE CRAP ON THE FLOOR. WANNA LEND A HAND, WREN?

PFFT. HELL, NO. I'M CHECKIN' THE DESK. WOULDN'T BE SURPRISED IF IT AIN'T SITTIN' RIGHT OUT HERE IN PLAIN--

OPEN MY UNNATURA OF DEATH

HEY. CHECK THIS OUT. THINK WE GOT A WINNER HERE.

WOW. SHE'S PRETTY.

HMM. AND HE'S... WELL, HE'S YOUNGER. AND NOT A ZOMBIE.

IT GETS BETTER. THERE'S A NOTE ON THE BACK.

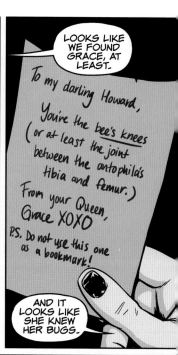

LOOKS LIKE WE FOUND GRACE, AT LEAST.

To my darling Howard,

You're the bee's knees (or at least the joint between the antophila's tibia and femur.)

From your Queen,
Grace XOXO

P.S. Do not use this one as a bookmark!

AND IT LOOKS LIKE SHE KNEW HER BUGS.

HEY, GUYS, C'MERE. I GOT SOMETHING ELSE YOU'LL WANNA SEE--

YOU FOUND THE BOOK?

NO, BUT, LOOK--DIDN'T DEAN OGDEN SAY HE WAS LOOKING FOR HIS COAT--

--AND SOMETHING CALLED A DYSON KIT?

YEAH, HE DID. YOU THINK--?

GIMME A SEC, AND WE'LL SEE WHAT THERE IS TO--

CRIKK CRAKK

AAAAAAAAAH!

NNAAAAAAH!

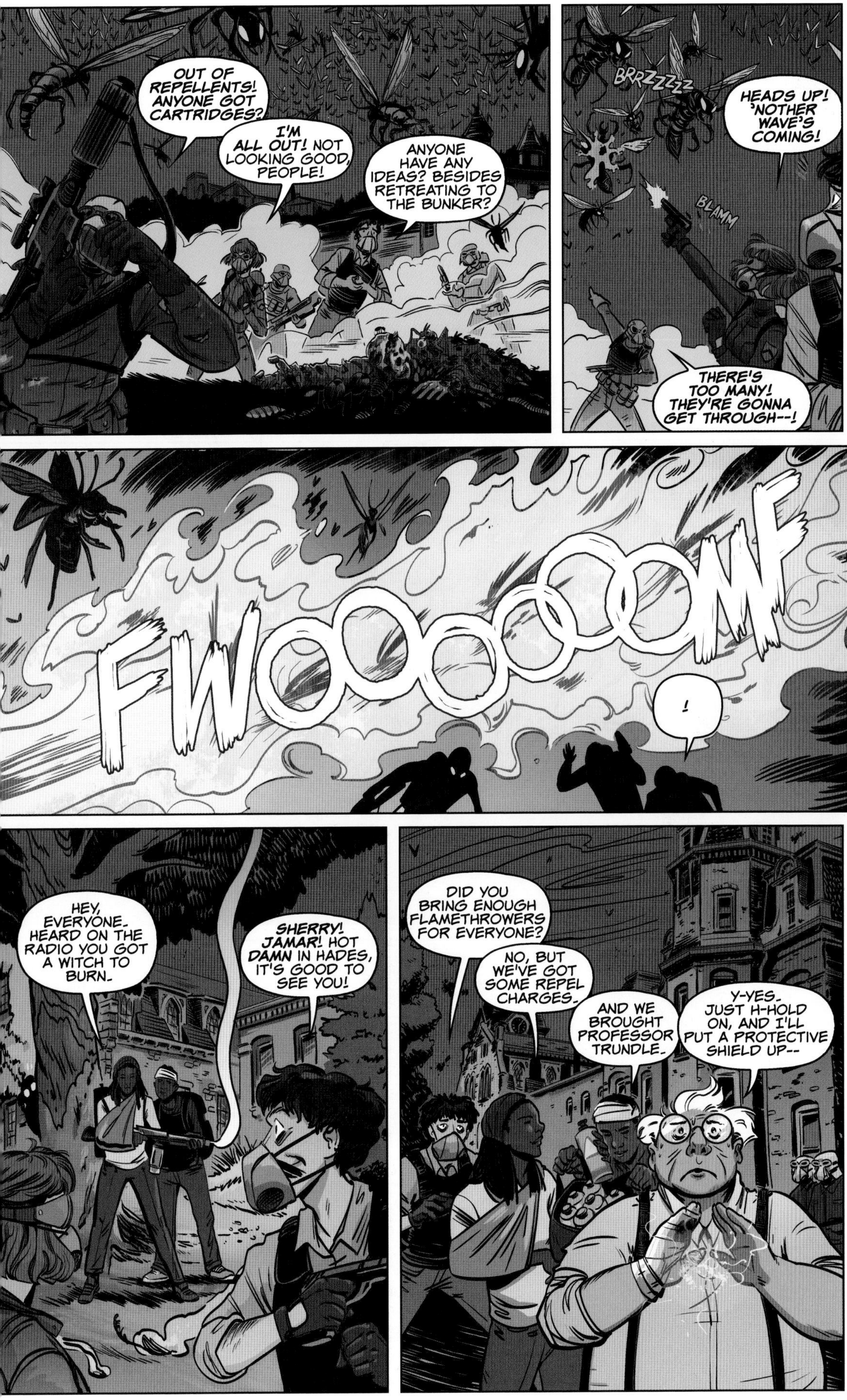
OUT OF REPELLENTS! ANYONE GOT CARTRIDGES?
I'M ALL OUT! NOT LOOKING GOOD, PEOPLE!
ANYONE HAVE ANY IDEAS? BESIDES RETREATING TO THE BUNKER?
BRRZZZZZ
HEADS UP! 'NOTHER WAVE'S COMING!
BLAMM
THERE'S TOO MANY! THEY'RE GONNA GET THROUGH--!
FWOOOOOOMF
!
HEY, EVERYONE. HEARD ON THE RADIO YOU GOT A WITCH TO BURN.
SHERRY! JAMAR! HOT DAMN IN HADES, IT'S GOOD TO SEE YOU!
DID YOU BRING ENOUGH FLAMETHROWERS FOR EVERYONE?
NO, BUT WE'VE GOT SOME REPEL CHARGES.
AND WE BROUGHT PROFESSOR TRUNDLE.
Y-YES. JUST H-HOLD ON, AND I'LL PUT A PROTECTIVE SHIELD UP--

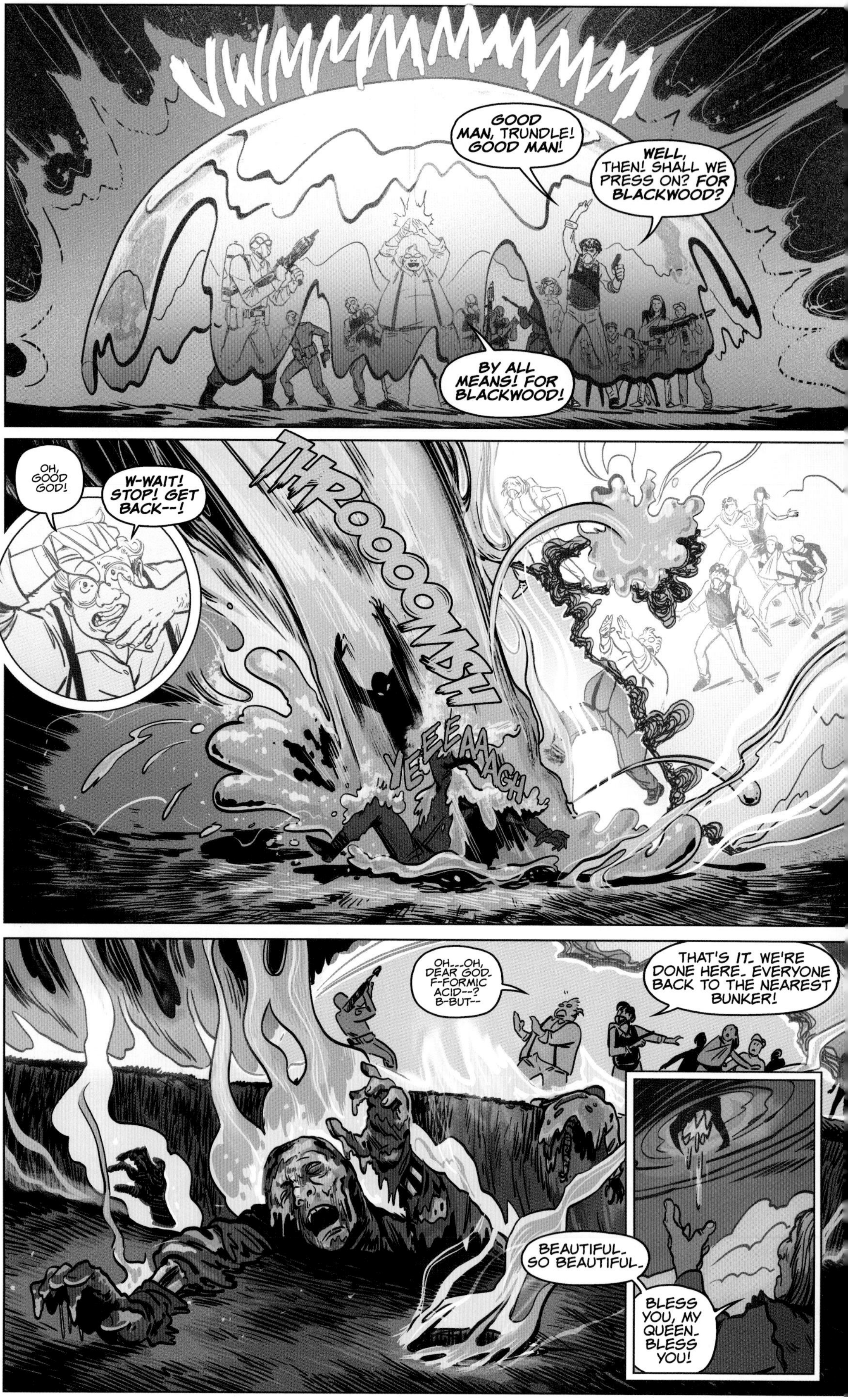
VWMMMMMMMM
GOOD MAN, TRUNDLE! GOOD MAN!
WELL, THEN! SHALL WE PRESS ON? FOR BLACKWOOD?
BY ALL MEANS! FOR BLACKWOOD!
OH, GOOD GOD!
W-WAIT! STOP! GET BACK--!
THROOOOOMSH
YEEEAAAAGH
OH... OH, DEAR GOD. F-FORMIC ACID--? B-BUT--
THAT'S IT. WE'RE DONE HERE. EVERYONE BACK TO THE NEAREST BUNKER!
BEAUTIFUL. SO BEAUTIFUL.
BLESS YOU, MY QUEEN. BLESS YOU!

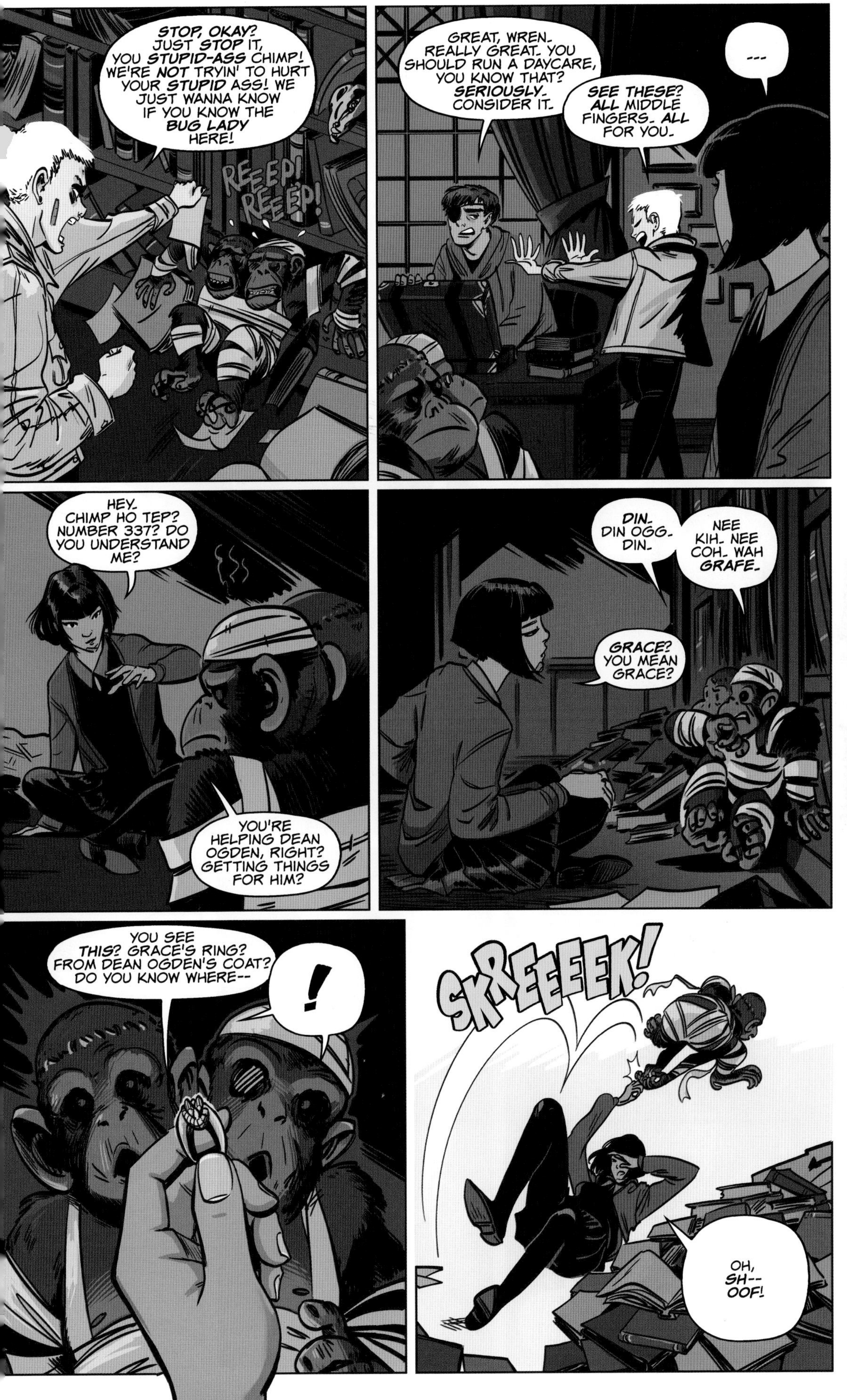
STOP, OKAY? JUST STOP IT, YOU STUPID-ASS CHIMP! WE'RE NOT TRYIN' TO HURT YOUR STUPID ASS! WE JUST WANNA KNOW IF YOU KNOW THE BUG LADY HERE!
REEEP! REEEP!
GREAT, WREN. REALLY GREAT. YOU SHOULD RUN A DAYCARE, YOU KNOW THAT? SERIOUSLY. CONSIDER IT.
SEE THESE? ALL MIDDLE FINGERS. ALL FOR YOU.
...
HEY. CHIMP HO TEP? NUMBER 337? DO YOU UNDERSTAND ME?
YOU'RE HELPING DEAN OGDEN, RIGHT? GETTING THINGS FOR HIM?
DIN. DIN OGG. DIN.
NEE KIH. NEE COH. WAH GRAFE.
GRACE? YOU MEAN GRACE?
YOU SEE THIS? GRACE'S RING? FROM DEAN OGDEN'S COAT? DO YOU KNOW WHERE--
!
SKREEEEK!
OH, SH-- OOF!

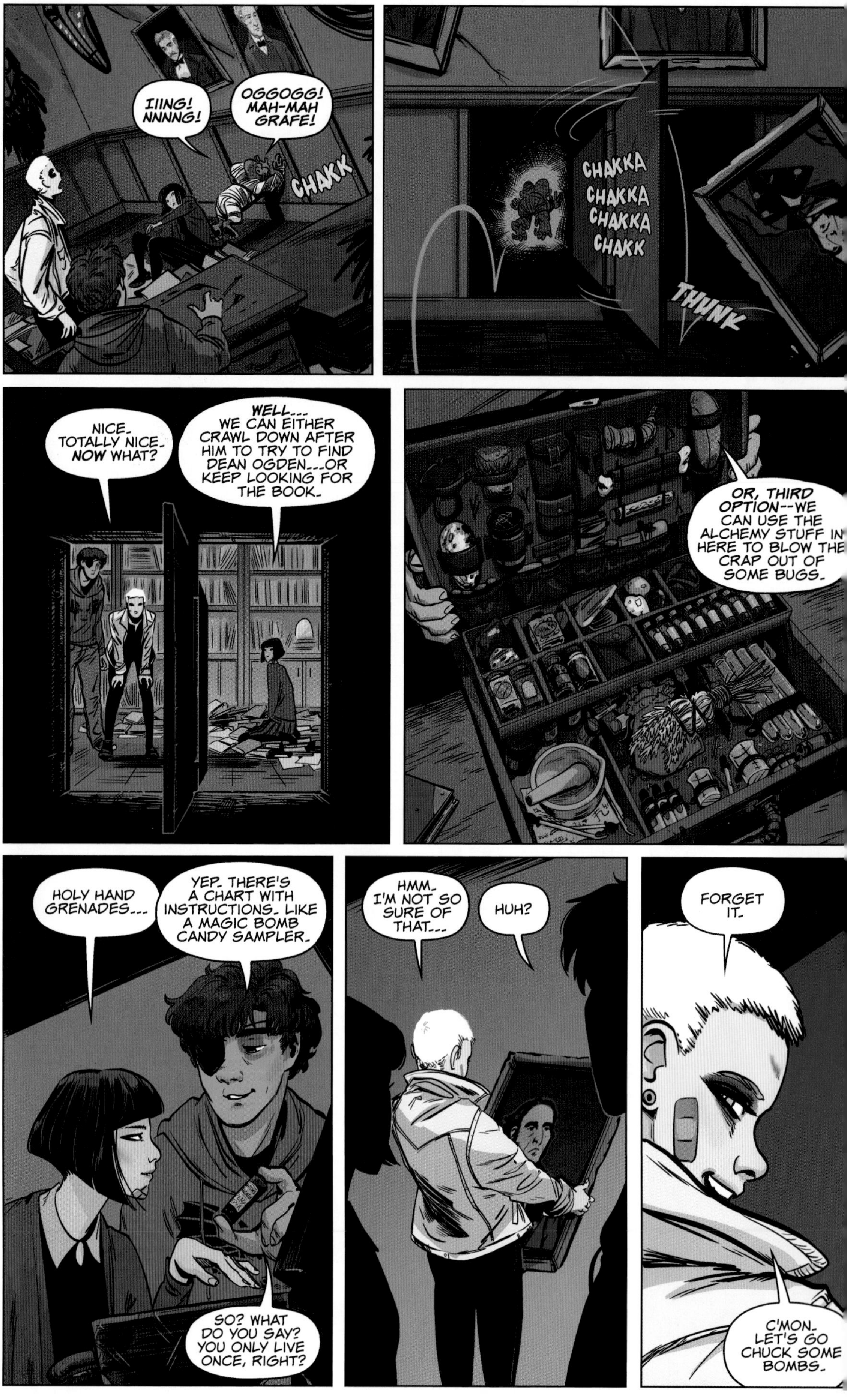
IIING! NNNNG!
OGGOGG! MAH-MAH GRAFE!
CHAKK
CHAKKA CHAKKA CHAKKA CHAKK
THUNK
NICE. TOTALLY NICE. NOW WHAT?
WELL... WE CAN EITHER CRAWL DOWN AFTER HIM TO TRY TO FIND DEAN OGDEN...OR KEEP LOOKING FOR THE BOOK.
OR, THIRD OPTION--WE CAN USE THE ALCHEMY STUFF IN HERE TO BLOW THE CRAP OUT OF SOME BUGS.
HOLY HAND GRENADES...
YEP. THERE'S A CHART WITH INSTRUCTIONS. LIKE A MAGIC BOMB CANDY SAMPLER.
SO? WHAT DO YOU SAY? YOU ONLY LIVE ONCE, RIGHT?
HMM. I'M NOT SO SURE OF THAT...
HUH?
FORGET IT.
C'MON. LET'S GO CHUCK SOME BOMBS.

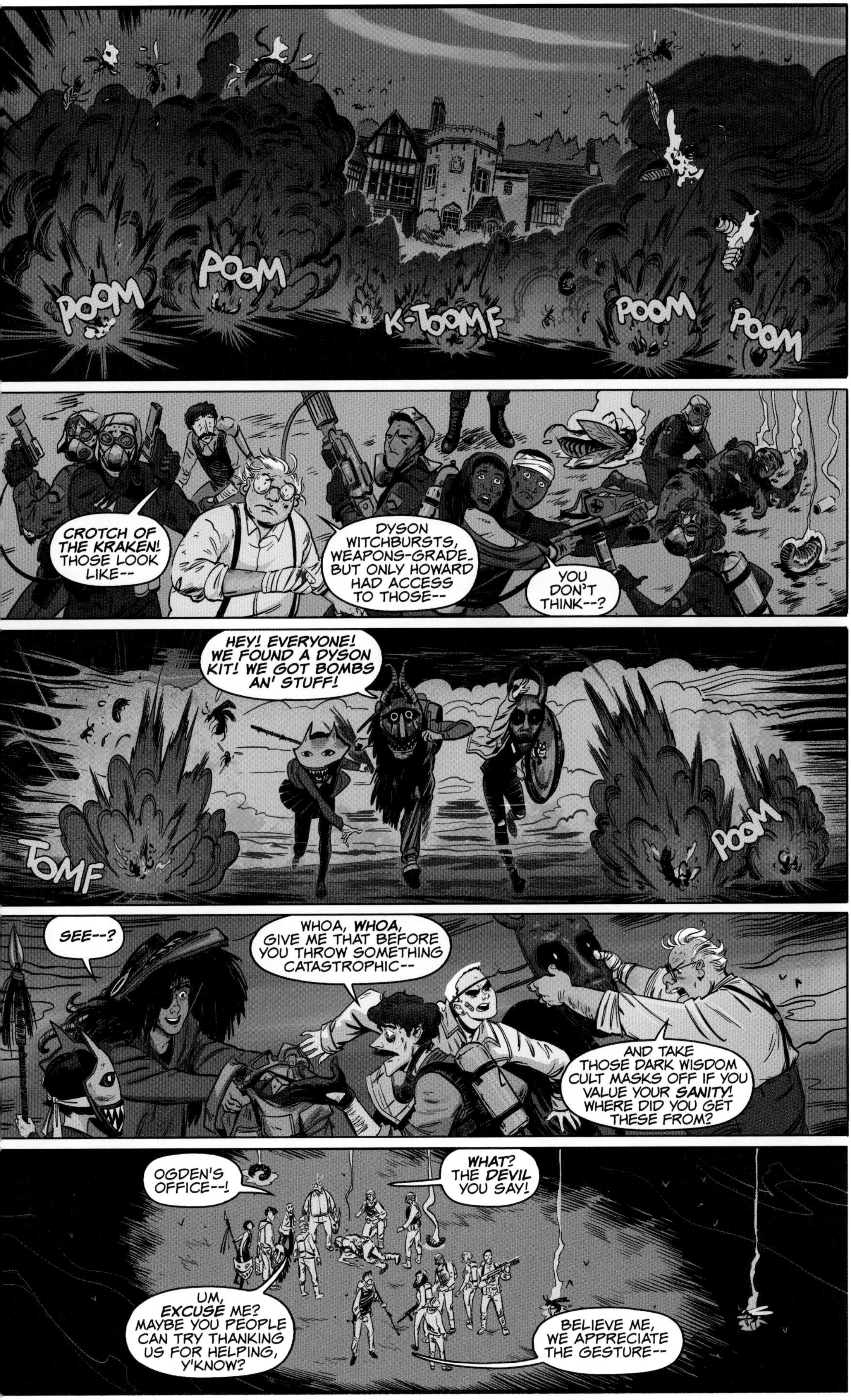
POOM
POOM
K-TOOMF
POOM
POOM
CROTCH OF THE KRAKEN! THOSE LOOK LIKE--
DYSON WITCHBURSTS, WEAPONS-GRADE. BUT ONLY HOWARD HAD ACCESS TO THOSE--
YOU DON'T THINK--?
HEY! EVERYONE! WE FOUND A DYSON KIT! WE GOT BOMBS AN' STUFF!
TOMF
POOM
SEE--?
WHOA, WHOA, GIVE ME THAT BEFORE YOU THROW SOMETHING CATASTROPHIC--
AND TAKE THOSE DARK WISDOM CULT MASKS OFF IF YOU VALUE YOUR SANITY! WHERE DID YOU GET THESE FROM?
OGDEN'S OFFICE--!
WHAT? THE DEVIL YOU SAY!
UM, EXCUSE ME? MAYBE YOU PEOPLE CAN TRY THANKING US FOR HELPING, Y'KNOW?
BELIEVE ME, WE APPRECIATE THE GESTURE--

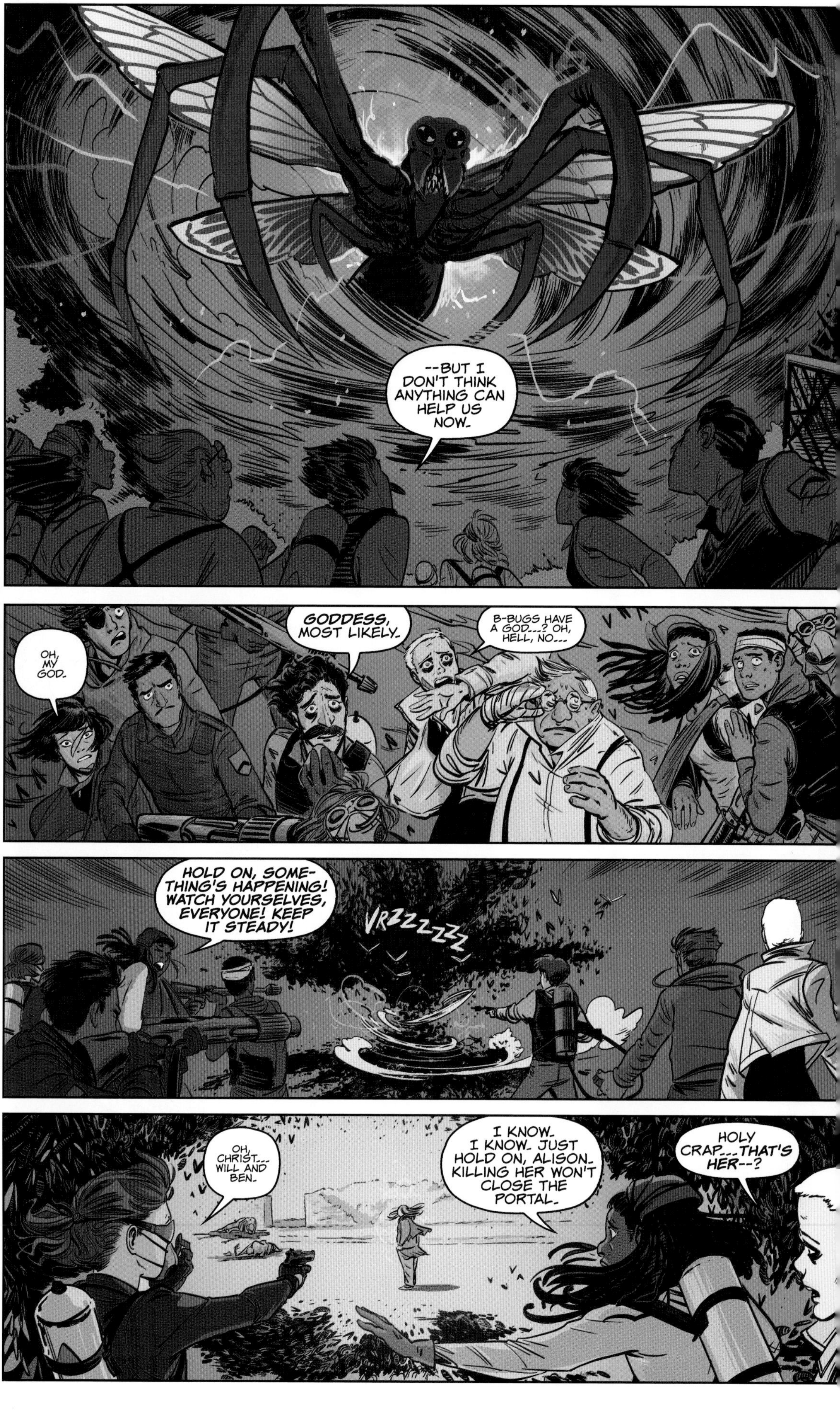
--BUT I DON'T THINK ANYTHING CAN HELP US NOW.
OH, MY GOD.
GODDESS, MOST LIKELY.
B-BUGS HAVE A GOD...? OH, HELL, NO...
HOLD ON, SOMETHING'S HAPPENING! WATCH YOURSELVES, EVERYONE! KEEP IT STEADY!
VRZZZZZZ
OH, CHRIST... WILL AND BEN.
I KNOW. I KNOW. JUST HOLD ON, ALISON. KILLING HER WON'T CLOSE THE PORTAL.
HOLY CRAP...THAT'S HER--?

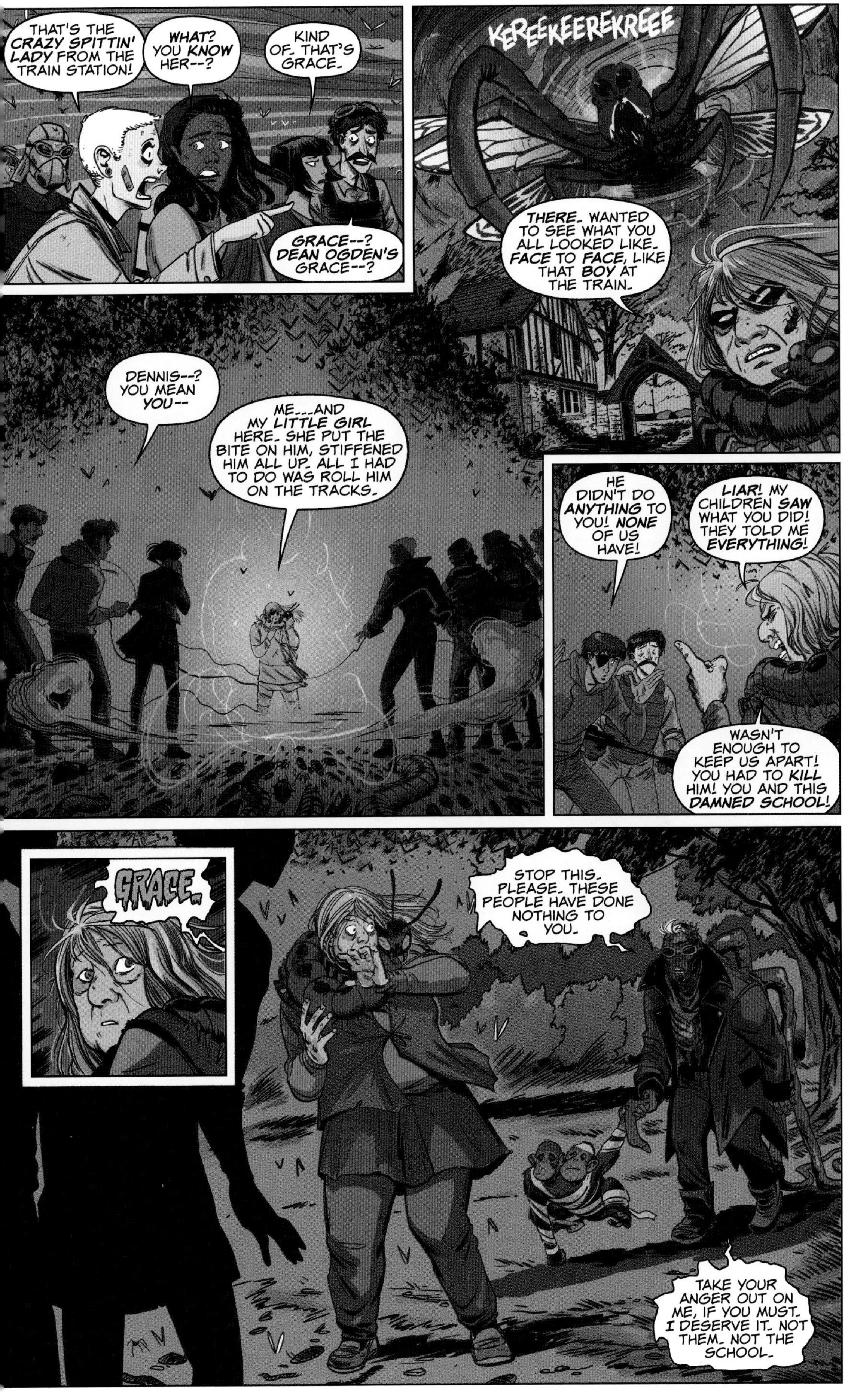

THAT'S THE CRAZY SPITTIN' LADY FROM THE TRAIN STATION!
WHAT? YOU KNOW HER--?
KIND OF. THAT'S GRACE.
GRACE--? DEAN OGDEN'S GRACE--?
KEREEKEEREKREEE
THERE. WANTED TO SEE WHAT YOU ALL LOOKED LIKE. FACE TO FACE, LIKE THAT BOY AT THE TRAIN.
DENNIS--? YOU MEAN YOU--
ME...AND MY LITTLE GIRL HERE. SHE PUT THE BITE ON HIM, STIFFENED HIM ALL UP. ALL I HAD TO DO WAS ROLL HIM ON THE TRACKS.
HE DIDN'T DO ANYTHING TO YOU! NONE OF US HAVE!
LIAR! MY CHILDREN SAW WHAT YOU DID! THEY TOLD ME EVERYTHING!
WASN'T ENOUGH TO KEEP US APART! YOU HAD TO KILL HIM! YOU AND THIS DAMNED SCHOOL!
GRACE.
STOP THIS. PLEASE. THESE PEOPLE HAVE DONE NOTHING TO YOU.
TAKE YOUR ANGER OUT ON ME, IF YOU MUST. I DESERVE IT. NOT THEM. NOT THE SCHOOL.

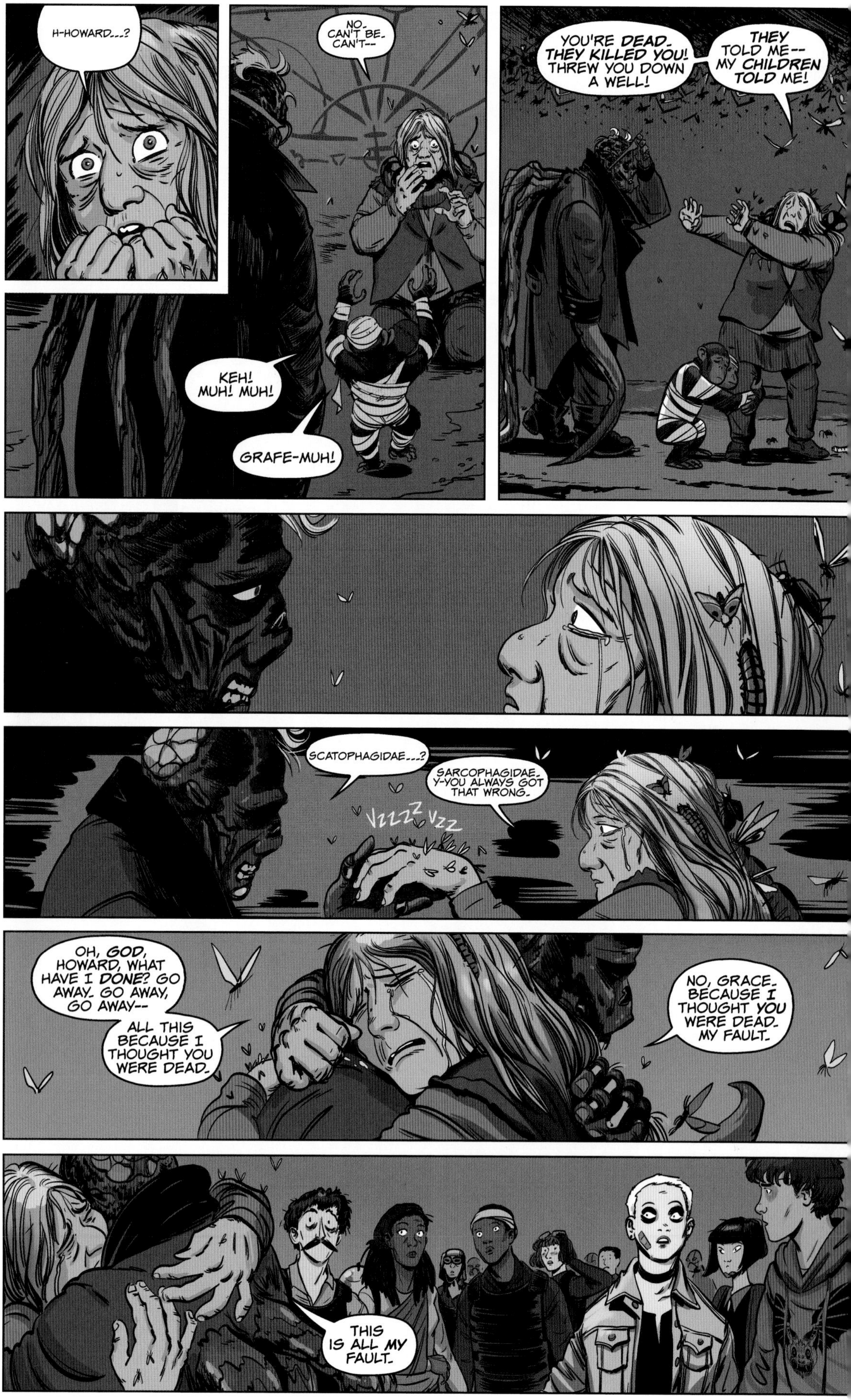
H-HOWARD...?
NO. CAN'T BE. CAN'T--
KEH! MUH! MUH!
GRAFE-MUH!
YOU'RE DEAD. THEY KILLED YOU! THREW YOU DOWN A WELL!
THEY TOLD ME-- MY CHILDREN TOLD ME!
SCATOPHAGIDAE...?
SARCOPHAGIDAE. Y-YOU ALWAYS GOT THAT WRONG.
VZZZZ VZZ
OH, GOD, HOWARD, WHAT HAVE I DONE? GO AWAY. GO AWAY, GO AWAY--
ALL THIS BECAUSE I THOUGHT YOU WERE DEAD.
NO, GRACE. BECAUSE I THOUGHT YOU WERE DEAD. MY FAULT.
THIS IS ALL MY FAULT.

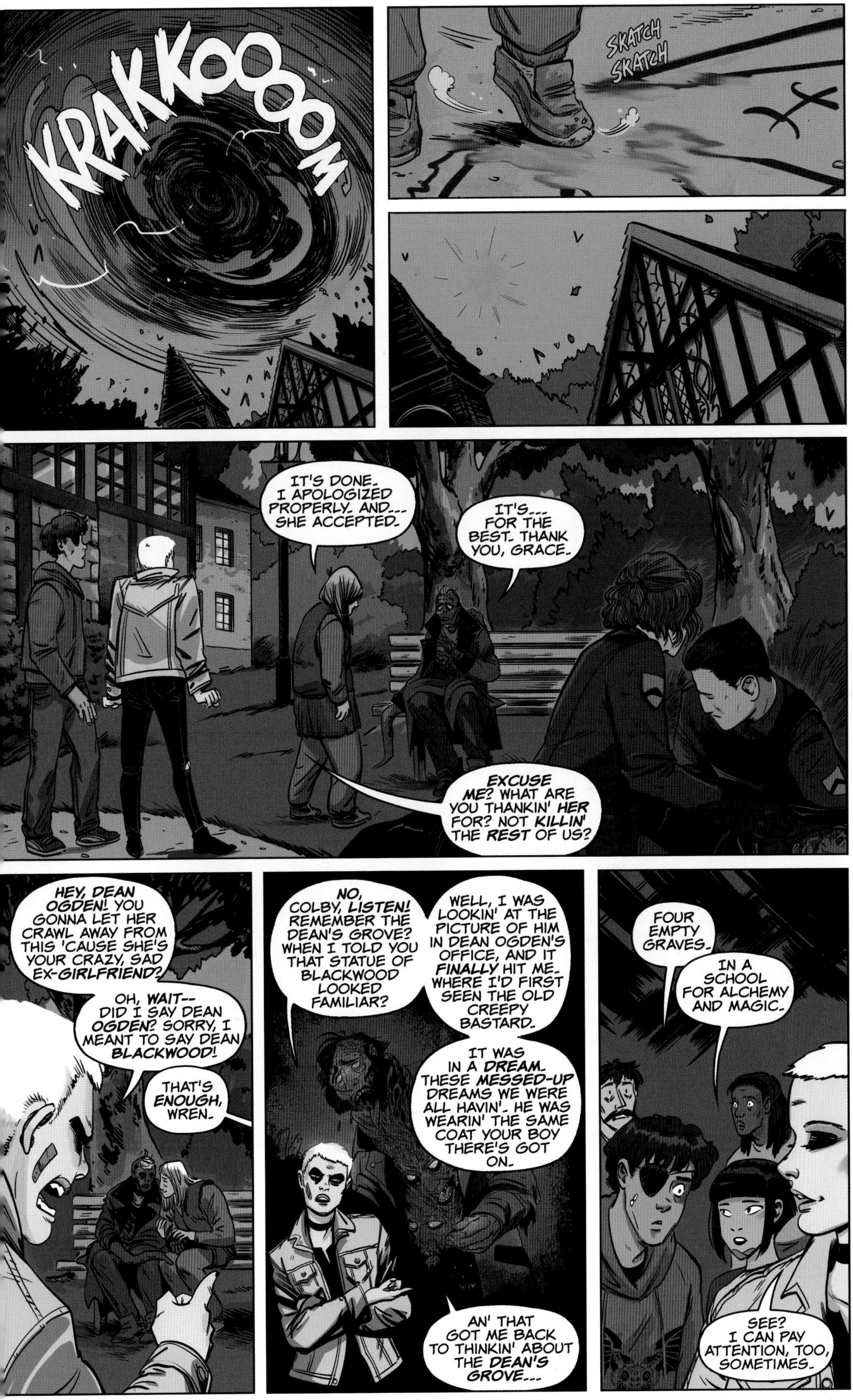
KRAKOOOOM
SKATCH SKATCH
IT'S DONE. I APOLOGIZED PROPERLY. AND... SHE ACCEPTED.
IT'S... FOR THE BEST. THANK YOU, GRACE.
EXCUSE ME? WHAT ARE YOU THANKIN' HER FOR? NOT KILLIN' THE REST OF US?
HEY, DEAN OGDEN! YOU GONNA LET HER CRAWL AWAY FROM THIS 'CAUSE SHE'S YOUR CRAZY, SAD EX-GIRLFRIEND?
OH, WAIT-- DID I SAY DEAN OGDEN? SORRY, I MEANT TO SAY DEAN BLACKWOOD!
THAT'S ENOUGH, WREN.
NO, COLBY, LISTEN! REMEMBER THE DEAN'S GROVE? WHEN I TOLD YOU THAT STATUE OF BLACKWOOD LOOKED FAMILIAR?
WELL, I WAS LOOKIN' AT THE PICTURE OF HIM IN DEAN OGDEN'S OFFICE, AND IT FINALLY HIT ME. WHERE I'D FIRST SEEN THE OLD CREEPY BASTARD.
IT WAS IN A DREAM. THESE MESSED-UP DREAMS WE WERE ALL HAVIN'. HE WAS WEARIN' THE SAME COAT YOUR BOY THERE'S GOT ON.
AN' THAT GOT ME BACK TO THINKIN' ABOUT THE DEAN'S GROVE...
FOUR EMPTY GRAVES.
IN A SCHOOL FOR ALCHEMY AND MAGIC.
SEE? I CAN PAY ATTENTION, TOO, SOMETIMES.

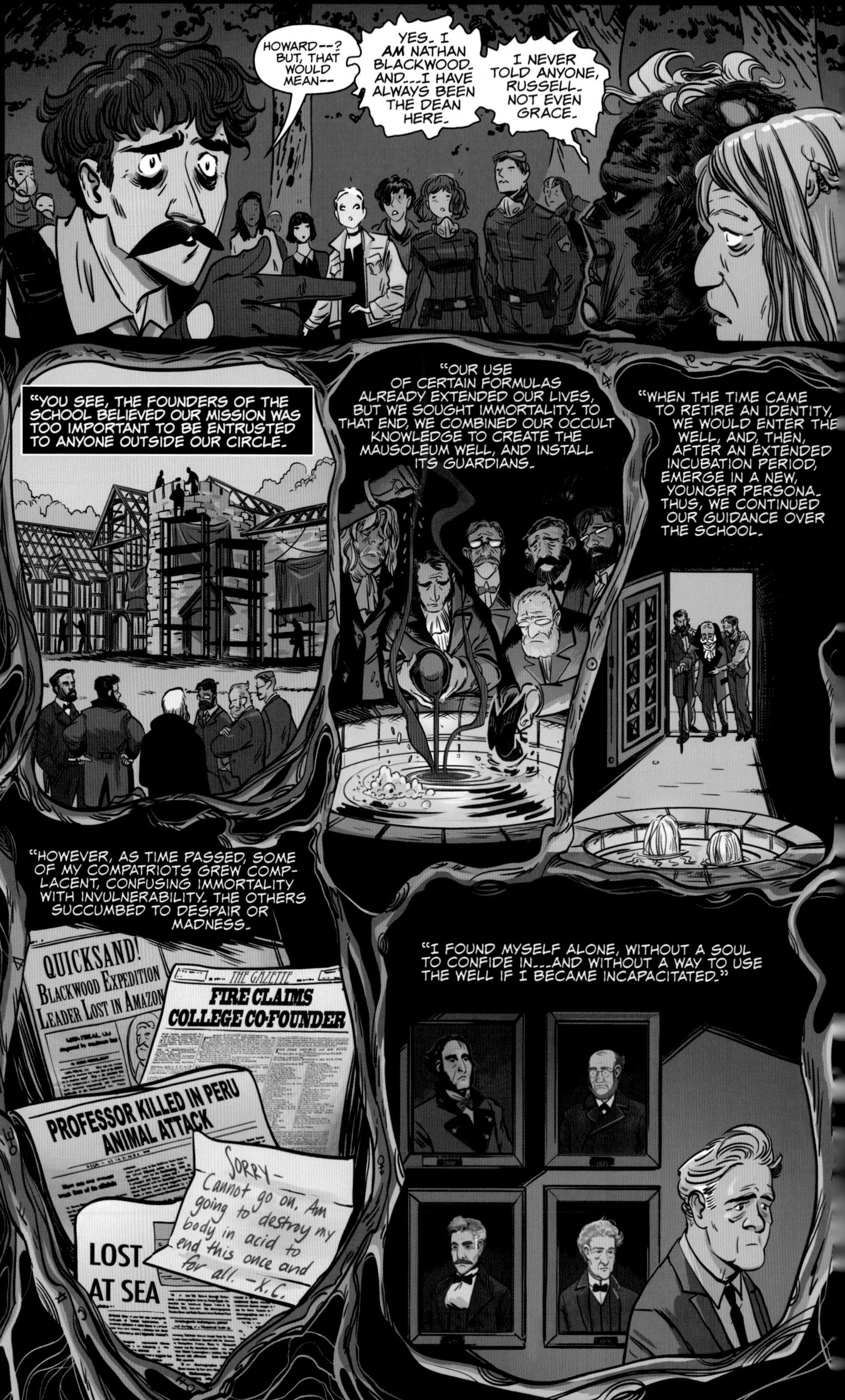
HOWARD--? BUT, THAT WOULD MEAN--
YES. I AM NATHAN BLACKWOOD. AND...I HAVE ALWAYS BEEN THE DEAN HERE.
I NEVER TOLD ANYONE, RUSSELL. NOT EVEN GRACE.
"YOU SEE, THE FOUNDERS OF THE SCHOOL BELIEVED OUR MISSION WAS TOO IMPORTANT TO BE ENTRUSTED TO ANYONE OUTSIDE OUR CIRCLE.
"OUR USE OF CERTAIN FORMULAS ALREADY EXTENDED OUR LIVES, BUT WE SOUGHT IMMORTALITY. TO THAT END, WE COMBINED OUR OCCULT KNOWLEDGE TO CREATE THE MAUSOLEUM WELL, AND INSTALL ITS GUARDIANS.
"WHEN THE TIME CAME TO RETIRE AN IDENTITY, WE WOULD ENTER THE WELL, AND, THEN, AFTER AN EXTENDED INCUBATION PERIOD, EMERGE IN A NEW, YOUNGER PERSONA. THUS, WE CONTINUED OUR GUIDANCE OVER THE SCHOOL.
"HOWEVER, AS TIME PASSED, SOME OF MY COMPATRIOTS GREW COMPLACENT, CONFUSING IMMORTALITY WITH INVULNERABILITY. THE OTHERS SUCCUMBED TO DESPAIR OR MADNESS.
QUICKSAND!
BLACKWOOD EXPEDITION LEADER LOST IN AMAZON
THE GAZETTE
FIRE CLAIMS COLLEGE CO-FOUNDER
PROFESSOR KILLED IN PERU ANIMAL ATTACK
SORRY- Cannot go on. Am going to destroy my body in acid to end this once and for all. -X.C.
LOST AT SEA
"I FOUND MYSELF ALONE, WITHOUT A SOUL TO CONFIDE IN...AND WITHOUT A WAY TO USE THE WELL IF I BECAME INCAPACITATED."
1800
1835

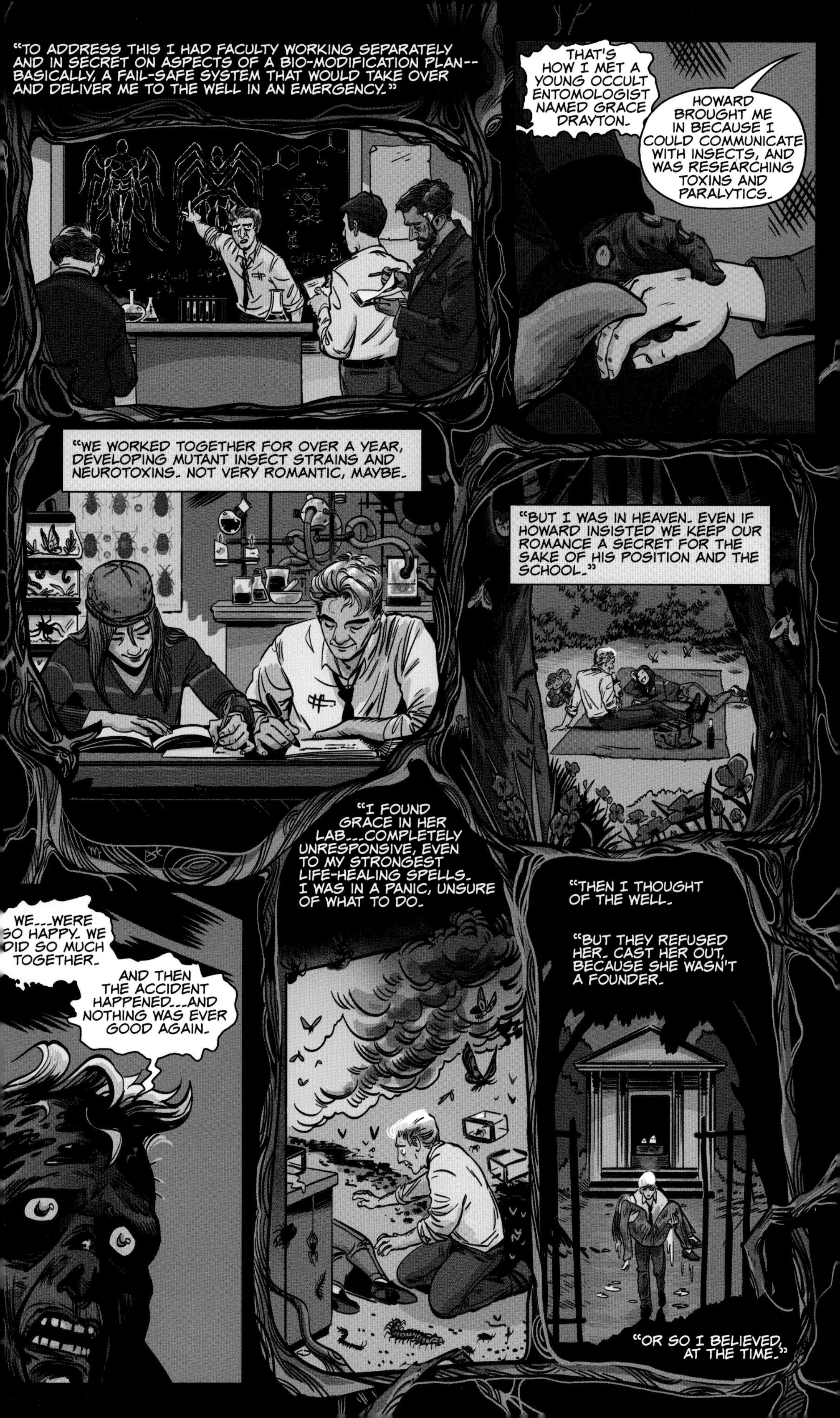
"TO ADDRESS THIS I HAD FACULTY WORKING SEPARATELY AND IN SECRET ON ASPECTS OF A BIO-MODIFICATION PLAN-- BASICALLY, A FAIL-SAFE SYSTEM THAT WOULD TAKE OVER AND DELIVER ME TO THE WELL IN AN EMERGENCY."
THAT'S HOW I MET A YOUNG OCCULT ENTOMOLOGIST NAMED GRACE DRAYTON.
HOWARD BROUGHT ME IN BECAUSE I COULD COMMUNICATE WITH INSECTS, AND WAS RESEARCHING TOXINS AND PARALYTICS.
"WE WORKED TOGETHER FOR OVER A YEAR, DEVELOPING MUTANT INSECT STRAINS AND NEUROTOXINS. NOT VERY ROMANTIC, MAYBE.
"BUT I WAS IN HEAVEN. EVEN IF HOWARD INSISTED WE KEEP OUR ROMANCE A SECRET FOR THE SAKE OF HIS POSITION AND THE SCHOOL."
WE...WERE SO HAPPY. WE DID SO MUCH TOGETHER.
AND THEN THE ACCIDENT HAPPENED...AND NOTHING WAS EVER GOOD AGAIN.
"I FOUND GRACE IN HER LAB...COMPLETELY UNRESPONSIVE, EVEN TO MY STRONGEST LIFE-HEALING SPELLS. I WAS IN A PANIC, UNSURE OF WHAT TO DO.
"THEN I THOUGHT OF THE WELL.
"BUT THEY REFUSED HER. CAST HER OUT, BECAUSE SHE WASN'T A FOUNDER.
"OR SO I BELIEVED, AT THE TIME."

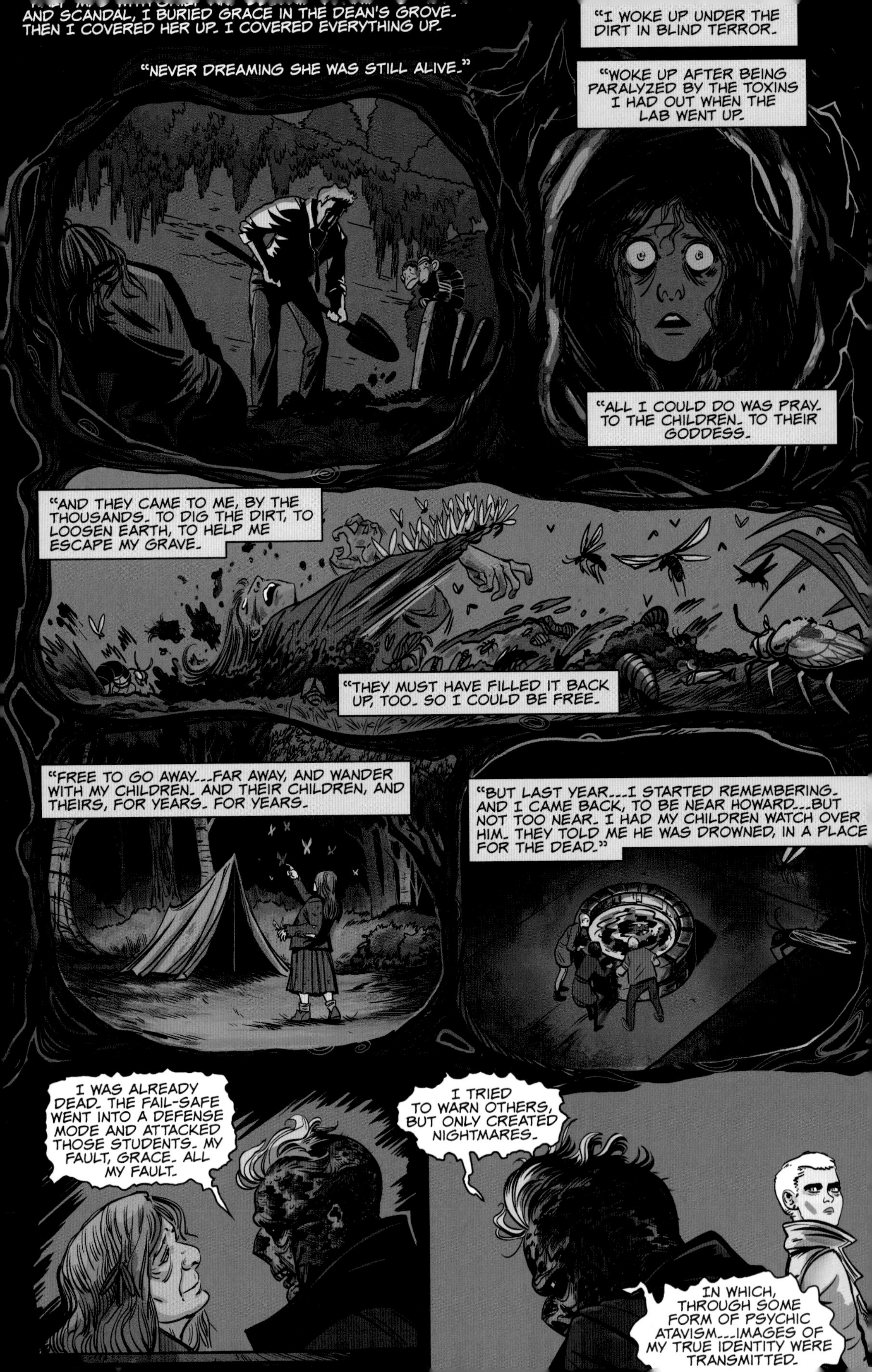

AND SCANDAL, I BURIED GRACE IN THE DEAN'S GROVE. THEN I COVERED HER UP. I COVERED EVERYTHING UP.
"NEVER DREAMING SHE WAS STILL ALIVE."
"I WOKE UP UNDER THE DIRT IN BLIND TERROR.
"WOKE UP AFTER BEING PARALYZED BY THE TOXINS I HAD OUT WHEN THE LAB WENT UP.
"ALL I COULD DO WAS PRAY. TO THE CHILDREN. TO THEIR GODDESS.
"AND THEY CAME TO ME, BY THE THOUSANDS. TO DIG THE DIRT, TO LOOSEN EARTH, TO HELP ME ESCAPE MY GRAVE.
"THEY MUST HAVE FILLED IT BACK UP, TOO. SO I COULD BE FREE.
"FREE TO GO AWAY...FAR AWAY, AND WANDER WITH MY CHILDREN. AND THEIR CHILDREN, AND THEIRS, FOR YEARS. FOR YEARS.
"BUT LAST YEAR...I STARTED REMEMBERING. AND I CAME BACK, TO BE NEAR HOWARD...BUT NOT TOO NEAR. I HAD MY CHILDREN WATCH OVER HIM. THEY TOLD ME HE WAS DROWNED, IN A PLACE FOR THE DEAD."
I WAS ALREADY DEAD. THE FAIL-SAFE WENT INTO A DEFENSE MODE AND ATTACKED THOSE STUDENTS. MY FAULT, GRACE. ALL MY FAULT.
I TRIED TO WARN OTHERS, BUT ONLY CREATED NIGHTMARES.
IN WHICH, THROUGH SOME FORM OF PSYCHIC ATAVISM...IMAGES OF MY TRUE IDENTITY WERE TRANSMITTED.

I HAVEN'T BEEN NATHAN BLACKWOOD IN QUITE SOME TIME. OR HOWARD OGDEN, FOR THAT MATTER. NOT SINCE BECOMING IMMERSED IN THE BOOK OF DESPAIR.

I LEFT THE WELL TOO EARLY... TO TRY TO SET THINGS RIGHT. BUT...YOU CAN SEE THE STATE I'M IN.

I NEEDED BUSIRUS HERE TO GATHER THE MATERIALS I NEEDED SIMPLY TO KEEP MYSELF ALIVE.

THAT'S WHAT KILLED ME. STILL....I OPENED THE DAMNED THING. I WAS RESPONSIBLE.

BLACKWOOD WAS BUILT ON TOO MANY SECRETS. NOT ALL OF THEM WERE NECESSARY. I KNOW THAT NOW.

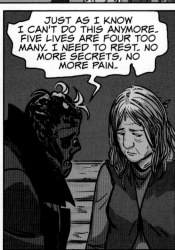

JUST AS I KNOW I CAN'T DO THIS ANYMORE. FIVE LIVES ARE FOUR TOO MANY. I NEED TO REST. NO MORE SECRETS, NO MORE PAIN.

I WAS A FOOL. AN OLD FOOL.

PLEASE DON'T HATE ME, GRACE.

GRACE.... YOU UNDERSTAND?

--SNIFF-- I DO. I DO, MY DARLING.

IT... HURTS...

SHHHH. IT'S OKAY. TRUST ME.

EVERYTHING'S GOING TO BE OKAY, NOW.

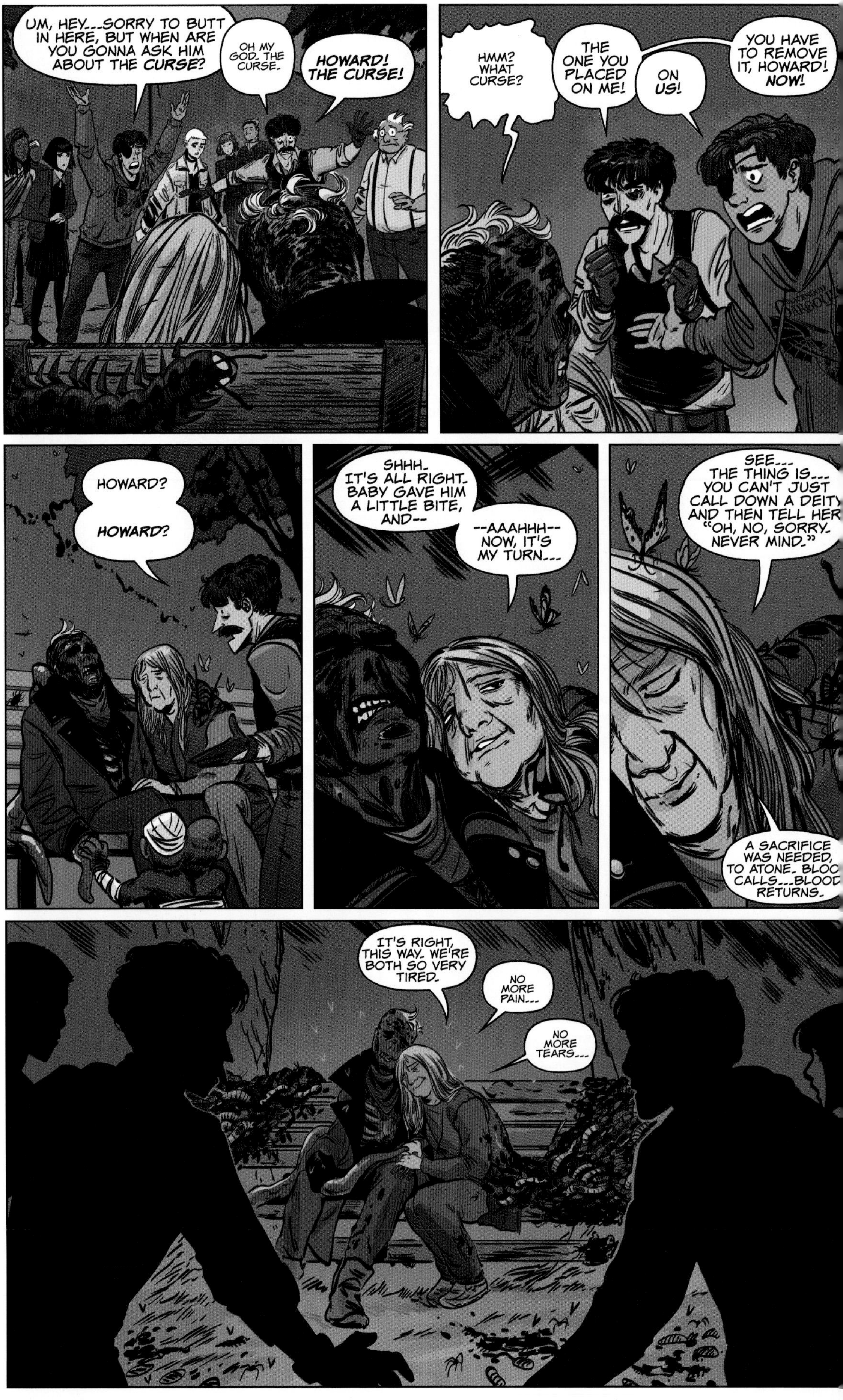

UM, HEY... SORRY TO BUTT IN HERE, BUT WHEN ARE YOU GONNA ASK HIM ABOUT THE CURSE?
OH MY GOD. THE CURSE.
HOWARD! THE CURSE!
HMM? WHAT CURSE?
THE ONE YOU PLACED ON ME!
ON US!
YOU HAVE TO REMOVE IT, HOWARD! NOW!
HOWARD?
HOWARD?
SHHH. IT'S ALL RIGHT. BABY GAVE HIM A LITTLE BITE, AND--
--AAAHHH-- NOW, IT'S MY TURN...
SEE... THE THING IS... YOU CAN'T JUST CALL DOWN A DEIT AND THEN TELL HER "OH, NO, SORRY. NEVER MIND."
A SACRIFICE WAS NEEDED, TO ATONE. BLOO CALLS... BLOOD RETURNS.
IT'S RIGHT, THIS WAY. WE'RE BOTH SO VERY TIRED.
NO MORE PAIN...
NO MORE TEARS...

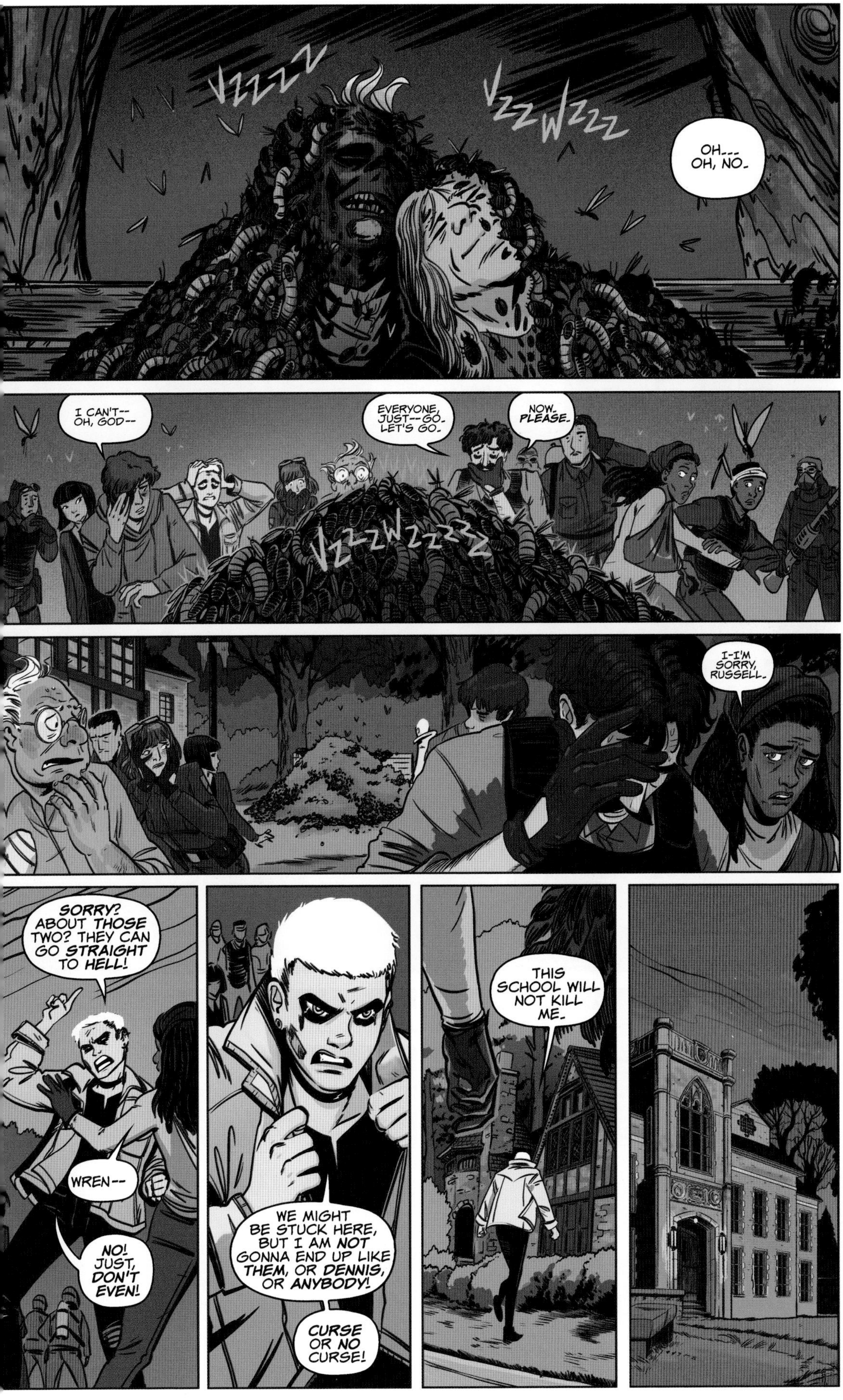
VZZZZZ
VZZWZZZZ
OH... OH, NO.
I CAN'T-- OH, GOD--
EVERYONE, JUST--GO. LET'S GO.
NOW. PLEASE.
VZZZZWZZZZZ
I-I'M SORRY, RUSSELL.
SORRY? ABOUT THOSE TWO? THEY CAN GO STRAIGHT TO HELL!
WREN--
NO! JUST, DON'T EVEN!
WE MIGHT BE STUCK HERE, BUT I AM NOT GONNA END UP LIKE THEM, OR DENNIS, OR ANYBODY!
CURSE OR NO CURSE!
THIS SCHOOL WILL NOT KILL ME.

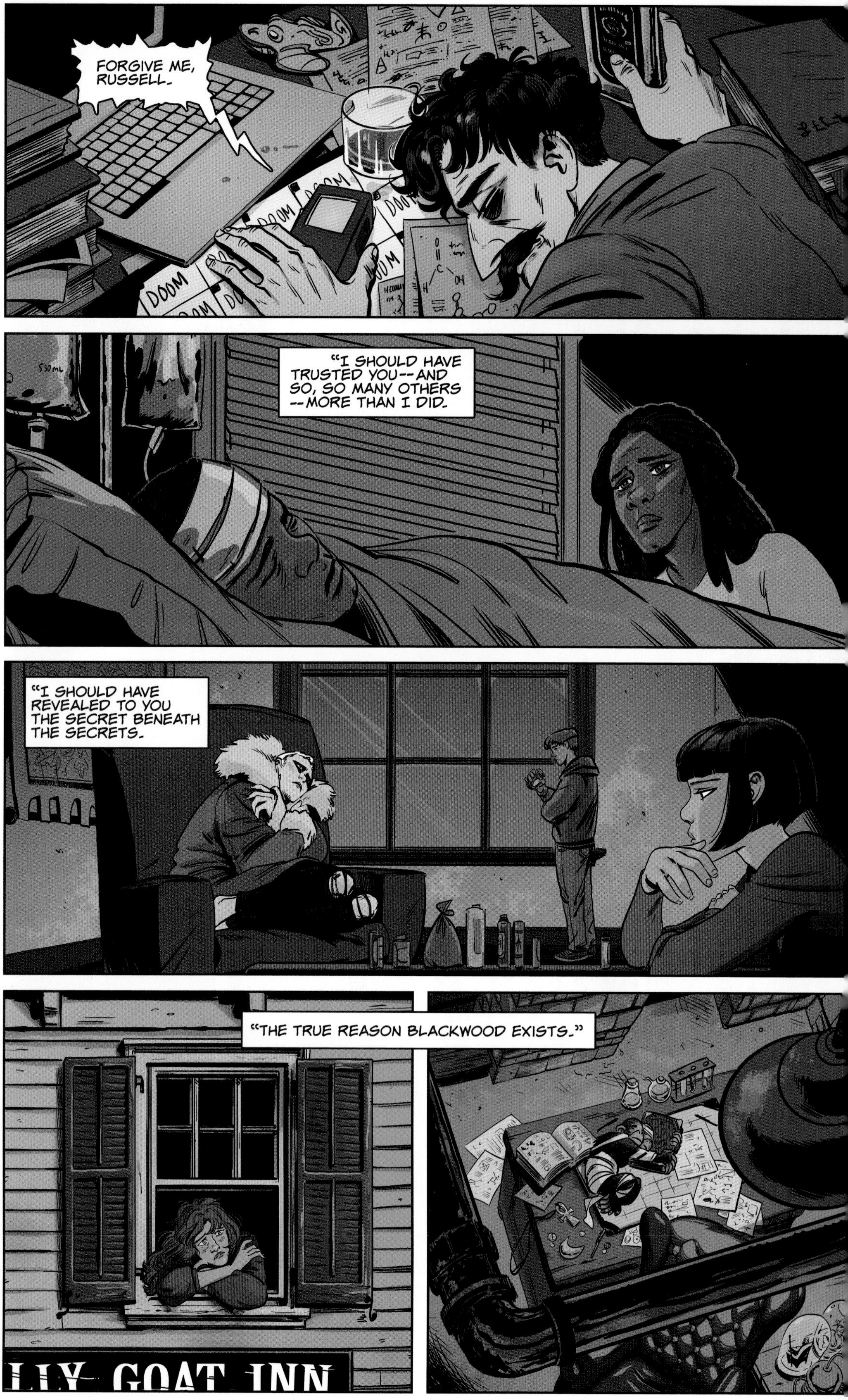
FORGIVE ME, RUSSELL.
"I SHOULD HAVE TRUSTED YOU--AND SO, SO MANY OTHERS --MORE THAN I DID.
"I SHOULD HAVE REVEALED TO YOU THE SECRET BENEATH THE SECRETS.
"THE TRUE REASON BLACKWOOD EXISTS."
LIY GOAT INN

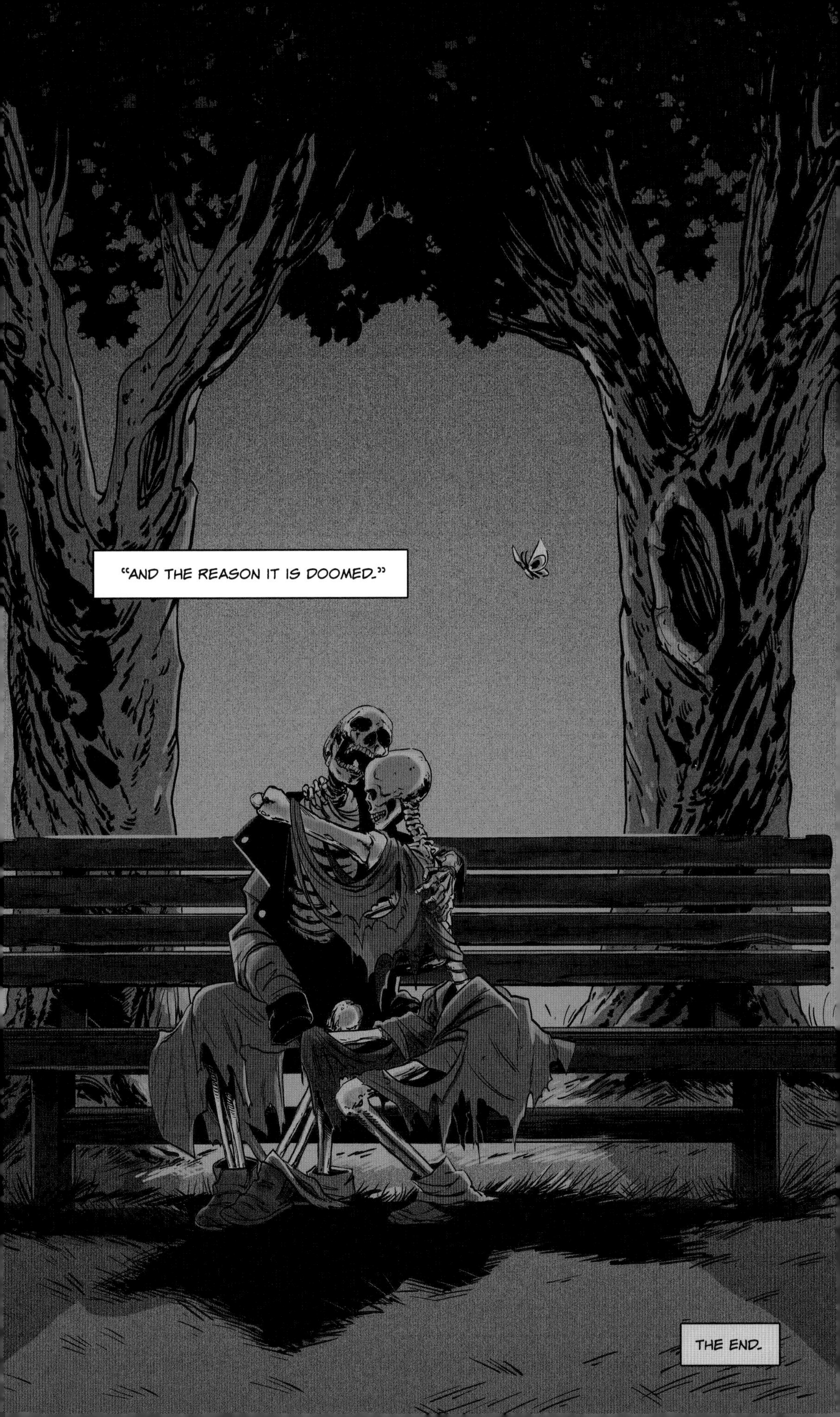
"AND THE REASON IT IS DOOMED."
THE END.

BLACKWOOD

SKETCHBOOK

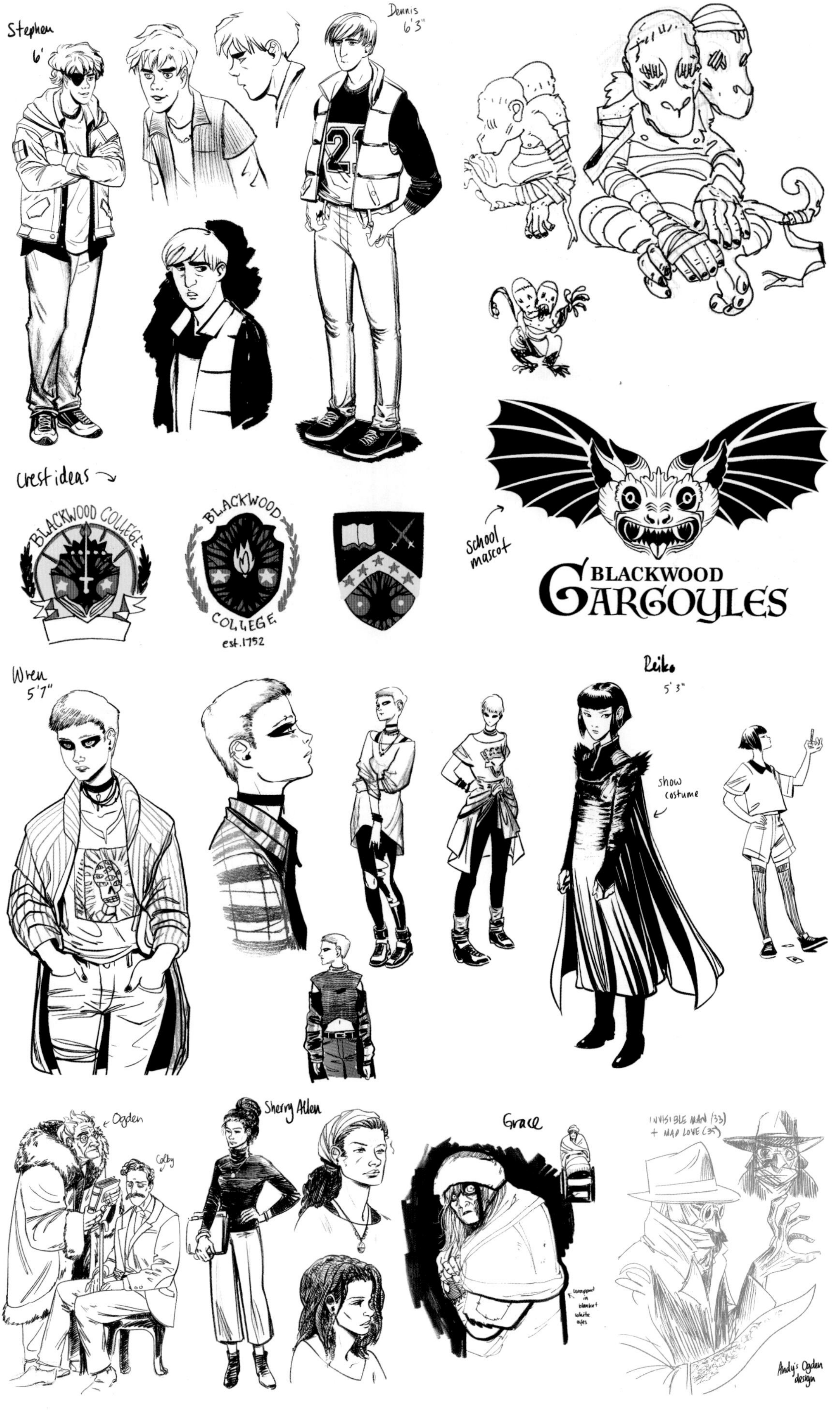
Stephen
6'
Dennis
6'3"
crest ideas →
BLACKWOOD COLLEGE
BLACKWOOD
COLLEGE
est.1752
school mascot
BLACKWOOD
GARGOYLES
Wren
5'7"
Reiko
5'3"
show costume
Ogden
Colby
Sherry Allen
Grace
wrapped in blanket
white eyes
INVISIBLE MAN (33)
+ MAD LOVE (35)
Andy's Ogden design

DINING ROOM TABLE ARRANGEMENTS

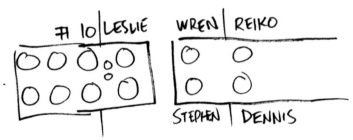

#10 LESLIE | WREN | REIKO

STEPHEN | DENNIS

CLOUDS ROIL IN
FORMERLY CLEAR SKIES

PG 1

KREEEEK REEE KREE~
KRA-KOOM

FOU?

BLOGDEN IN ADMIN HALL - OGDEN'S DOOR / A + J
2 GUARDS AT THE WELL →

CHIMP HO TEP →

F6 CRAWLING INSECTS ON GROUND

FLYING INSECTS

THIN SILK FILAMENTS LIKE MOTHRA SILK FALL

PORTAL OPENS W/A SONIC BOOM TYPE SFX

← SHERRY W/ JAMAR IN HOSPITAL RM

← TRUNDLE IN SURGERY W/ DOCTOR

OGDEN IN LAB SECURITY CAMERAS

GRACE

3 | STUDENTS IN COMMON RM   ↑ CRAWLERS GOING TO GRACE

SHUTTLE VAN MAP

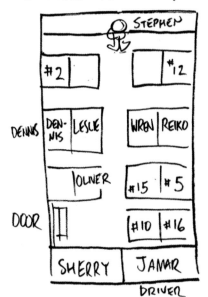

STEPHEN

#2 | #12

DENNIS | DEN-NIS | LESLIE | WREN | REIKO

OLIVER | #15 | #5

DOOR | #10 | #16

SHERRY | JAMAR

DRIVER

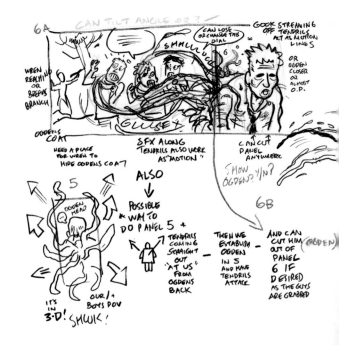

6A   CAN TILT ANGLE OR ?

WREN REACHING OR BREAKS BRANCH

CAN LOSE OR CHANGE THIS DIAL

SHLLLU

GOOK STREAMING OFF TENDRILS ACT AS MOTION LINES

OR OGDEN CLOSER OR ALMOST O.P.

GLUSE

OGDENS COAT

NEED A PLACE FOR WREN TO HIDE OGDENS COAT

SFX ALONG TENDRILS ALSO WORK AS "MOTION"

CAN CUT PANEL ANYWHERE

SHOW OGDEN? Y/N?

6B

ALSO
↓
POSSIBLE * WAY TO DO PANEL 5 +

5
OGDENS HEAD

TENDRILS COMING STRAIGHT OUT "AT US" FROM OGDENS BACK

THEN WE ESTABLISH OGDEN IN 5 AND HAVE TENDRILS ATTACK

AND CAN CUT HIM (OGDEN) OUT OF PANEL 6 IF DESIRED AS THE GUYS ARE GRABBED

IT'S IN 3-D! SHWK!

OUR/+ BOYS POV

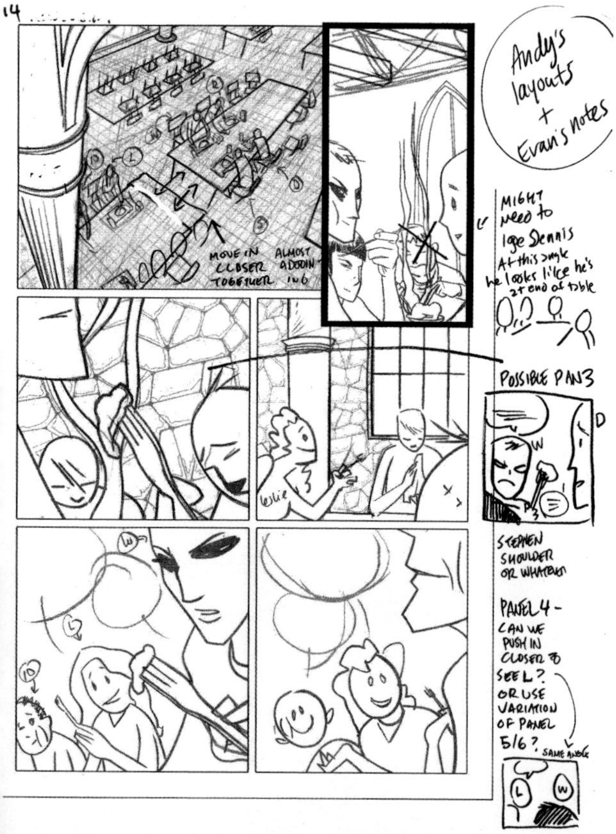
14
Andy's layouts + Evan's notes
MIGHT need to
At this angle he looks like he's at end of table
MOVE IN CLOSER TOGETHER
POSSIBLE PAN3
STEPHEN SHOULDER OR WHATEVER
PANEL 4 - CAN WE PUSH IN CLOSER TO SEE L? OR USE VARIATION OF PANEL 5/6?
SAME ANGLE

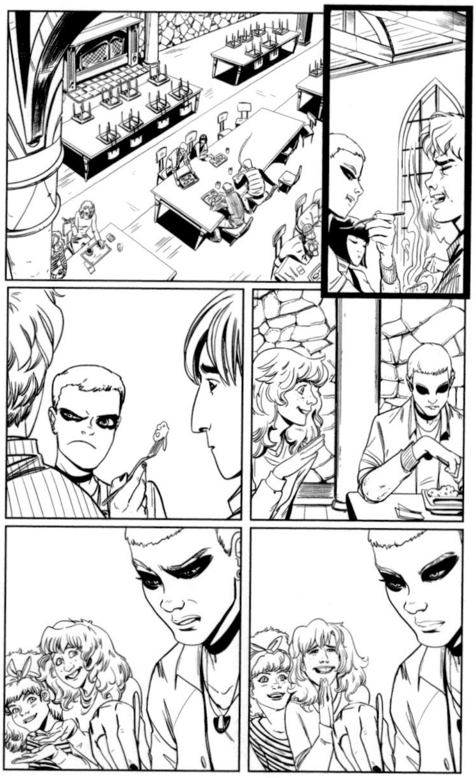

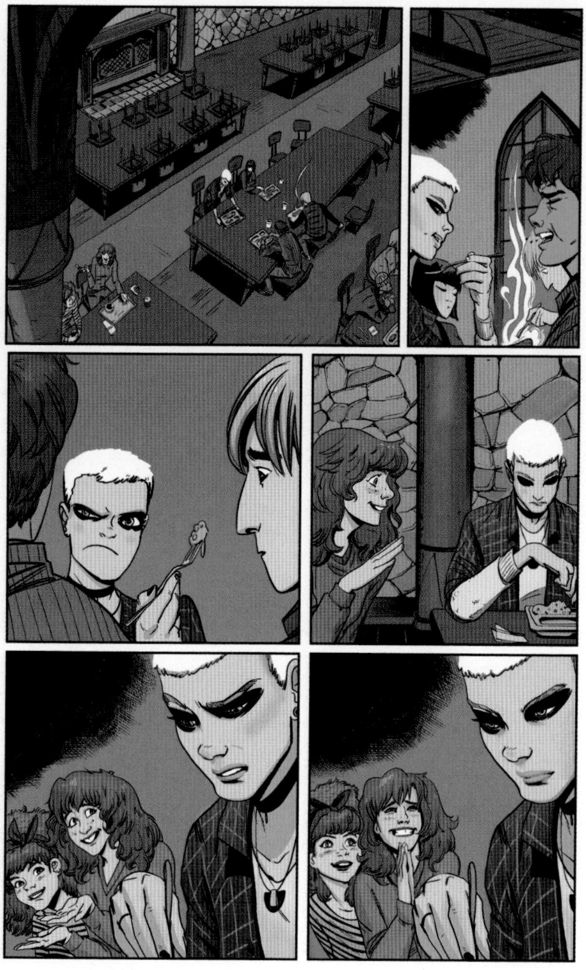

The process for *Blackwood* typically starts with Andy and myself creating roughs together and sending in for notes. Evan would then draw some ideas over our layouts and we'd amend in the penciling stage. Andy would tackle perspective and other tough panels while I go chronologically. Then I'll ink and do finishes, Andy takes them for color flatting and lettering, then back to me for final colors.

—Veronica

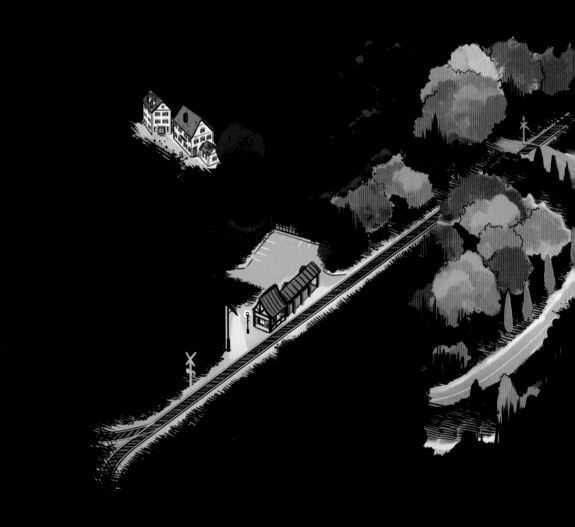

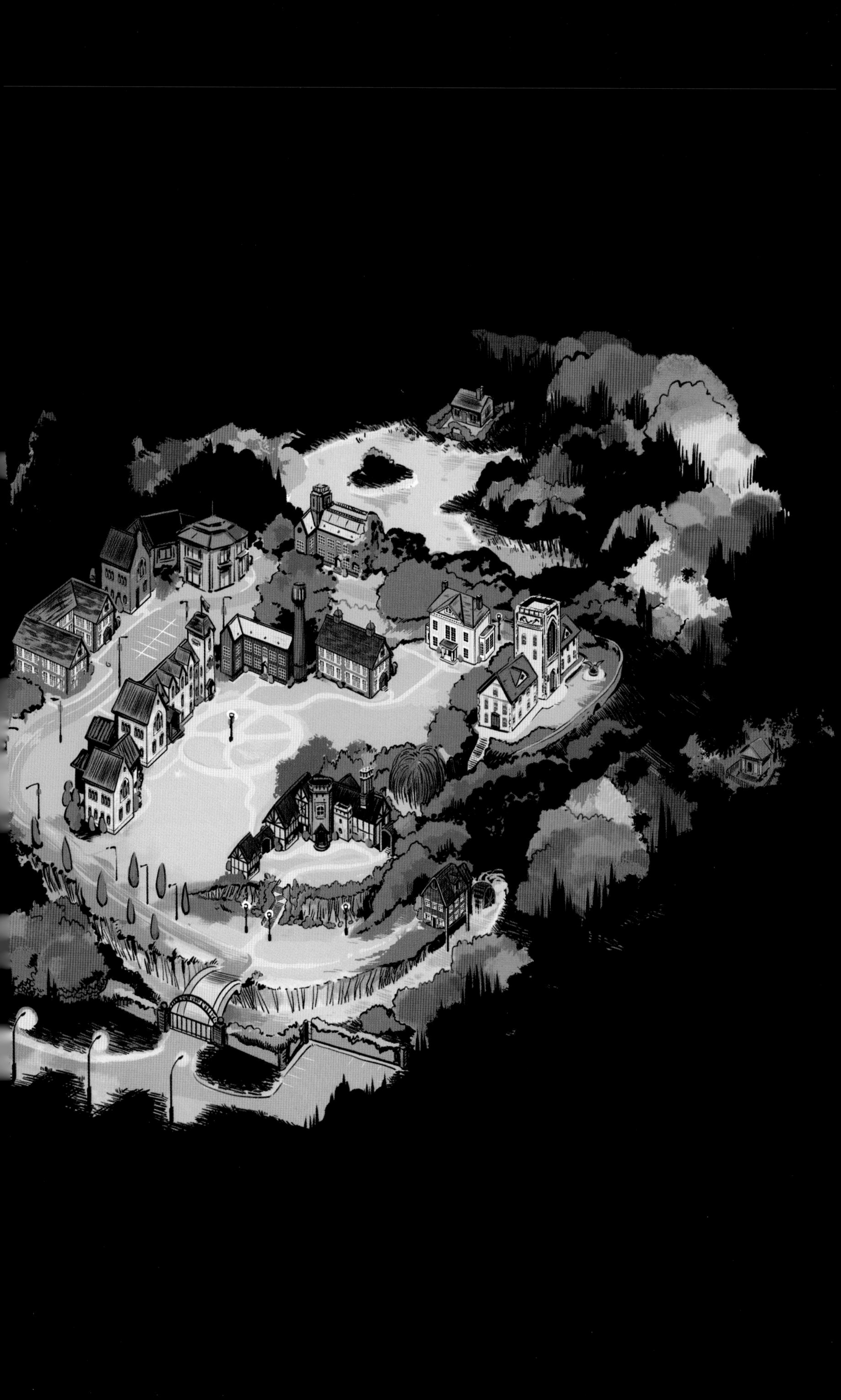

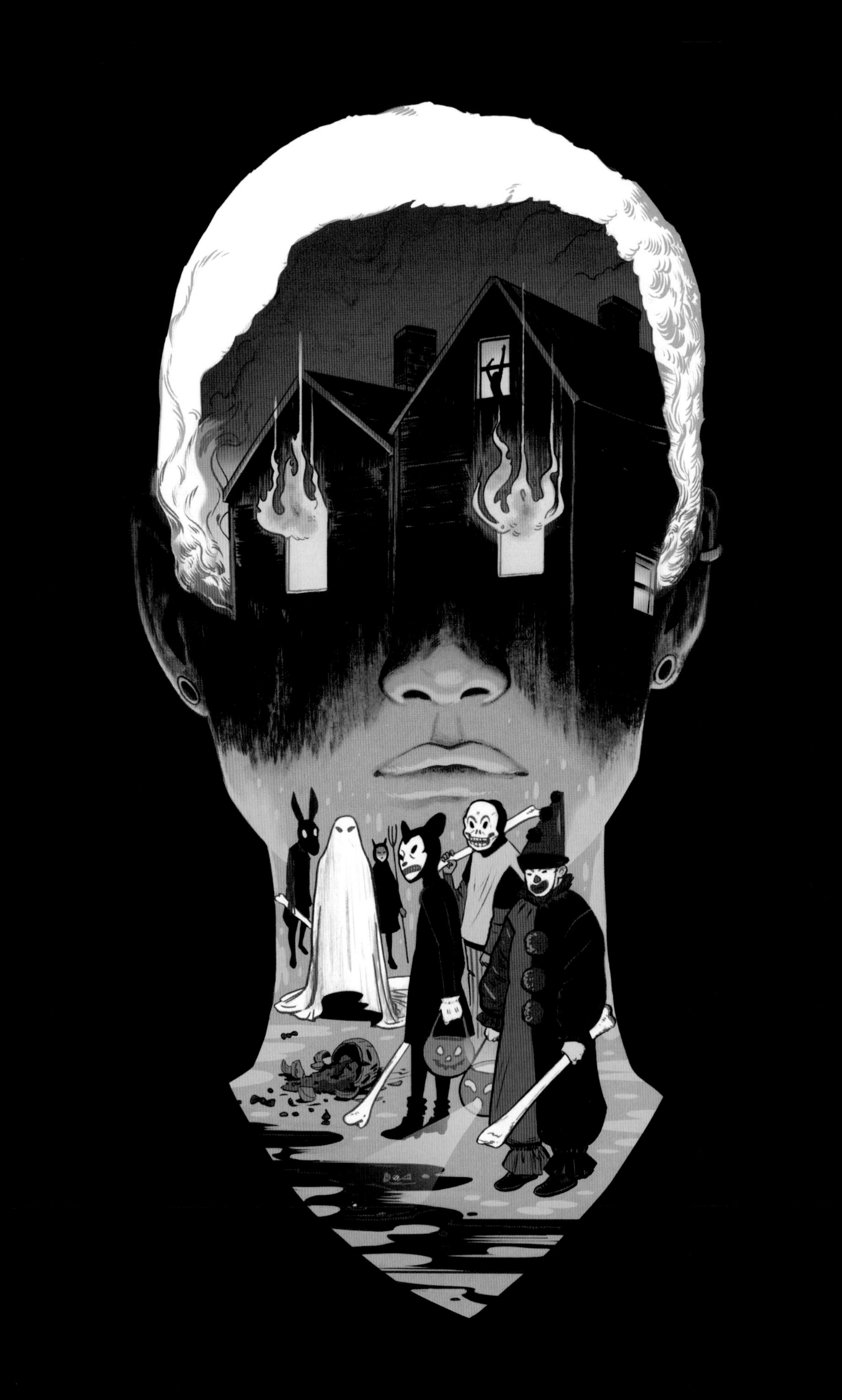

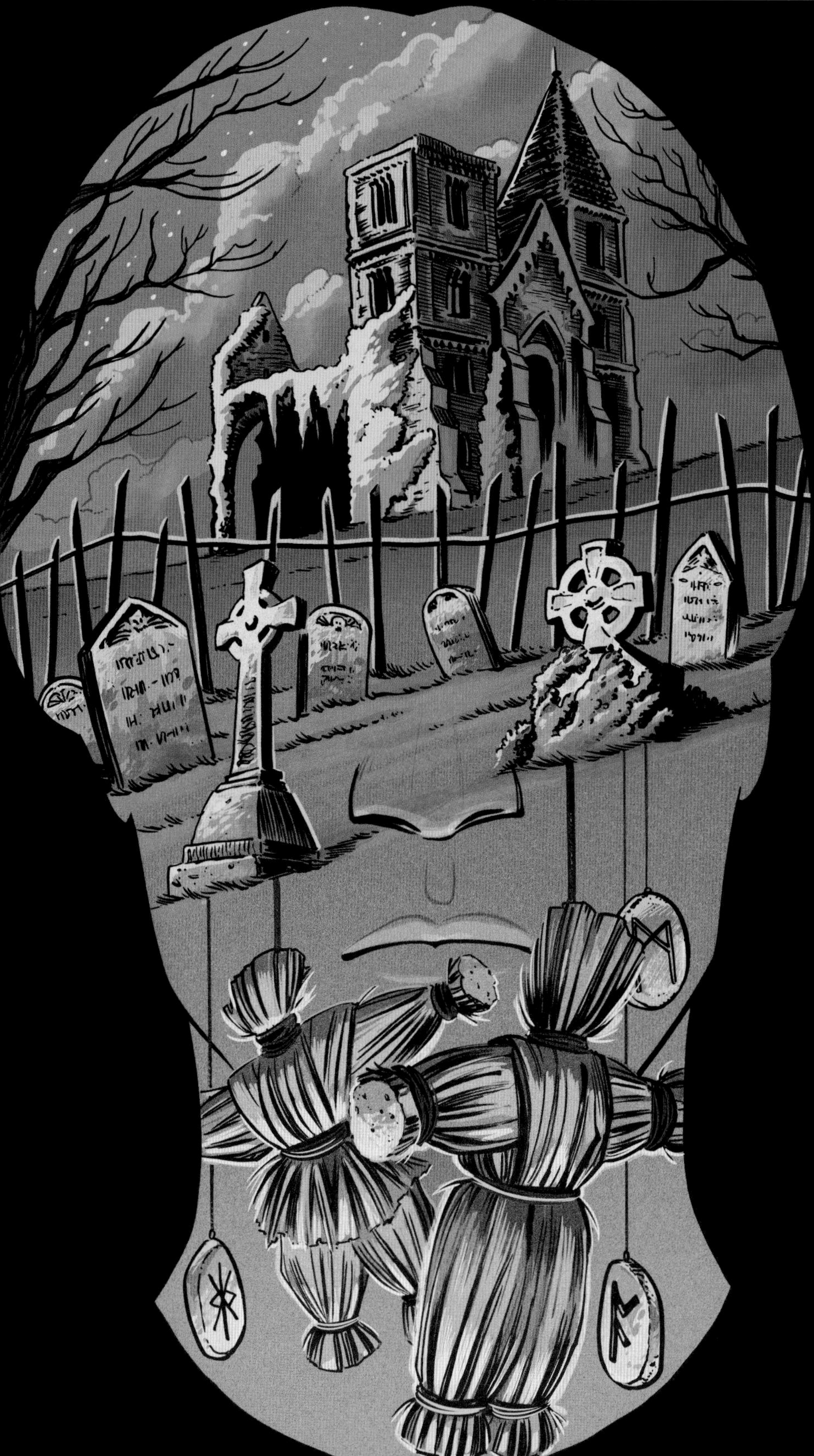

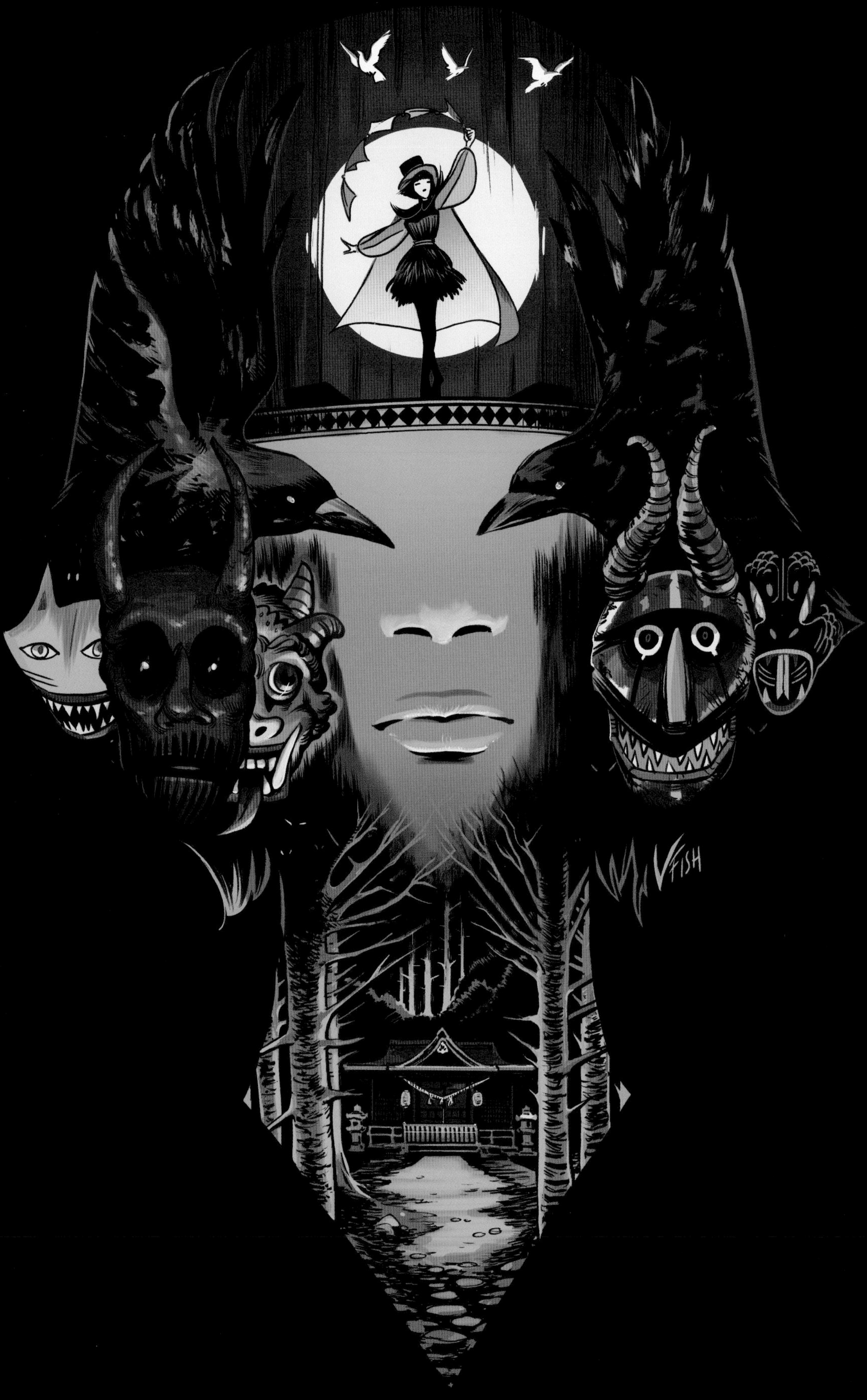
VFISH

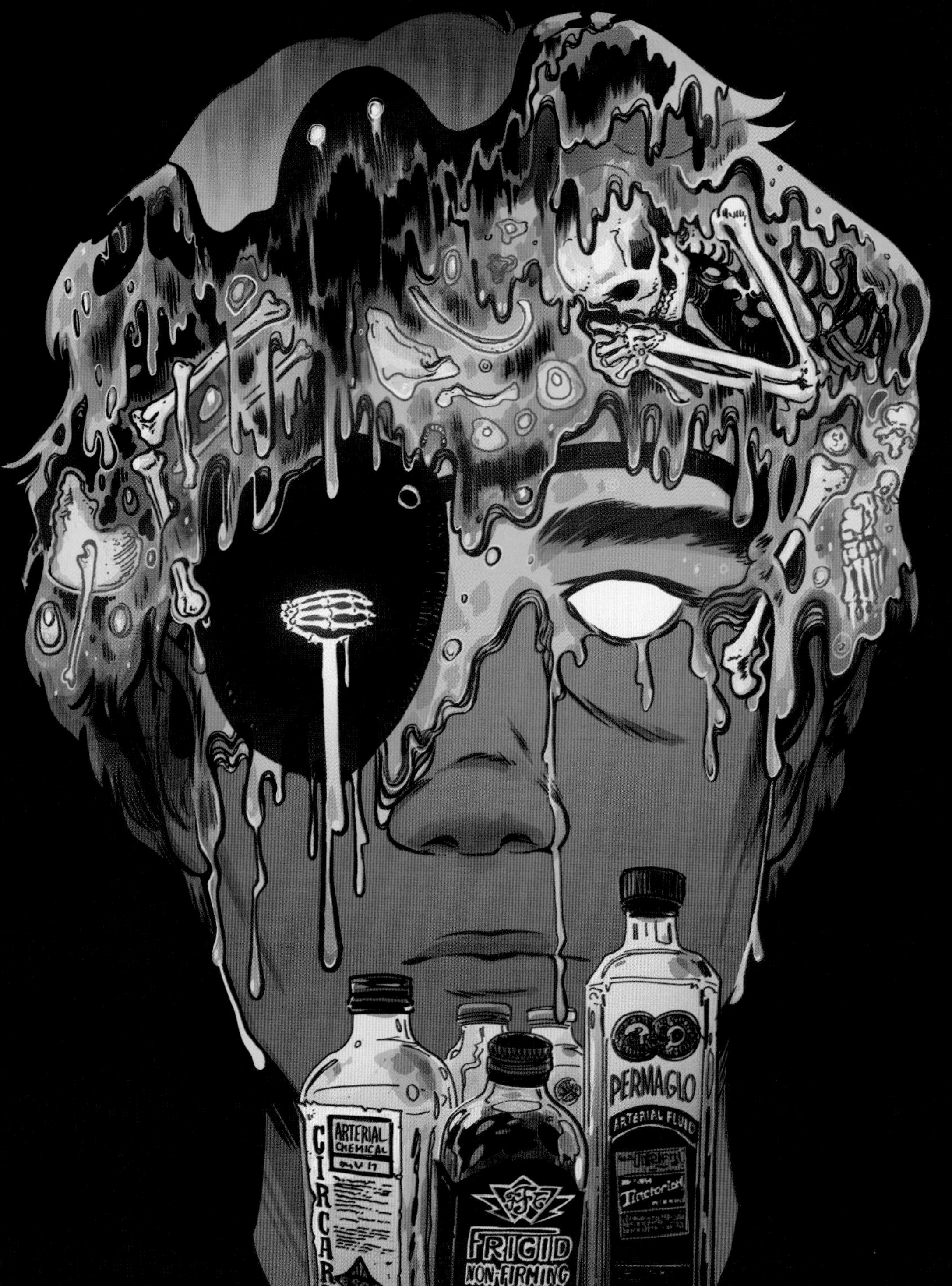
ARTERIAL CHEMICAL
CIRCART
FRIGID
NON-FIRMING
ARTERIAL
EMBALMING FLUID
PERMAGLO
ARTERIAL FLUID

BECKY CLOONAN

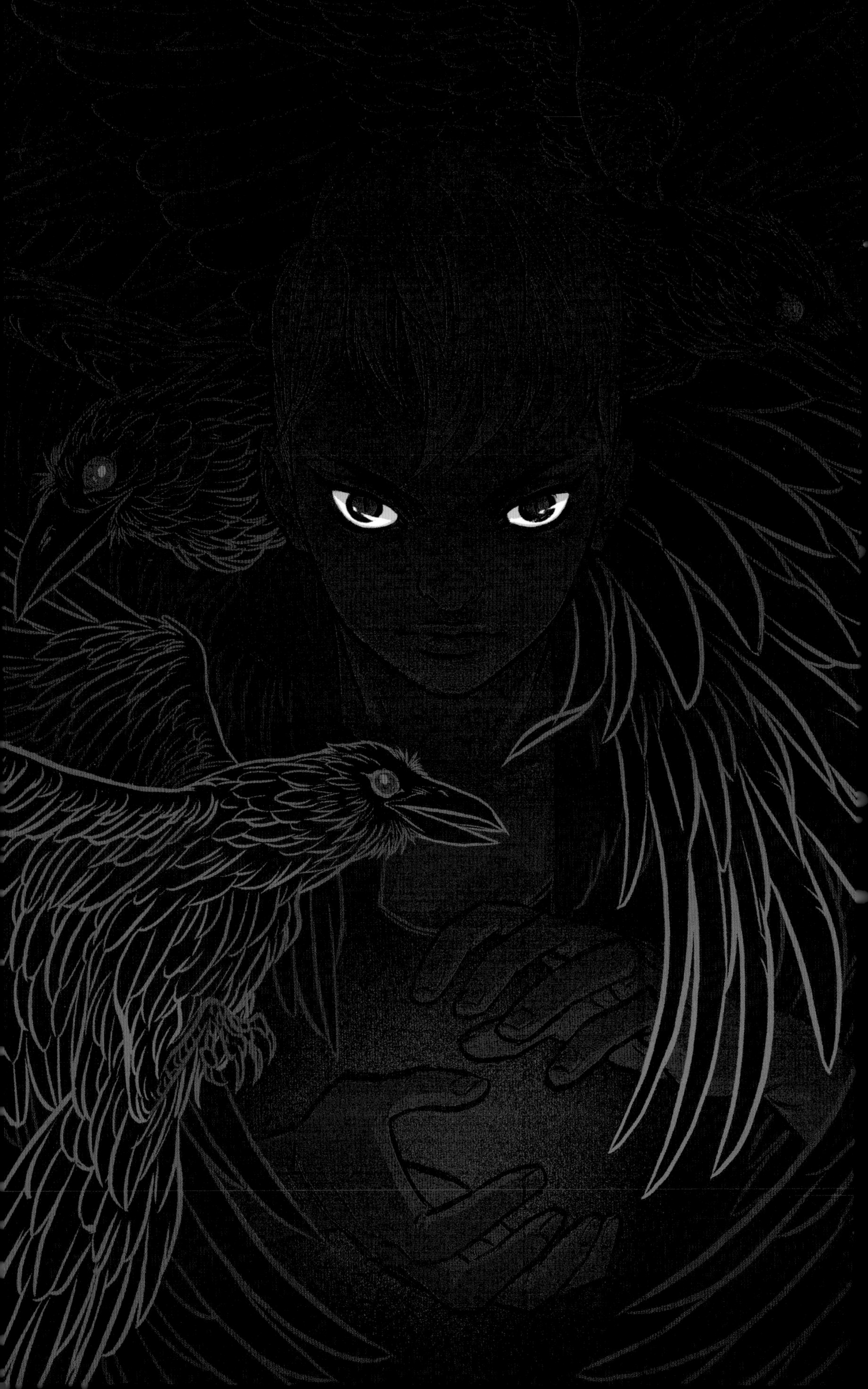

DECLAN SHALVEY AND JORDIE BELLAIRE

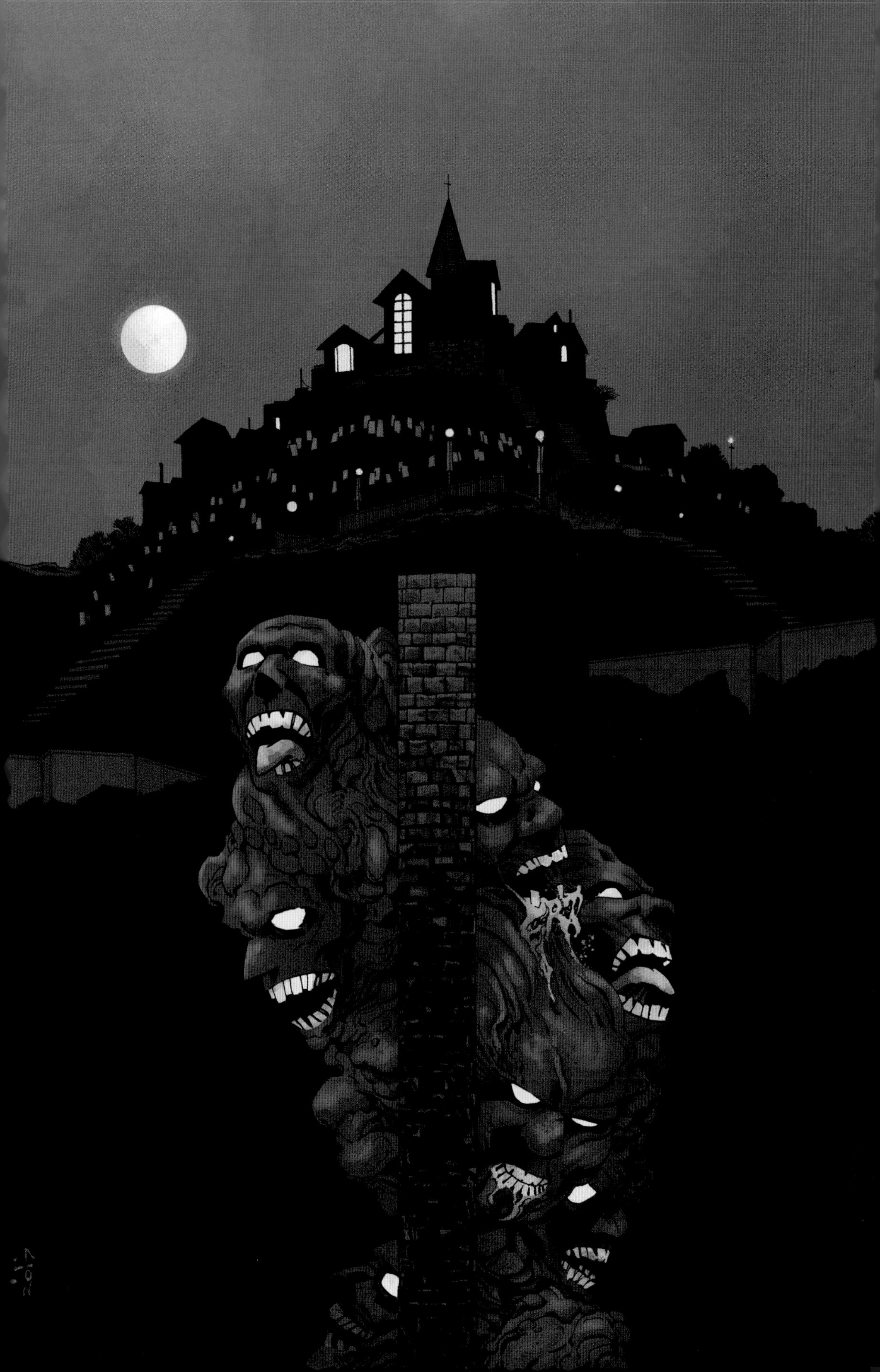

TYLER CROOK

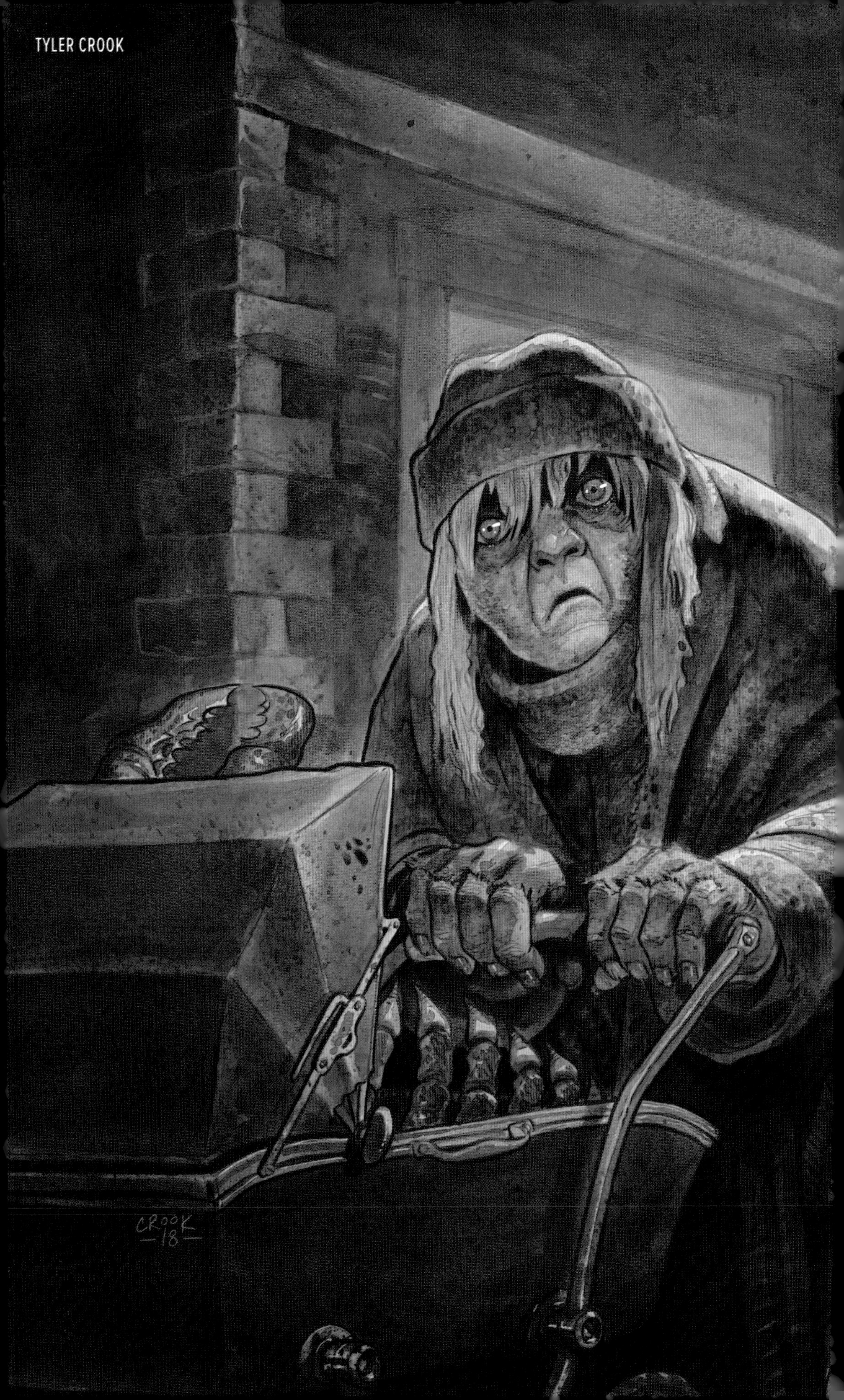
CROOK
18

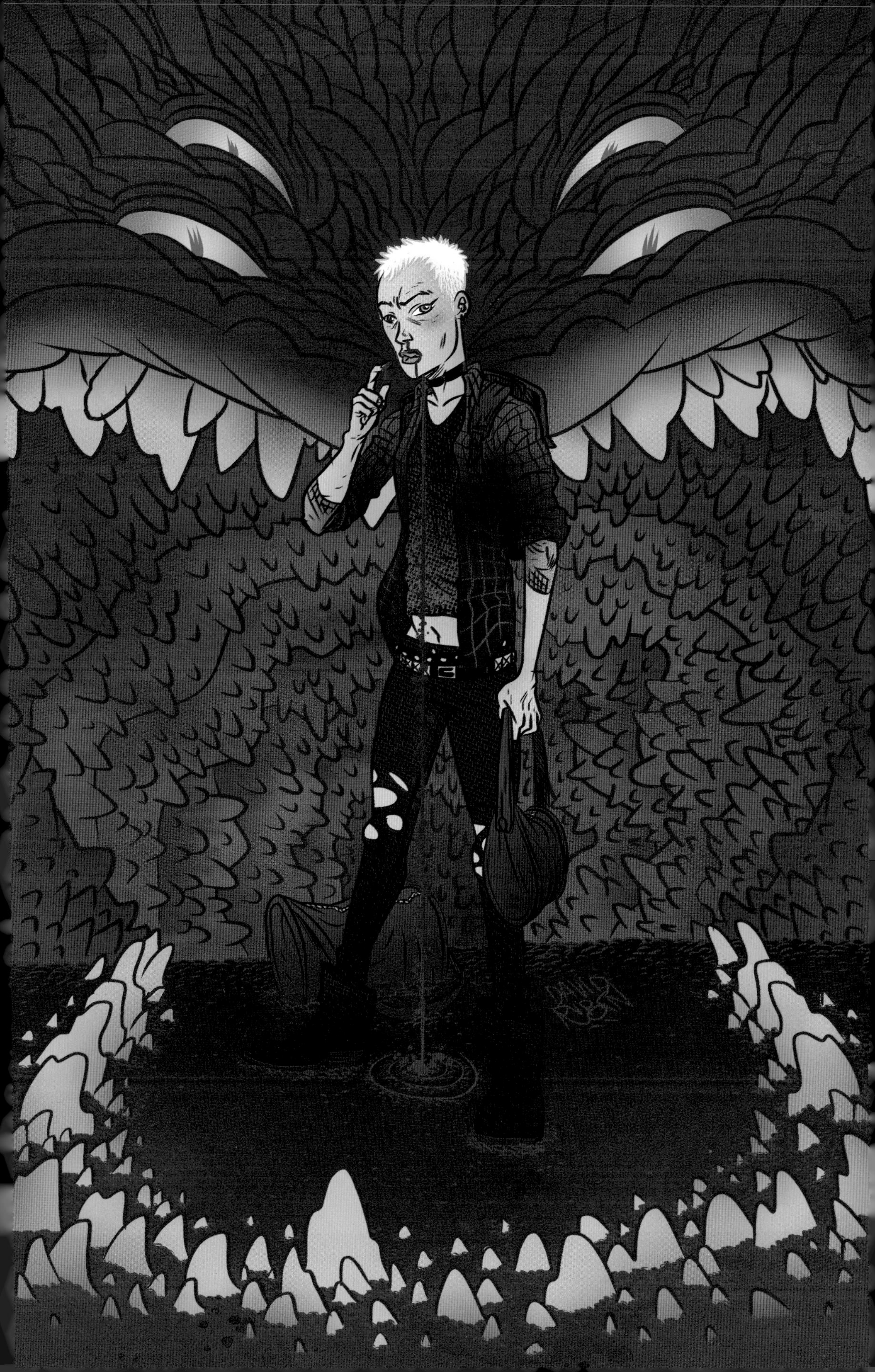

EVAN DORKIN

EISNER AND HARVEY AWARD WINNER

"BRILLIANT."—*FORBIDDEN PLANET INTERNATIONAL*

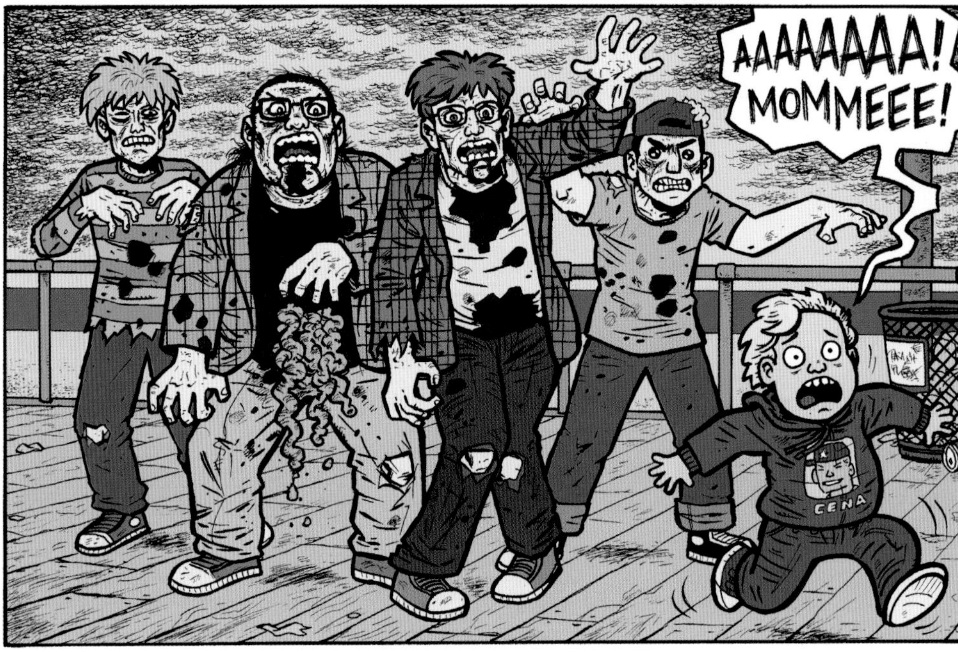
AAAAAAAA! MOMMEEE!
CENA

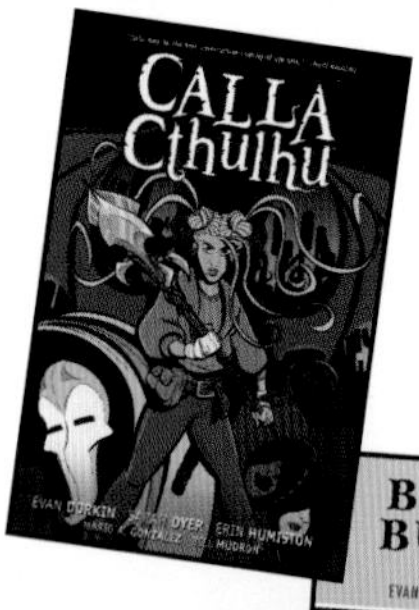
CALLA Cthulhu
EVAN DORKIN

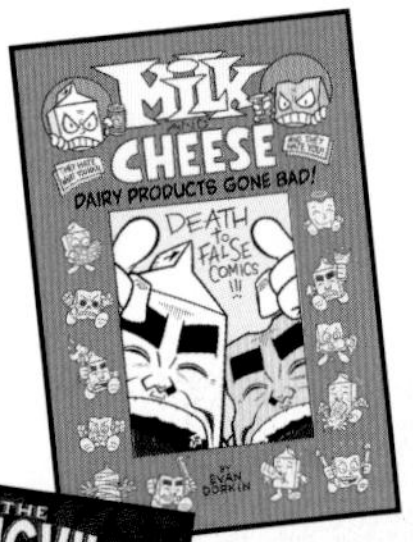
MILK CHEESE
DAIRY PRODUCTS GONE BAD!
DEATH TO FALSE COMICS!!!
EVAN DORKIN

BEASTS OF BURDEN: ANIMAL RITES
Written by Evan Dorkin, art by Jill Thompson
978-1-50670-636-8 | $19.99

CALLA CTHULHU
Written by Evan Dorkin and Sarah Dyer
Art by Erin Humiston, Mario A. Gonzalez, and Bill Mudron
978-1-50670-293-3 | $12.99

MILK AND CHEESE: DAIRY PRODUCTS GONE BAD
By Evan Dorkin
978-1-59582-805-7 | $19.99

THE ELTINGVILLE CLUB
By Evan Dorkin
978-1-61655-415-6 | $19.99

DORK!
By Evan Dorkin
978-1-50670-722-8 | $19.99

BLACKWOOD
Written by Evan Dorkin, art by Veronica Fish and Andy Fish
978-1-50670-742-6 | $17.99

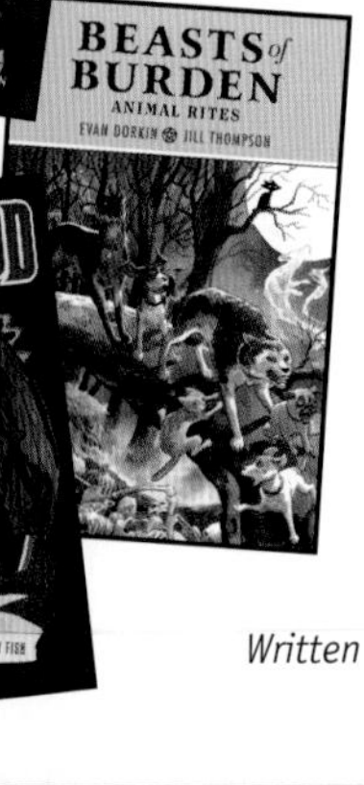
BEASTS of BURDEN
ANIMAL RITES
EVAN DORKIN JILL THOMPSON

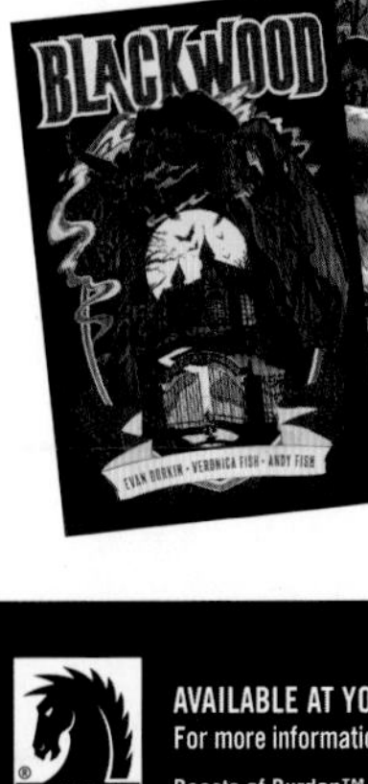
BLACKWOOD
EVAN DORKIN • VERONICA FISH • ANDY FISH

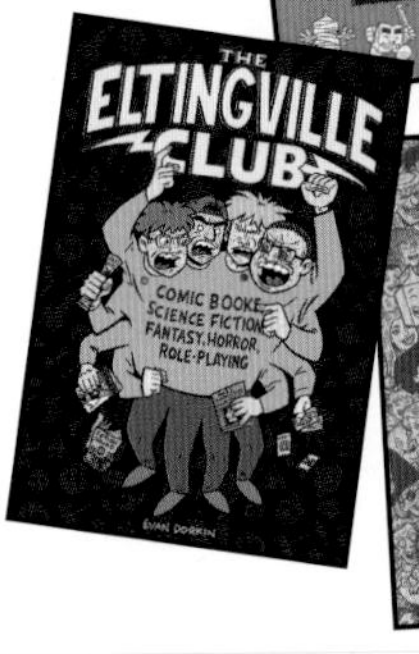
THE ELTINGVILLE CLUB
COMIC BOOKS SCIENCE FICTION FANTASY, HORROR ROLE-PLAYING
EVAN DORKIN

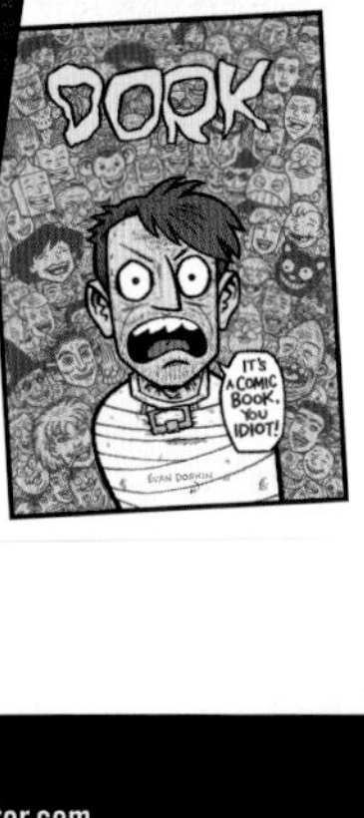
DORK
IT'S A COMIC BOOK, YOU IDIOT!
EVAN DORKIN

DARK HORSE BOOKS

AVAILABLE AT YOUR LOCAL COMICS SHOP OR BOOKSTORE! • TO FIND A COMICS SHOP IN YOUR AREA, visit comicshoplocator.com
For more information or to order direct visit DarkHorse.com or call 1-800-862-0052 Mon.–Fri. 9 AM to 5 PM Pacific Time. Prices and availability subject to change without notice.

DARK HORSE HORROR

drawing on your nightmares

HELLBOY IN HELL VOLUME 1: THE DESCENT
Mike Mignola
ISBN 978-1-61655-444-6 | $17.99

EDGAR ALLAN POE'S SPIRITS OF THE DEAD
Richard Corben
ISBN 978-1-61655-356-2 | $24.99

GRINDHOUSE: DOORS OPEN AT MIDNIGHT DOUBLE FEATURE VOLUME 1
Alex de Campi, Chris Peterson, and Simon Fraser
ISBN 978-1-61655-377-7 | $17.99

HARROW COUNTY VOLUME 1: COUNTLESS HAINTS
Tyler Crook and Cullen Bunn
ISBN 978-1-61655-780-5 | $14.99

ALABASTER: WOLVES
Caitlín R. Kiernan and Steve Lieber
ISBN 978-1-61655-025-7 | $19.99

DEATH FOLLOWS
Cullen Bunn, A. C. Zamudio, and Carlos Nicolas Zamudio
ISBN 978-1-61655-951-9 | $17.99

HOUSE OF PENANCE
Peter J. Tomasi and Ian Bertram
ISBN 978-1-50670-033-5 | $19.99

JOE GOLEM: OCCULT DETECTIVE - THE RAT CATCHER & THE SUNKEN DEAD
Mike Mignola, Christopher Golden, and Patric Reynolds
ISBN 978-1-61655-964-9 | $24.99

WEIRD DETECTIVE: THE STARS ARE WRONG
Fred Van Lente, Guiu Vilanova, and Mauricio Wallace
ISBN 978-1-50670-038-0 | $17.99

H.P. LOVECRAFT'S THE HOUND AND OTHER STORIES
Gou Tanabe
ISBN 978-1-50670-312-1 | $12.99

GARY GIANNI'S MONSTERMEN AND OTHER SCARY STORIES
Gary Gianni
ISBN 978-1-50670-480-7 | $19.99